W. D. Northup To R. W. Sailor
with the compliments
of the Editor

Vol. I NOVEMBER, 1927 No. 1

THE FRENCH REVIEW

Devoted to the Interests of Teachers of French

Published by the
American Association of Teachers of French

CONTENTS

THE AMERICAN ASSOCIATION OF TEACHERS OF FRENCH, *Charles A. Downer* 5

FRENCH ART IN AMERICA, *Paul Claudel* 11

A FRENCH TEACHER'S LANGUAGE SCALE, *A. G. H. Spiers* 13

EN MARGE DES EXAMENS D'ENTRÉE AU COLLÈGE, *O. T. Robert* 29

FRENCH TEACHERS' FORUM 40

WHY TEACH FRENCH, *Colman Dudley Frank* 41

FRENCH CLASS-TEXTS PUBLISHED IN THE U. S., *Alexander Green* 53

VARIA, *J. F. Mason* 63

BOOK REVIEW (BOUDDHA VIVANT), *René Taupin* 69

BIBIOGRAPHY, *Hélène Harvitt* 71

THE LIBRARIAN'S CORNER 75

A. A. T. F. NEWS 76

The *French Review* is the official journal of the American Association of Teachers of French and is published four times during the year.

Application made for second-class mailing privilege.

The annual dues of the American Association of Teachers of French, including subscription to the *French Review*, are $2.50. Applications for membership should be addressed to E. A. Méras, the Secretary of the Association, Adelphi College, Brooklyn, New York.

Communications to the editors, manuscripts, etc., should be addressed to the Editor of the *French Review*, Cornell University, Ithaca, N. Y.

All correspondence concerning advertising should be forwarded to Edward O. Perry, Business Manager of the *French Review*, George Washington High School, 192nd St., New York City.

All books, texts, publications which may interest the teacher of French will receive mention in the bibliography or critical comment, if a copy is sent to a member of the editorial staff. Literary and scholarly works should be forwarded to A. G. H. Spiers, Columbia University, New York City, while texts and other publications should be sent to Dr. Hélène Harvitt, 1309 Carroll Street, Brooklyn, N. Y.

Exchange of the *French Review* with other journals may be arranged by addressing the Editor of the *French Review*, Ithaca, N. Y.

74242

THE FRENCH REVIEW

VOL. I — NOVEMBER, 1927 — No. 1

THE AMERICAN ASSOCIATION OF TEACHERS OF FRENCH

By CHARLES A. DOWNER

The officers of the American Association of Teachers of French join in sending greetings to all members, present and prospective, of the new Association, and to all persons interested in the language and literature of France under whose eyes this first number of the *French Review* may fall. It is their hope that ere long, in a year or two at most, this society may have flourishing Chapters in every State of the Union, bound together in a well-knit organization, actively and effectively devoted to the maintenance of the highest standards of culture among the teachers, to the study and application of the best methods of instruction, the pursuit of the best conditions for teaching, and the creation of the spirit of solidarity and mutual helpfulness without which these aims cannot be realized. We are the last of the four nation-wide associations of foreign modern language teachers to come into existence.

We hope to work side by side in friendly rivalry with those whose example we have followed, and whose names we have imitated in our own. It has been stated in the editorial and in the presidential utterances of two of them that no teacher can owe allegiance to more than one language; the statement is doubtless extreme. Fairly numerous cases might be cited of teachers who have worked ably, faithfully and successfully, in more than one field. But it is true here, as in every human activity, that concentration and specialization are essential to the best results.

Modern language teachers ought to know other languages than the one they teach; if it be a Romance language, Latin also, and they should have considerable knowledge of linguistics in general. But as the acquisition of a thorough knowledge of one language, literature, and culture is more than sufficient to occupy a lifetime, it seems inevitable that the main effort of each of us must be centered upon his specialty. The new organization, then, has for its chief purpose to aid each one and all of us in this effort for thoroughness and excellence.

A divergence of views in regard to these separate associations exists, of course, and these are good arguments to be adduced in favor of the system of a nation-wide modern language society. One of the chief arguments against it would be its unavoidable large size and unwieldiness, and especially the difficulty of maintaining in its periodical a proper balance in apportioning the subjects treated therein according to the needs of the separate groups. In a national language journal that concerns itself with all the languages taught and all the periods of any one language, the reader has to search carefully for articles likely to interest him, and is repelled by the much larger mass of matter, remote from his interest, that he is sure to find in every number. This difficulty might be met by the creation of local modern language periodicals, but here again, when four languages are represented, the reader feels that a large part of the text before him is devoted to subjects in which he takes a minor interest or no interest at all. The strongest argument for a union of all modern language groups lies in their having one great object in common, the promotion of the study of foreign modern languages in this great American democracy as a needed element in the culture of the American people; and in the consequent necessity of presenting a united front. A further corollary to this proposition is that no dissension should be allowed to grow up among them. The question therefore presents itself as follows: Can a number of separate associations work side by side without hostility, conscious that the good of each is bound up with the good of all? Two things there are that militate against this ideal harmony, one on a lower plane than the other. The lower one arises from the instinct to fight for one's group, one's interest, one's job, the other from the sincere conviction that one's group really represents the higher, nobler, and more important interest of the nation or community. Some of us have been guilty of claiming for the language and literature we teach a glory like that of the sun, which obliterates all the other lights in the heavens. But we, as guides and guardians of the young, as men and women of trained minds and superior culture, should look at the facts objectively, avoid comparisons not based upon complete knowledge, remembering that comparisons are not only odious in a passive sense, but that they excite hate in others.

In our Father's house are many mansions; these are not divided into hotels and hovels. The motto of each Association might well be: no conflict, friendly emulation, solidarity in the defense of the common interest. Questions are bound to arise, none the less, that easily lead to conflict. One, for example, presents itself continually. A small school cannot offer a wide choice of languages; which languages shall they be? It can offer only one; which shall it be? Shall utilitarian or shall cultural considerations prevail? Who shall decide, the students, the parents, the principal, the faculty, the board of education? Here is a problem that has to be solved. It is more likely to be solved properly by getting together than by fighting. If there is only one champion in arms, he, of course, wins. If his opponent arms, as he is likely to do in self-defense, then the quarrel is on. But as it takes two to make a quarrel, so it takes two to make peace and keep the peace. Can we teachers rise above prejudice and study a question like this calmly, objectively, with mutual good-will! Chi lo sa?

The small school also presents another problem, namely, the problem of the teachers who are obliged to do work in more than one subject, to teach more than one language, and so are asked to join several associations, attend numerous meetings, subscribe to various periodicals. The individual is here in a sort of internal conflict. All such difficulties are inherent in life itself. We teachers ought to possess two qualities that help smooth them out, intelligence and kindliness. Are not all teachers supposed to be intelligent and kind?

The credit for the founding of the A.A.T.F., as of the A.A.T.G., goes to Dr. William R. Price, Supervisor of Modern Languages in the State of New York. These two associations, like the A. A. T. S., have their beginnings in New York. The first annual meeting of the American Association of Teachers of Spanish took place December 29, 1917, at the College of the City of New York. The first meeting of our own Association, after its organization meeting, took place this year at the same institution, where our Président d'Honneur, Dr. John H. Finley, former President of the College, made the first address delivered before the Association. Dr. Price, who had long since become convinced of the need in New York State of an association of teachers of German, and one of teachers of French, in November of last year issued a call for the formation of the German Association and in December sent out a call for the French Association. This he did in each case after consultation with leading teachers in all parts of the State. The German Association having started with a Metropolitan Chapter. he and those he consulted deemed it wise to lay the foundation of our Association in a Metropolitan Chapter also. Preliminary meetings of committees were held in January, and on February 26 the organization meeting was held at the *French Institute in the United States,* 20 East 60th St., at which officers were elected and a temporary constitution adopted.

This constitution is valid until such time as the nation-wide association is adequately organized. Meanwhile the officers of the Metropolitan Chapter will serve in the main as those of the general association. The governing body is a Board of Directors, Directors being delegated by each Chapter as it is formed, one Director for every forty members. The organization of the Chapters of New York State has been achieved, that of Chapters in other States begun, and it is expected that within this school year every State in the country will be represented in the Association. The Association, although founded in New York and in charge for the present of the Metropolitan Chapter, is a democratic organization; the faster it grows, the wider its extent, the more evident this will become. Two ways lay open before the organizers; to attempt a nation-wide association at once with members and officers in all parts of the country, or to begin with a single chapter as founder and organizer. The latter course was chosen. The ultimate goal is to enroll all the teachers of French in the United States, and to have them organized in Chapters whose influence shall be proportionate to their size or to the abilities of their members.

These teachers fall naturally into three categories, those who teach in Universities, those who teach in Colleges, those who teach in High Schools, or Elementary Schools. The first two are often grouped together, and while it is true that no marked line of distinction is drawn between them, the present writer believes that in the field of literature some line ought to be drawn. Dr. Von Klenze, first President of the A. A. T. G., in his Preliminary Bulletin addressed to all teachers of German, making an appeal for enthusiastic co-operation among them, puts the two together and declares that their "main" business is to keep abreast of new currents in the higher life of Germany. It would seem, however, that the College teacher's "main" business is to present the great and splendid pieces of literature that have stood the supreme test of time, taking account of the present, if you will, but keeping steadily before his students the difference between achieved excellence and mere novelty and change, and that the "main" business of the University teacher is the search for truth in the past as well as in the present, because the present is to be explained by the past. There can be, there is, over-emphasis on new currents; many of these are slender indeed and are lost in the great stream when considered from a point of vantage.

The teachers in the schools are mainly concerned with language teaching itself, but language is studied as a means, and for the vast majority of our students as a means of acquiring first of all the power to read understandingly and appreciatively. Hence the need of all teachers for a knowledge of literature. All possible contacts are therefore desirable among the three categories. University and college professors ought to know all there is to know about the teaching of language, for well are they aware that not all students who come before them are in possession of a complete mastery of the language they have been taught, or even of the art of reading. Our Association has therefore as one of its chief objects the mutual advantage that comes of contact among those who are performing different parts of the same general task. It seeks to help each and every teacher to complete his personal equipment, to enrich his mental life, to solve his individual problems.

We wish to justify our existence in the eyes of the community by demonstrating that we serve a great cause, a cause that involves mutual good-will between our own country and France. We must show that we are competent teachers of the French language, knowing it well and able to teach those entrusted to our care to understand it through the ear and through the eye, to speak it acceptably, and to appreciate and enjoy the great literature to which it is the key.

We must prove that we are endeavowing to make them acquainted with the best and finest the French have to contribute to human civilization, for America needs to know and to assimilate the best from all sources in order to lag behind none in the forward march of humanity. The aims of our Association reduce to one; namely, to adopt every means that can be proven practicable to lead us toward the realization of these ideals, to keep us at the level of each upward step achieved, and to help us to climb higher.

College of the City of New York.

FRENCH ART IN AMERICA[1]

By H. E. Paul Claudel

Ambassador of France to the United States

I thank you for your kind invitation. I am greatly honoured to sit to-night at the same table with the President and your other distinguished guests. I was delighted to see Pittsburgh and to have an opportunity to come in touch with the powerful and beautiful city which is the great workshop and shape maker of America. But there are other shapes than contrivances of cement and metal,—frail dreams of line and colour which somehow are never more pleasant to the eye and to the heart than when they are shining against a perpetual background of smoke and toil. I remember when I visited Manchester in England two years ago how the water colours of Turner looked full of strange and wistful meaning as they appeared revealed to me by a touch of electric light in the deep gloom of the Museum like treasures in an Arabian cave. The masterworks of Titian have a more spiritual significance in the pure light of Spain. I enjoyed more Japanese art in Boston than in Japan. And here in Pittsburgh the fresh and bright colours of our impressionist painters have acquired for me a new charm, the charm of exoticism. They are not only for me a memory, they not only make me see what I had only looked at, I feel they have a message.

(1) *Upon a request for a contribution to the first number of* ***The French Review,*** *Mr. Paul Claudel, the French Ambassador at Washington, very kindly sent a copy of the speech he recently delivered at the Carnegie Institute, Pittsburgh, on the occasion of the well known French painter, Henri Matisse receiving the first prize in painting at the annual art exhibition.*

A message can be conveyed from one mind to another mind not only in words but in colours. There is in America a kind of proverbial advice to shy lovers: Say it with flowers. Well, we feel we have many things to say to you about France which it is better to say with flowers, even with painted flowers. And what are our modern pictures, and specially this one of our great artist, Mr. Matisse, which received to-day the medal of Carnegie Institute, but intellectual flowers born from the marriage of the sun and the mind?

Gentlemen, the same is true of French Art and American Art as of French and American individuals: it is because they are so different that they like each other and they need each other. Works of art exchanged between different countries are not only models, they are challenges. They challenge us not to do the same thing but to do as well with other means, with our particular means. Well, we know that the friendly challenge which French Art addresses to American Art has not remained unanswered. You treasure many French masterworks in your galleries but ours are by no means poor in American names. One of the glories of the Louvre is the picture of his mother by your great painter Whistler. We hope that such institutions as the Carnegie medal and the Carnegie Institute will help to develop that spirit of mutual curiosity and beneficent competition. I thank you in my name and in the name of my countryman Matisse.

A FRENCH TEACHER'S LANGUAGE SCALE

By A. G. H. Spiers

For the past three years the Department of French in Columbia College has been using a French Language Scale of its own invention for measuring the achievement of students in French. Although this Scale has been applied in some 4000 cases, both in school and college, it has never been publicly described. It is explained here in the belief that the premises on which it is built, the detail of its form and the usefulness of its results will prove of interest at a moment when similar tests, often based on other principles, are being tried throughout our country.

The nature of this Scale was determined by certain definite considerations. Many of these have been either ignored or differently applied in tests now appearing elsewhere. We give a few of these considerations, accompanied by occasional comparisons with these other tests.

The first of these considerations is that a French test, to be satisfactory, should be planned and executed by persons possessing at least two qualifications: they must be thoroughly competent and constant users of French and they must be experienced in giving class-room instruction in that language. Neglect of this consideration has been responsible for mistakes not only in the preparation of new tests, but also in the criticism of tests already published.[1]

1). Every kind of mistake has been made by persons lacking these qualifications. Those coming most frequently to the attention of the writer are, however, of two kinds. In criticising the examinations prepared by others, these persons fail to recognize either the nature or the degree of difficulty of the points raised in these examinations. A mistake of this kind weakens, for instance, the results of the recent calculations on the reliability of the old-type Regents Examinations of New York State. On the other hand, when such persons prepare tests of their own, they err in another way. Starting with English as a basis, they transpose their questions into a semblance of French by means of a dictionary and a grammar. The results of such a procedure, especially in the preparation of questions

Our second consideration is this: a good foreign language test should test the language and, as far as possible, nothing but the language. If Professor Terman is right, then Mr. Wilkins is, in all probability, wrong. The "mixed sentences" which the former uses to test the minds of students should not be used by the latter to gauge their knowledge of French[2].

Good mental ability will, of course, help the student to answer the questions of any test; but tests should be so constructed that two students possessing the same technical linguistic accomplishment, though differing in mental calibre, should receive. as nearly as possible, the same score. Riddle questions or those obviously introducing elements of mental confusion should most evidently be avoided;[3] it would seem further, that examiners should avoid also other forms of questions in which the mental difficulty is less obvious. Thus experience proves the paragraph-statement form not to be as satisfactory as might naturally be expected.[4] Our present-day school and college student suffers from

---

of the true-false type, is often disastrous. On a set of questions thus prepared, the late Professor De Bacourt made a worse score than certain college freshmen. The better the examined knew French, the less he understood the questions!

2). "Mixed sentences" are sentences the words of which are given out of their proper order. Thus, in Terman Group Test of Mental Ability for Grades 7 to 12 (Form B): "is it all away throw wisest money to one's"; and in Wilkins (Le Petit Journal, February 1, 1924); "sans partout regardé voir rien avait-il."

3). Can it be that Professor Weeks's amusing "Boys' Own Arithmetic" is influencing modern language instruction? One might be led to think so by the following question in which the mention of the father is nothing but a mental obstacle. *"Hier soir mon père est rentré à dix heures, et moi je suis rentré à huit heures. Si mon frère Jean est rentré trois heures plus tard que moi, à quelle heure Jean est-il arrivé à la maison?"* (Wilkins in "Le Petit Journal".).

4). In this form of question, students read a paragraph of French. Having done so, they indicate the truth or falseness of a list of statements based upon the facts given in the paragraph. An experiment finally convinced us of the danger of such a test. Taking three such paragraphs and sets of questions as they appeared in The Meras-Roth-Wood French Scale for the Junior High School (special New York City edition), we translated mental hazards which we, of another generation, do not experience. This, at least, is a possible explanation for the unexpected difficulty presented by questions of the true-false type.[5] No matter how straight-forward the question, students invariably look for a "catch".[6]

A good test, and this is our third consideration, should gauge the student's ability to handle French in the conditions of actual use. We do not care how he has learned the foreign language. Whether he has acquired his French by years of conversation with careful speakers in France or by study in the schools of our own country, whether he has learned it by the direct method or the indirect, whether he names his tenses as they are called in the older grammars or the new, what we wish to know is simply how well he can read, write, and generally understand French. It would therefore seem a mistake to allow the results of a test to depend upon his familiarity with technical terms[7] or his ability to give a correct translation of isolated words.

---

both the paragraphs and the statements into English. Having thus eliminated all difficulties arising from the use of a foreign language, we set these questions in a class of Columbia College students. The average score obtained by these students was only 83.5 per cent.

The authors gave up this type of question in the more recent Regents' Examination in French for June 1925.

5). In questions of this type the student is asked to show his knowledge of French by indicating whether a statement made in French is true or false, the statement bearing on a fact of common knowledge, e. g. *Tous les chevaux sont blancs.* Unfortunately it is not easy to find many sentences at the same time sufficiently hard in expression and sufficiently clear in thought to test any but elementary language. The temptation is great to quote from recent examinations certain gems worthy of a first class nonsense book.

6). This habit, which certain of our colleagues find to be equally strong in students of other subjects than French, has been the subject of many talks between the writer and individual students. As a result, the only explanation he can give, besides the naturally "disputatious" spirit of the times, is the possible influence of the mental tests so much used in our schools and colleges.

7). We are thus tempted to find fault with the use of grammatical terms in the American Council French Tests, while recognizing fully the extreme care with which they are employed. e. g. "Write on the dotted line at the right the proper possessive adjective (*mon, son,* etc.)"

Our fourth consideration has to do with the foreign words to be used as a basis of a good French test. What words may we expect our students to know and what is the relative importance, for the students, of these various words as compared one with another? Much hard and energetic work has been done by certain investigators in an endeavor to establish vocabulary lists based on a count of words and phrases. As developed up to the present time, however, such lists must be used only with extreme caution: necessarily based on a strictly limited observation, they lead to disastrous results in the hands of any but discriminating and experienced users of French. Special care is necessary in the case of such lists when derived from a frequency count of words as they appear, not in the text, but in the dictionary sections of a number of school texts.[8] More reliable than these, but still requiring the greatest caution, are word lists based on a painstaking count of the frequency with which words appear in the running text of a great variety of well-chosen passages of language and literature. We have nothing but admiration for the enormous labor performed by Professor Henmon and his associates, and for the modesty and scientific conscientiousness with which they have published their unmodified results and nothing but these results. Their little volume is an interesting document in itself and a reliable contribution towards a still more elaborate investigation; but no one can maintain that its data can be successfully used by any but an experienced teacher of French, in the construction of a test. Can we believe, for instance, that *mardi, mercredi* and *jeudi,* the names of

8). Instruction in the schools of our country is so lacking in uniformity that the choice of school texts to be used in this count is itself difficult to make. Furthermore, the necessities of grammar explanation and example-giving lead, in the case of grammars, composition books and texts containing exercises, to the introduction of many words of little general value to the student. We are apt to forget, too, that increasing the number of texts studied does not eliminate the fundamental vice of working from the vocabulary of a text book rather than from the running text itself. In a vocabulary, the word occurring once in the book is as prominent as the word occurring a hundred times. In that of "Le Voyage de Monsieur Perrichon", for instance, *l'arrosoir* is the equal of *le dîner* and the thoroughly unimportant *sieur* is the peer of *dieu.* Though the rejection of words not common to several vocabularies reduces the magnitude of this error, it does not wipe it out.

the three middle days of the week, should be learned by our students only after they have already learned 3900 other French words?[9]

This frequency count of running words in discourse is now being extended under the able direction of Professor Coleman of Chicago; it is to include not only the 400.000 running words used as a basis of the Henmon list, but a total of 1.200.000 words in more than thirty categories. We are awaiting the publication of this list with much interest.[10] But whatever may ultimately be the results of such further investigations, today it is still true that the best source of words for a vocabulary test is the knowledge and intuition of the experienced teacher who will take the trouble to jog his memory by turning over the pages of a dictionary and is willing to learn by the lessons of careful experimentation. To collect, on a large scale, the material offered by such sources would be a difficult, but a most meritorious undertaking worthy of the support of an important foundation.[11]

A fifth consideration determining the nature of our French Language Scale is the belief that, important as the knowledge of words may be, other matters are more important. Every real teacher of French knows this to be a fact, and neglect of this fact has been one of the mistakes of those who, without knowing French teaching and its problems, have sought to construct French tests.[12] French educators have for many years recognized the

9). These three words do not appear at all in Professor Henmon's "A French Word Book". This volume contains other surprises also. The non-French *groschen* for instance has, in this list, the same frequency as *rideau. Nain* is certainly less useful to our students than either *adieu* or *gras;* in this list, however, it has a frequency double that of the second and three times that of the third.

10). For an account of a little experiment with the Henmon list, see note 19 below.

11). One of the most satisfactory educational French word lists to come to the attention of the writer was prepared by a Committee of Five appointed by the New York Syllabus Committee and published by the New York State Department in 1913.

12). The late Professor Méras, in spite of his great interest in vocabularies, felt very strongly on this point. His indignation was great, some years ago, when he learned that, in the correction of a test which he had helped to prepare, the correctors paid attention only to those sections which involved vocabulary.

relative unimportance of vocabulary; in their foreign language examinations they allow the student to use dictionaries or supply him with a text, in the foreign language, from which he may draw his words. A French sentence is anything but a word for word translation of an English sentence. If "John's father does not want him to go there" is to be translated into French, the translator must first grasp the thought of the English sentence; and then, reviewing mentally or intuitively the mechanism of the French language, he must apply to the expression of this thought whatever processes this mechanism offers. He must use at least seven different processes, in which the French differs from the English, before he arrives at the proper result: *Le père de Jean ne veut pas qu'il y aille.*[13] Within limits, it may be stated that, from the student's point of view, words may be picked up at any time; they are materials to be found, when and as needed, in the storehouse of the dictionary. On the other hand, syntax, accidence and, to a certain extent, characteristic idiom constitute a stock of tools and machinery necessary whenever work of any kind is to be done. To possess power in French is to know what these tools and machinery are and to have developed the technical skill necessary to use them. A good test then, especially for elementary classes, must emphasize above all syntax, accidence and idiom.

A last consideration, and one of much importance in view of the widespread search for objectivity, rapidity and ease of scoring, runs as follows: it is impossible to construct an adequate French test in such a manner that it can be corrected throughout by persons incapable of recognizing accurately a written word or set of written words. The need of mass correcting by unskilled persons is no doubt a real need in the present state of education in our country; but it must not be heeded to the extent of impairing the efficiency of a test. In testing a certain few points of language knowledge, it is perhaps possible so to contrive questions that the correctness of the reply may be determined by noting whether the student has put down on a certain line, a+, a— or a 0; or by insisting that he shall underline a word to be found

13) e. g. *de* possessive, definite article, negation, finite for infinitive clause, subjunctive mood, position and use of conjunctive.

at a certain spot on a printed page. In reality, however, the effective use of such methods is limited and the effort to apply them on a large scale is responsible for many evils. Most common among these evils are an indirection leading to mental puzzles such as have already been mentioned and a strong tendency to test passive knowledge rather than active knowledge.[14]

* * *

The French Language Scale of the French Department of Columbia College is an attempt to observe the considerations explained above in the construction of a test fulfilling the desiderata developed by contemporary conditions, namely standardization of different editions and objectivity, ease and rapidity in scoring. It may be corrected with uniform results by anyone who can compare students' entries with correct forms appearing on a corrector's slip. It may be given within the limit of a classroom hour, taking but fifty minutes of the student's time and five or six minutes of the time of the corrector. It has proved sufficiently comprehensive and accurate to be used successfully in placing new students in any one of four different classes and to serve as a gauge of their progress at the end of each semester's work.

14). Both these evils exist simultaneously, for instance, in questions which offer to the student a long list of possible answers only one of which is correct. Students themselves complain of the bewilderment produced by such questions; and it is evident that recognition of a correct answer is by no means as good a proof of knowledge as an ability to produce this correct answer without suggestion from the question itself. The following examples show these methods when applied, first, in the testing of grammar and, secondly, in testing vocabulary. The American Council French Test, not unmindful of Monsieur Jourdain, asks the student to identify the proper translation for "Our friend must leave at once" and suggests:

Notre ami faut partir tout de suite.. Il faut que notre ami part tout de suite.... Il faut que notre ami parte tout de suite.... Il faut notre ami partir tout de suite. Similarly, the Columbia Research Bureau, testing a knowledge of words, asks the student to identify the English word which best translates the French word given at the left and presents *à la queue leu leu* no less than a hundred lines like the following:

menton	1 Chinese	2 chin	3 dog	4 shine	5 give
dormir	1 door	2 sleep	3 give	4 shine	5 go away

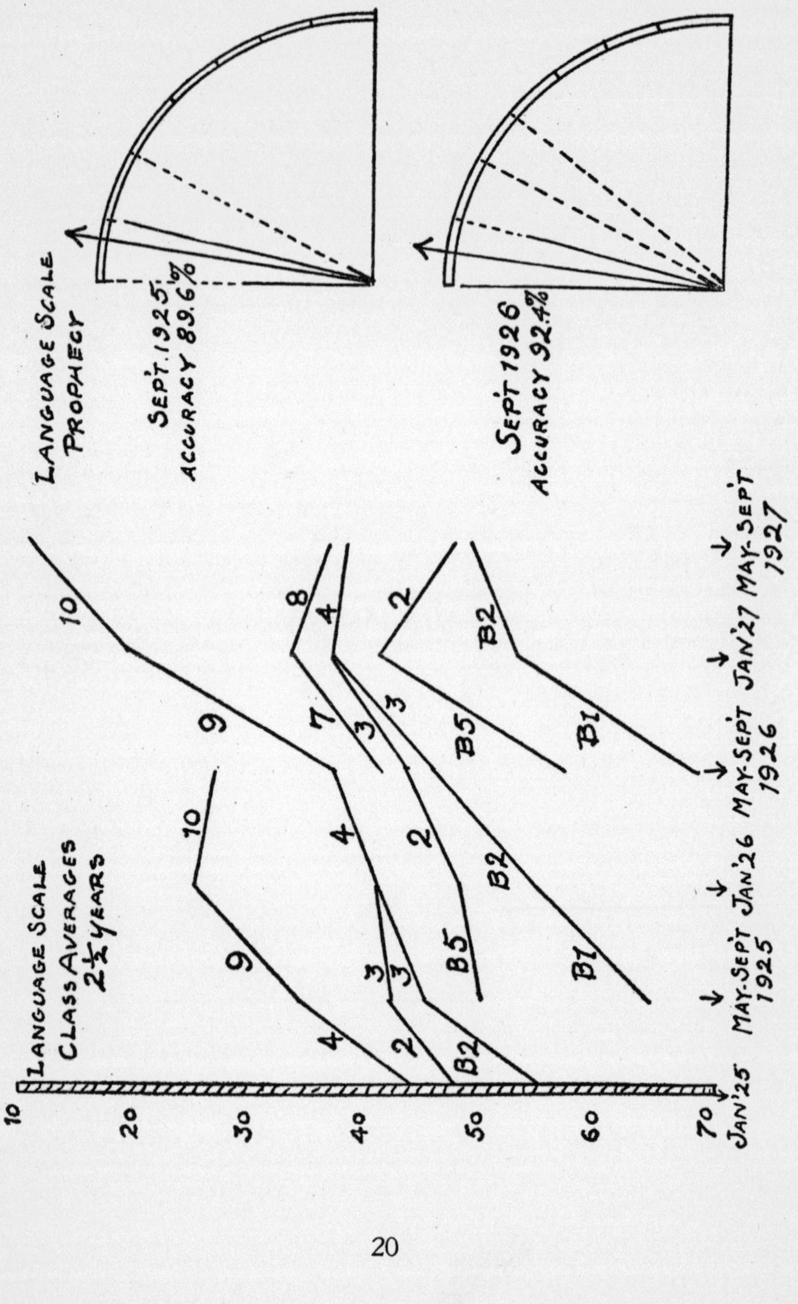
LANGUAGE SCALE
PROPHECY
SEPT. 1925
ACCURACY 89.6%
SEPT 1926
ACCURACY 92.4%
LANGUAGE SCALE
CLASS AVERAGES
2½ YEARS
10
20
30
40
50
60
70
JAN '25
MAY-SEPT 1925
JAN '26
MAY-SEPT 1926
JAN '27
MAY-SEPT 1927

Many teachers, and we may one day find ourselves among their number, may find that the way in which this Scale presents its material is of more lasting value than this material itself, especially, as we have already explained above, in its vocabulary sections. We therefore explain this method of presentation in some detail.

Two fundamental features characterize this method. The first of these consists in conditioning every point to be tested by means of its context in a sentence. Every difficulty from French into English is set in a French sentence. Thus, to test vocabulary, our questions read as follows:

> Work out, mentally, the meaning of the French passages; then write, on the numbered lines below them, a good English translation of the italicized words. Be sure the numbers at the left of the lines correspond with the numbers of the words you are translating.
>
> Puisque vous désirez voyager cet *été,*[1] vous devriez me *louer*[2] votre maison en me faisant *un prix d'ami.*[3] Que pensez-vous gagner à la laisser *inhabitée?*[4]

Every difficulty from English into French is not only set in an English sentence, but is also accompanied by partial French translation of that sentence. This feature eliminates the mental puzzle and reduces to a minimum variations in results which might otherwise arise from differences in the mental calibre of the students. In matters of vocabulary, it has two further advantages: it permits us to focus the attention of the student upon a particular meaning of the French word;[15] and may be extended to show the student's ability to handle French of different styles.

The second feature distinguishing our method of presentation is the use of several blank spaces *some of which alone* call for in-

15). One of the many questions to be carefully considered in carrying further the establishment of educational vocabulary lists arises from the great variety of meanings possessed by certain words. Is the dictionary form, after all, a proper basis for frequency counting? A student may well be expected, even in his first year of French, to understand the verb *tenir* in *Je tiens un crayon;* whereas a knowledge of its meaning in *Ces crayons tiennent tous dans cette boîte* is a far less elementary matter.

sertions. Although, in its origin, this is but an extension of the sentence-completion device, in reality it amounts to a very different method. The older device, using carets or bracketed blanks, warned the student of the number of insertions to be made and of the positions in which they should be put. Our arrangement does not do this. Moreover, one single set of directions is used, and one set only, in all questions requiring translation from English into French, whatever may be the nature of the difficulty to be tested. These directions read:

> Supply, in each French sentence below, the word or words necessary to make this sentence a complete translation of the English sentence given above it. (Strike out nothing.) Write the missing word or words at the right of the page, putting in front of them a number corresponding to the numbered space or spaces in which they belong. Correct numbers are as important as correct words. Examples:
>
> I am giving my sister my father's pen. — [2] à
> [1] je donne [2] ma sœur [3] la plume [4] père [5] — [4] de mon
> Whom were you talking to?
> [1] qui parliez-vous [2] — [3] à

In the first versions of this Scale, students made insertions directly in the blanks. Experimentation later proved that the use of numbers introduced no mental hazard. Its convenience from the corrector's point of view is obvious.

The advantages of this arrangement of additional blanks will be fully appreciated by the experienced teacher; for he realizes how important in French and how difficult for the American student are questions of omission and position. In addition to the facilities which it has in common with the older devices of carets and brackets,[16] it presents also others allowing us

16). Like these older devices, it can focus the attention of students as definitely as the examiners may require ([1] *il est content que la guerre* [2] *finie*), or it may test an ability to solve simultaneously several difficulties (There is nobody left in the street: [1] *il n'y a* [2] *dans la rue* [3]).

It is an essential condition for the proper correcting of this scale that it be corrected directly from the corrector's slip. Correctors pay no attention whatsoever to students' insertions other than those bearing the into test difficulties which these devices cannot test at all or can test only in a cumbersome and, in our opinion at least, less effective manner.[17] Among these difficulties are the following: the use of adjectives varying in sense according to their position, the position and the relative order of pronouns, the position of certain adverbs, the characteristic omission or insertion of connectives, articles and prepositions, and the general ability of the student to sense, without suggestion from special captions or other indications in the questions themselves, the necessity of applying rules or observing habits of the language unlike those of English.[18]

---

sertion number as given on the slip. (As a matter of fact, superfluous insertions have proved to be exceedingly rare). This Scale is a carefully balanced test, not a lesson in French composition. A student may, in a particular sentence, make mistakes which are not counted against him in that sentence; but his weakness is not ignored by the test as a whole. It is shown by other sentences given expressly to detect this weakness.

17). Of all grammatical points, none is more important or more characteristically French than the positions of two pronouns with one verb. (*Je me le donne, je le lui donne, je me donne à lui*). Yet the Columbia Research Bureau French Test (Form B) for High Schools and Colleges contains not a single question to test the student's knowledge of this point. The American Council Alpha French Test devotes to this matter a whole division including three separate questions; but finds it necessary to introduce it as follows:

Rewrite on the dotted lines the following sentences, substituting the proper personal pronouns for *all noun objects, direct and indirect.* For example:

J'écoute le professeur. *Je l'écoute.*

18). The use of bracketed blanks or carets forces the examiner either to abandon the complete isolation of the single difficulty, as in the test of the Columbia Research Bureau e. g. *Nous craignons qu'il* (ne vienne), or to put the student on his guard thus: *Nous craignons qu'il* (ne) *vienne.* A still stronger warning to the student is conveyed by a separate set of directions in the American Council Test which tests omission, insertion and choice (though solely for prepositions) in a division headed thus: Write on the following dotted line the proper *preposition,* if a preposition is needed. In case *none* is needed, put a *cross mark* on the dotted line.

Examples of insertion, position and word order:

We fear he will be late.
^{1} nous craignons qu'il ^{2} soit en retard ^{3}
She will buy a red (*rouge*) pencil.
^{1} elle achètera un ^{2} crayon ^{3}
They gave them (*les*) to me.
^{1} ils ^{2} me ^{3} ont donnés ^{4}

In the above questions, the corrector's slip bears, for each sentence respectively, the following entries: ^{2} *ne;* ^{3} *rouge;* ^{3} *les.*

In many cases the examiner will find it convenient to test a second difficulty also in each sentence. The incomplete French sentences, and correct insertions, might then read:

^{1} désirez-vous^{2} voir^{3}	Correct: 1 *qui,* 2 (*blank*)
^{1} nous^{2} qu'il^{3} soit en retard^{4}	Correct: 2 *craignons;* 3 *ne*
^{1} elle^{2} un^{3} crayon^{4}	Correct: 2 *achètera;* 4 *rouge*
^{1} ils^{2} me^{3} ont^{4}	Correct: 3 *les;* 4 *donné* (*e*)*s*

The material used as a basis of this Scale is divided in the proportions of 2 to 1 between accidence, syntax and characteristic idiom, on the one hand, and vocabulary and accidental idiom, on the other.

The first suggestions for questions on accidence, syntax and characteristic idiom were derived from class-room experience ranging from college preparatory teaching to the teaching of advanced college classes in writing and speaking French, classes to which were admitted only those students having successfully made their way through five or six years of study of the language. These suggestions were checked by an examination of the various divisions of the same material as it appears in the more complete grammars of France and our own country. From each of these divisions (conjunctives, partitives, negation, etc.) a number of points have been included in each edition of the Scale, a careful record being so kept that each succeeding edition may present an equal number of points, equally distributed both as to range of difficulty and variety of subject.

The material for questions of vocabulary and accidental or unrelated idiom is drawn primarily from the intuition of the teacher who has reviewed the most frequent needs and the most frequent mistakes of students and jogged his memory by means of a dictionary. It should be added, however, that the accuracy of this intuition has been checked up and its errors corrected at various times and by various means. Before constructing even the first edition of this Scale, certain vagaries of college entrance examinations were not forgotten; the power of prophecy of translation sections in certain old-line examinations were tested, and experiments were made, and still continue to be made, with word lists prepared by members of the French Department of Columbia College or by persons outside this department.[19]

This Scale is used for two purposes: to place new students in college classes suited to their accomplishments and to gauge periodically the progress of students already in our classes.

As a means of placement it permits us to separate in-coming students into seven divisions according to their prognosticated ability to carry unusually well, with average success, or poorly,

19). Thus, to cite but two of the simpler examples of this experimentation, it was found possible to draw up intuitively a list of 24 words, so arranged in three columns that the 8 words in each column should differentiate between the better and poorer students belonging respectively to each of three different classes: second year, third year and fourth year French. Furthermore when all 24 words were given to the students included in all three classes, it was found that the division into columns according to difficulty corresponded satisfactorily with the conditions of student knowledge. The average student knew 68% of the words in column one; 47% of those in column two; 28% of those in column three.

When the Henmon list appeared, a somewhat similar experiment was made. The singular assemblages of this list, to which we have already referred (*groschen* having the same frequency count as *rideau*) made it impossible to include in each column only words having the same frequency. We therefore made a choice of our own, observing however in a general way three main divisions. For the first column we chose words, not too easy, yet appearing only among the 900 having the highest frequencies: *pays* 167, *sourire* 81, *malgré* 84, *dos* 53, *habit* 46, *neige* 50, *affreux* 38, *digne* 36; in the second column only words having a frequency of 20 or 21: *piquer, constater, voie, frémir, outre, souffle, ménage, mépris;* in the third column, only words having the frequency 7: *congé, contrarier, entamer, peigner, tourbillon, avaler, pli, nœud.* The average student knew 87% of the words in column one; 47% of those in column two; 31.9% of those in column three. Total number of students: 399.

the work of college classes varying in difficulty. The accuracy of this prognostication, as computed by a comparison with the college grades received by these same students at the end of one semester's work, is shown in the accompanying drawings. In September 1925, it was 89.6%; in September 1926, 92.4%.[20]

At the end of each semester this Scale is given to all college French classes in which any attention whatsoever is paid directly to matters of language. In certain of these classes, the principal object of study is literature; in others, at least two-thirds of the time is devoted to reading and writing French. The Scale has permitted us to keep a check on these classes and to see to it that students studying literature should retrograde linguistically as little as possible and that those occupied with language should advance with satisfactory speed.

Charts such as that reproduced here, based upon the results furnished by the Scale, thus become records of our linguistic endeavor—its difficulties, its successes, its failures and the effect of its efforts at improvement.[21] It is evident, for instance, that the schoolboy material taken into our classes in September 1926 was inferior to that of September 1925; it is equally plain that, in consequence of this deterioration, we found it necessary in our teaching to stress language with unusual vigor during the following semester, September 1926 to January 1927. (As a matter of fact, we introduced a new feature into our teaching). The des-

20). The marks on the circumference of the quadrant represent the seven divisions. The arrow shows the degree of accuracy of the prognostication as a whole. In case of complete failure, it would lie horizontal; if every student had made, during the college semester, a record in complete agreement with the prophecy of the Scale, it would stand vertical. The heavy lines represent, by their length, the number of students; by their direction, the agreement or the extent of divisional deviation between the prophecy and the standing of the students at the end of the semester. Thus, in September 1926, out of 168 students tested, the prophecy was exact for 88 students, one division out for 69 students, two divisions out for 9, and three divisions out for 2.

21). Classes are half-yearly. The language Scale contains 100 possible mistakes. Points on the chart are determined vertically by the average number of mistakes made by each class; horizontally, by the date at which the Scale was given.

cent shown by French 4 and French 3 from January to May 1927 is due to an inopportune neglect of linguistic matters: French 4 was devoted to rapid reading in class and literary appreciation, and French 2 to outside reading and literary discussion. The chart reveals this mistake, especially in the case of the less advanced of these classes, French 2; we have now given up this latter course, offering the work of rapid outside reading and literary discussion only to more advanced students whose linguistic power is more firmly established. French 9 and 10 are advanced courses in writing and speaking French. The contrast between their records in 1925-1926 and 1926-1927 is explained by a very severe selection made in the latter year and resulting in the retention only of the most able students; many of the students rejected in this selection entered the new course French 7-8. Their limitations are evident: when, in French 8, they were taught by very much the same methods and by the same instructor as their abler brethren in French 10, they were not only incapable of advancing, but even fell back considerably.[22]

It is of course possible to make, from the data supplied by this Scale, equally instructive studies of a great number of kindred matters; the progress of an individual student, for instance, or of a particular group of students. Thus, desiring to see what advance had been made by a certain eighteen students over a period of one and a half years, we found the following record: September 1925, 66.05; January 1926, 50.8; May 1926, 47.0; January 1927, 42.1.

This record of eighteen identified students presents an interesting problem. Their total progress, 24 points, is satisfactory; but their half yearly advance is puzzling. If we compare this record with the record, as given by the chart, of the classes through which this group passed (B1, B2 and 3), we see that these students, starting 2 points below the average, were 4 points better than the average at the end of B1; they were, however, 1 point

22). It should be added that less frequent instruction undoubtedly had something to do with these results: French 7-8 met only twice a week; French 9-10, three times. One of the abler students, however, who for certain reasons entered 7-8 instead of 9-10, did make real progress during both semesters.

worse than the average at the end of B2 and had fallen 5 points behind at the end of 3. The causes of this initial spurt, followed by a gradual slowing up, must be looked for in conditions peculiar to these students and to our teaching. What are these conditions? How can we make the most of them? Such questions, raised by the use of our Language Scale, have helped us to a better understanding of our students and of ourselves.

Columbia University.

EN MARGE DES EXAMENS D'ENTRÉE
AU COLLÈGE

By O. T. Robert

The four examinations in French set by the College Entrance Examination Board were this year printed separately under clearly indicated titles. This obviated for the candidate the necessity of picking out what was intended for his use and permitted him to give his whole attention to the answering of the questions from the moment the examination began.

The examinations themselves differed in no essential respect from those of previous years. Apart from the translation into French which tests the candidates active knowledge of vocabulary and grammar, they remain in the main tests of the candidates' passive knowledge of written French, and of his memory of verb forms and of grammatical rules.

The free composition, (for which no small part of the vocabulary is provided in the instructions), is too short—125 and 150 words respectively for Cp3 and Cp4—to be considered a serious test of the candidates' ability to express himself in French. To deal with any of the subjects proposed in so few words, requires the concentration of expression of a great poet, or the use of a style reminiscent of a bargain sale list. It is the latter mode of expression which the candidates generally use.

Question C (Cp2) calling for the use of dates, numbers, expressions used in referring to places and the seasons, is to be highly commended. A question of the same type, but a little more difficult, in the more advanced examinations, would do much to discourage the abandonment of such all important matters after the first year or two. Students who have passed the Cp3 and Cp4 examinations are rarely capable of reading a date correctly and without hesitation, and not infrequently they show regrettable unfamiliarity with the correct use of the prepositions *dans, en,* or *à* before place names.

D1 (Cp4) was in our estimate rather cruelly hard for College *entrance* candidates. There could be no objection to any of the expressions if they had occurred in a prescribed text, even though *ne faire que de* is seldom met with nowadays. But taken, as they were, from the almost infinite number of French idiomatic expressions, they were exceedingly difficult, because the use of idiomatic expressions cannot be learned from lists, and there is little likelihood that just those expressions had been come across frequently enough in the reading, and had been sufficiently studied to have ceased to be impossibly difficult. We tested the question by submitting it to an advanced course composed of two graduate students and of six seniors who had spent a year in France and had done work there which their French professors had judged satisfactory. The average mark obtained was 3,7 out of 8, or 46% of the maximum. When questions are so difficult, the readers are obliged to be very lenient, with the result that the marks obtained cease to be a true measure of the students' attainments, for the weak students obtain marks almost as high as the strong.

The indications of what was to be done in D3 (Cp4) seemed to us rather awkwardly and not too clearly stated, and should, we think, have included a demand for the use of the words in sentences illustrating their meaning and their use. Knowledge of isolated forms when not accompanied by an exact knowledge of their meaning, and ability to use them in the kind of sentence in which they usually occur, is worth very little.

In Part 3 of Cp3 (which is also Part I of Cp4)—the question in which infinitives were to be replaced by verbal forms in certain moods and tenses—the preponderance of the subjunctive gave a very fair chance to the candidate who guessed that he was in presence of the usual question on the subjunctive, to get passing marks and even very good marks by doggedly putting subjunctives everywhere.[1] The test was therefore essentially one of the

1). The tenses called for were hinted at in a number of cases by indicating that an auxiliary verb was to be used, and, where a participial form was wanted, the candidate was told to use it. We feel that Cp3 and Cp4 candidates ought to be familiar enough with the syntax of the verb (including participial constructions) not to have to be prompted in this manner.

candidate's knowledge of grammatical forms. A similar paragraph in which infinitives were to be replaced by indicative, subjunctive, or participial forms *according to the meaning of the text,* would have made the question much more valuable.

On the other hand, question D2 (Cp2) was, in the estimate of the writer of these remarks, one of the very best. One would have been glad to see it increased to ten examples instead of five, with a heavy mark assigned to it, heavy enough to jeopardize the success of the candidate who failed to do it satisfactorily. It involved four points of syntax, laid stress on the use of tenses and not merely on their formation, did not hint (as was done in part III of Cp3) at what was to be done, nor permit a single good guess on the part of the candidate to get him through by a not necessarily intelligent application of rules; it involved some grammatical reasoning based on meanings, and gave to the candidate who had read his texts observingly and practiced imitating what he had read, an advantage over the one who had merely crammed for the examination. Had the first part of D been so set as to permit the candidate to show that he knew *how to use* the verbal forms asked for, as well as how to form them, the marks obtained for the whole of D would have been a reliable measure of the student's knowledge of syntax. Such a question would not have been out of place in the Cp3 or even in the Cp4 paper if one may judge by the amount of syntax still unknown to candidates who have obtained passing marks at those examinations.

The question on pronunciation remains utterly inadequate as a test of the candidates' pronunciation, and the proportion of marks assigned to it is too small to make it worth while for the teachers to spend much time on oral work. By the form in which the answers to this question were given, one could gauge whether or not the candidates had acquired habits of orderliness in setting out their work, but no conclusions could be drawn as to the manner in which they pronounced French.

How much more enlightening would be a transcription into phonetic script of any three or four lines of one of the passages set for translation, and what a stimulus to the teaching of pronunciation the expectation of such a question would be! The candidate would thereby be given an opportunity of indicating, by means of a few easily mastered signs, the pronunciation of the consonants and vowels of the selected passage, not merely in isolated words, but in word groups. He could, at the same time, indicate stress, quantity, elisions, *liaisons* and word groups, all of which are as much part of the pronunciation of a language as the opening or closing of vowels or the omission of consonants. What is more, the practice (so dulling to the intellect, so prolific of absurd inaccuracies, so deadly to the interest of the pupil') of learning word lists and rules in the attempt to prepare for this part of the examination, would soon be eliminated as utterly unprofitable.

One fails to understand why any examining board should hesitate to demand that candidates be familiar with the values of the International Phonetic Alphabet symbols. Objections to their use generally come from people who have never taken the trouble to learn them and who, more often than not, make use of phonetic systems of their own invention: systems which are without exception inferior to the International. The use of phonetic symbols for the teaching and testing of pronunciation has passed beyond the experimental stage, and its rejection seems as reactionary as would be the rejection of formulas in the teaching of Physics, or that of the staff in the teaching of Music.

Last year, in a similar article, the present writer expressed regret that no measures were taken by the Board to test the candidate's ability to understand spoken French. He repeats his expression of regret this year. Knowledge of a foreign modern language surely includes ability to understand it through the ear as well as through the eye, and ability to express oneself with the mouth as well as on paper. A knowledge of a foreign language which does not include ability to understand it when it is spoken is as incomplete as an American's knowledge of spoken English would be if, having been born deaf, he suddenly, through a miracle, acquired the power of hearing.

In insisting upon this, the writer is not particularly concerned with the student's mortification at being unable to converse when he happens to be abroad, nor is he particularly thrilled by the thought that our pupils might some day experience the triumph of astonishing some foreign waiter or their own intimate friends by the ease with which they order Virginia ham or ask for a clean glass. He is thinking rather of the incompleteness of a student's preparation for work in literature, if his ear and his mouth have not been trained to hear and to pronounce French in the manner of the authors he studies. There is more, we know, in French poetry than mere sounds, but sounds nevertheless play an important part in all French poetry as well as in much French prose, and the glory of Parnassus is witheld from the profane who massacre those sounds. Why does not the Board recognize, as other examining bodies have done both here and abroad, the importance of aural and of oral work, when serious writers on the question of modern language pedagogy are unanimous in the recommendation of such work? Even if an oral examination is impracticable because the candidates are so widely scattered, aural tests would not be impossible. And aural tests would necessitate oral preparation, and oral work would give time and opportunity for ten repetitions of a correct construction where only one is possible when all the work is done in writing; and students would thereby learn their vocabulary and its use, and acquire a vast store of intelligible grammatical examples and of idiomatic expressions purposefully used, faster and better than they now do. As matters stand at present, pupils who have been well trained are not given a full opportunity of proving to the examiners the superiority of their training over that of others.

With regard to the translation into English, we feel that the length of the selections, and the number of marks apportioned to that work, give to a merely passive knowledge of the language a value out of all proportion to the intelligence and the work required to attain it. In their present form, the examinations put a premuim upon extensive reading, with a view, no doubt, to encouraging the cultivating of a "reading knowledge" of French. This is done at the expense of any training in thoroughness and —as we shall show later,—at the cost of the pupils' English and of their active knowledge of French. It is true that theorists, who ought to know, have told us that Modern Languages are to be classed as "tool subjects",—an obiter dictum which, of course, brooks no reply, and which disposes once for all of any illusions which we may have entertained with regard to the educational value of our work. We exist solely to get pupils ready to read foreign works on Natural Science, History, or Sociology,—subjects which represent the Absolute in Education. *Pauvre de nous!* Two things stand out pretty clearly however: the first is that this estimate of the very relative usefulness of our work did not emanate from language specialists who had given earnest thought to the possibilities of their work; the second is that such an estimate is evidently the result of the common but regrettable confusion of a "reading knowledge" of a foreign language with a real knowledge of it.

The Board does not seem to endorse that estimate unreservedly since it examines in grammar, composition, and the meaning and use of idiomatic expressions. It is evident, however, that it is not whole—heartedly with those who regard modern French as a language to be read, written, understood, and spoken; and one suspects it of having affinities with those whose ideal is a "reading knowledge", else why should it recommend as desirable an amount of reading which crowds out any serious study of the texts read, and makes it necessary to teach grammar as a separate subject having little or no connection with the texts read?

It is so evident that extensive reading as practised in our schools is a hindrance to the formation of those habits of thoroughness of understanding and exactness of expression which characterize the scholar, that one hesitates to insist; and yet every year, after marking the C. E. E. B. papers one feels that it ought to be shouted on the housetops.

If in three short years hundreds of pages of French have to be gone through and done into English—in addition to the memorizing of an infinite number of grammatical rules and the writing of composition exercises (which by their nature necessarily lead to the committing of errors upon the correction of which much time has to be spent)—the close study of French texts, the observation of them, the use of them as models; in a word, the application of laboratory methods to the teaching of French, and the mental training gained by such work,—all that becomes impossible. Time fails also for the rendering of those texts into adequate and readable English and the result is what one sees illustrated in the majority of the translations sent in by the Board candidates.

We quote below some typical examples of the results obtained by an excessive amount of rapid oral translation. They are culled from the translations of the passages set in the Cp3 paper of last June. We have refrained from quoting the worst examples of sustained gibberish which showed that the candidate was mentally, as well as linguistically, unprepared for college.

A. Misuse of English vocabulary:

A meeting of the *most importance* (for *of the greatest importance*).

For *"Juliet had spent there years which had seemed to her all too short, and of which she cherished the memory although she had almost died there of a malignant fever"*, we found the following renderings.

Juliet spent there *at the most, short years,* which she *guarded the most dear* in her memory.

Juliet had spent there years which *were too short* and which she *garded* as her dearest *remembrance* although she *had died* there *from* a malignant fever.

.... although she had *failed to die* there of a malignant fever.

.... too short years which she *cherished to remember.*

.... which she *considered most dear to remember.*

.... the memory of which she cherished most dearly *since she had failed in dying* there of *an insidious* fever.

Juliet had stayed there *too many short years,* which she *guarded the dearest to remember although she had failed to die,* etc.

For "they were few in number" we found: they were a *small* number, or, they were *small* in number.

The life they were *doomed* (for destined) to *hold.*

It was necessary that (for "I had to") change my dress.

I *believed* (for "I thought") that you never failed... etc.

How charming she must have been in all the *burst* (for "bloom" or "glory") of her youth.

How charming she *ought to be* in all the *state* of her youth.

"Mr. Boissy, at any rate, understood me when I congratulated him" was rendered:

Well, Mr. Boissy *agreed* with me, *where* I questioned him.

We also found: Mr. Boissy *compromised* me (*even him*) when I begged for it. (We wish to give our word of honor that there was nothing in the text or context, to justify, or even to suggest, such a rendering.)

"By caring for their beauty or their voices" was rendered:

In drawing out their beauty or their *voice* (variant: *in following* their beauty, etc.)

B. Syntax.

Some of the above quotations, to which one may add:

Mr. Boissy *has told* me that when I *congratulated* him;

Mr. Boissy *understands* me when I *have congratulated* him;

Mr. Boissy *has understood* me, *he,* when I *offer* my congratulations;

..when I questioned him *of* it.

The young people of the boarding school, appeared to be happy in *an* extreme *by gentle life* (the rendering should have been: seemed to have enjoyed a very quiet and pleasant existence).

The expression "C'est qu'elle persiste à nier et à rougir" seems to have given the candidates a great deal of trouble. Comparatively few succeeded in finding an adequate readering. By far the commonest was: *It is that she persists...* and very few indeed had any idea of the construction to be used with "persists". We found countless examples of "persists *to deny";* we even found: "persists *to denying it"*.

C. Careless reading of the French text resulting in nonsense which was nevertheless cheerfully written down:

"des traces plus ineffaçables que *les nuits de veille"* was frequently rendered: *old nights,* and sometimes: *knights of old.*

"son journal dont le ton a plu à Chateaubriand" yielded: her diary the *tenure* (for *tenor* or *tone*) of which has *spread to* (quite frequently: *has rained at*) Chateaubriand.

"les *jeux* avec ses *compagnes*: *cheeks* with her *countries.*

It may be contended that the quotations under C betray as much ignorance of French as of English, but that cannot be said of the majority of those under A and B. The Readers were sometimes in doubt as to whether the text had really been understood, and, I think, more often than not gave the benefit of the doubt to the candidate, although the onus of the proof that the passage has been understood surely lies with the candidate who is told to use "clear and idiomatic English" in his translation. Students who have been trained to examine their texts closely and to translate them adequately do not make use of that hybrid language which is neither English nor French but a monstrous offspring begotten in the French class room by Hurry upon Slovenliness and nurtured on a mixed diet of English and French.

By rapid reading and slovenly translation (when I say *reading* c'est une manière de parler for there is no time to read aloud the French text, pupils are made to develop very rapidly what Harold Palmer calls bilingual consciousness—a state of greater or lesser incapacity to distinguish between what is English and what is French—and their already precarious hold upon the constructions and usages of the mother tongue is still further loosened. The time comes when the most glaring departures from accepted English forms of speech fail to shock them. If only, by going over hundreds of pages of French text, one succeeded in forming the pupils' French style, the loss of feeling for the mother tongue would still be a heavy price to pay, but one would have at least something in return, but in rushing through texts, the pupil gives his whole attention to making out their meaning; he has neither time nor inclination to study French modes of expression and to contrast them with the corresponding English ones. That suffices to explain why the French vocabulary and constructions of the candidates are as English in meaning, form, and usage as the English of their translations is French.

In France and in England, but especially in France, the study of ancient and of modern languages has for one of its objectives the learning of the mother-tongue. But in order to achieve that, one reads very slowly and observingly and one translates very carefully what is read. It is hardly an exaggeration to say that our young people are made to gulp down in one dose of homework preparation a page of text for every two or three lines of translation which a French boy has to do. And he would be a bold wag who suggested that the French boy works less than the American. But the French boy leaves school with a mental discipline which our young people have not, with a better, and also a more lasting, knowledge of the languages he has studied, and with a much better grasp of his mother-tongue.

Translation from French into English is, for the English speaking pupil, much more of an English than of a French exercise, and all such work, after being carefully prepared in the French class to insure a thorough understanding of the text, should be written out and then handed for correction to an English specialist, who would be quicker than any French teacher can be, to detect inadequate renderings, strained constructions and other traces of gallicisms in the work submitted. Some years ago, the writer of these remarks experimented in the manner indicated with an English colleague. The conditions in which the work was done resembled those which prevail in our High and Preparatory Schools today, insofar as literary English was more or less of a foreign language to the majority of the pupils. The results obtained fully justified the little trouble one was put to in organizing the work with a view to that collaboration. Other conditions were favorable to the experiment. The same group of boys who took French with one master took English with the other, and the English master was far too intelligent a man to imagine that when he was correcting a translation from the French he was necessarily doing the French master's work.

Is there a remedy to the present state of affairs? There would be if French Teachers and their Superintendents could be made to see that extensive reading, valuable though it may be to add to the general information of the pupils, is greatly overrated as a means of imparting an active knowledge of French, and that intensive reading has to be resorted to if one wishes to interest pupils in the study of a language as such, and to make them observant (i. e. intelligent) readers. Much could also be done by Examining Boards to encourage (or rather, let us say, not to discourage) teachers who wish to inculcate in their pupils habits of scholarly thoroughness. They might, for instance, make it clear that poor English is not excusable by the mere fact that it is used in French classes or in French examinations. They might also abstain from making any recommendation with regard to the amount of reading to be done, and so leave the teacher perfect freedom in the choice of the method which seems best adapted to his purpose.[1] Furthermore, one might cut down to not more than twenty-five per cent of the maximum, the mark assigned for translation into English, since the understanding of a written passage constitutes but one fourth of a full knowledge of the linguistic material used in that passage.

The remaining seventy-five per cent of the marks could then be assigned for proficiency in written, aural and oral French. The extent of the candidates' active vocabulary and their practical knowledge of grammar could be ascertained by a free composition of three or four times the importance of the one usually asked for; by a translation into French, or by any exercise which tested the candidates' understanding of the relation between meanings and grammatical forms. Ability to understand spoken French could be tested by the reproduction in English or in French of a passage read aloud by a competent person, and, if oral examinations are really out of the question, the candidates' pronunciation could be seriously and accurately gauged by the phonetic transcription of a short paragraph. A dictation would test ability to understand spoken French, knowledge of grammar, and power to reason to boot.

There would be some chance, under such conditions, of students receiving, before they came to college, a training in all the fundamentals of the French language: a minimum of fully possessed vocabulary and of thoroughly practised grammatical principles, as well as training of ear, eye, and mouth. Such a preparation would make corrective courses unnecessary (and that is where the time is lost), and would permit the students to start immediately on a study of French literature which could be thorough, penetrating, and intellectually honest.

Smith College.

1). The present recommendations of the Board compel teachers, often against their better judgment, to substitute rapid sight tranlation for the reading and serious study of texts.

THE FRENCH TEACHERS' FORUM

Resolved that students in our High Schools are not sufficiently advanced to read with profit the French classics of the seventeenth century such as Corneille, Racine and Molière.

Readers of **The French Review** *are invited to comment favorably or unfavorably upon the above resolution. The most interesting replies will be published in the next issues. Comments must be limited to* 200 *words; they must bear the name and address of the sender and be sent to* **The French Review Forum,** 306 *Hamilton Hall, Columbia University, New York City.*

WHY TEACH FRENCH?

By COLMAN DUDLEY FRANK

Why this investigation? What was the aim and purpose of it?

At a faculty meeting of the De Witt Clinton High School a few years ago, the principal (now a superintendent), always a thought-provoking and inspirational leader, turned suddenly to the Head of the Mathematics Department and said "Mr. A., why should Mathematics be taught in this High School? Justify yourself. Prove that you and your teachers of Mathematics have a right to your jobs."

The same question has often been asked for French. Why should French be taught in a city high school? The answers to this question are as various as the dominating qualities of the persons to whom it is put. Ask it of a conservative and he answers, "Because it always has been so." Ask it of a radical and he will reply, "Because the Socialists are a dominant party in French politics and have even succeeded in electing a socialist premier." One French teacher sees in it a job and a monthly pay-check; another sees in it an opportunity for creative culture. A teacher of science would reply: "No reason at all to teach languages; let the pupil take science. The language barriers that separate peoples will be melted away by the gases of the chemists". A distinguished Teachers' College professor has compiled statistics to show the harm French (and other modern languages) do in high schools by causing failures, with the ensuing discouragement and leaving school.

And so I decided to go directly to the students themselves to find out their own justification for the subject which they, of their own free will, had elected. And in order to get a judgment that was seasoned, ripened, and mature, I directed my inquiry to graduates who had been out in life some ten years or more.

The second purpose of this investigation, for it had a double purpose, was to find out, in case that French was justified as a high school subject, whether the course of study, the types of teachers, and the methods used at De Witt Clinton gave the pupils what was of most value to them. In other words, if they justified our being, did we justify their high hopes of us?

The questionnaire was purposely made as succinct and definite as possible, in order that the personal reaction of the individual would be as little in evidence as possible, and in order that the questionnaire might be of most practical benefit. Most of the questions can be answered by "yes" or "no", the type of question most appealing to the busy business and professional man, whose time is limited, and the type that is readiest of quick tabulation.

In order to get a fuller, more varied point of view, the questionnaire was submitted for revision to the Assistant Principal, to a Head of an Annex, and to the Chairman of a Science Department. Their suggestions are incorporated into the final form.

The questionnaire was sent out to some 400 graduates, but such is the migratory character of the New York population that 350 were returned marked "Not Found", "Moved", "Not there", "Address Unknown". It was discovered that neither the school records, the Department records, nor the Alumni Association were able to keep up with the moves made by its shifting graduates. Consulting the city directory gave little help. It was impossible to tell whether the Morris Cohen who as a boy of fourteen lived with his parents at 106 Goerck Street was the Morris Cohen now listed as "Fairy Dresses" at 239 West 35th Street or as "Choice Delicatessen" at 2297 Broadway. It is however indicative of the great interest this questionnaire evoked that no one who received it failed to answer it.

It should be here stated that De Witt Clinton is one of the largest high schools in the country, that it is a school exclusively for boys, that it gives an academic course, preparatory for college, that it counts an enrolment of from 6000 to 8000 boys, that the Department of French counts from 2500 to 3000 students, and that the school has its graduates in practically every college of the country.

While the questionnaire was answered by a total of only 50,

these 50 are a thoroughly representative cross-section of the student body. It is doubtful whether a larger number of answers could have given any better replies. These men were average students who won average marks, some attaining distinction in French, some failing from time to time. They have been out of their Clinton class-rooms from ten to sixteen years. The majority have been to college. They represent every profession and walk in life. Almost all are now typical "better" citizens of New York, tho one sent his reply from his home in California. Among them are to be found five teachers, seven doctors, nine lawyers, six dentists, eight business-men, two publishers, two realtors, one army officer, two editors, one band-leader, one financier, one accountant, two insurance brokers, one radio announcer, one hotel manager, one engineer. Included among them are the President of a well-known publishing house, the President of the Real Estate Board of New York, an Assistant District Attorney, an army officer, a band leader, the maker of a well-known brand of hosiery, and a celebrated radio announcer.

THE QUESTIONNAIRE

Question 1. *Of what value, if any, has French been to you?*

On the practical side, 39 found it of immediate value for college entrance, 19 in business, 35 in the practice of their professions, 34 in travel; on the more cultural side, 24 found it of value in improvement of their English, 35 in enhancing their enjoyment of reading (in English), 30 in the enjoyment of their leisure, 36 in their appreciation of literature, 6 found it of great help during the war, one as a liaison officer, and one "to get out of a very disagreable assignment." One of those Clinton service-men fought his war in a small town of France where he trained his mitrailleuse of French conversation on a certain lovely French maiden, conquered her, and convoyed her to this country as his wife. French is now the language of their New York home and children. One graduate found French of "social and restaurant" use. One writer, and only one, bravely confessed that he found French of no earthly use.

Question 2. *Would you have had just as much pleasure, satisfaction, success, had you had no French?*

9 confess frankly that they would have had just as much satisfaction out of life without French, 4 remain neutral on the subject, unable to measure the exact influence of French on their happiness, and the overwhelming majority of 37 vote emphatically for French as a factor in promoting their enjoyment of life.

Among the contributions of French to the fullness of life are "it broadened my scope of understanding and appreciation", "it permitted me to enjoy another civilization than that of the U. S.", "without French I could not enjoy English to the extent that I do now", "I would consider it a handicap not to have studied French", "for travel and the enjoyment of literature I have found the knowledge of French indispensable", "I enjoy reading French and find it valuable in reading scientific journals", "to know a language is to understand a people", "it opened up to me another source of history and philosophy", "it brought me into contact with a thing of beauty, the French language", "cultural advantages, music, plays, comedies", "a knowledge of French for me meant an appreciation of European (world) culture", "I find much enjoyment in reading French books in the original, Jean Christophe, Emile, Les Misérables, Le Petit Chose", "it has been a constant source of pleasure and satisfaction to me. I do not feel that every subject a boy takes should be chosen solely to contribute towards his business or professional success".

Question 3. *If you had it to do over again, would you now again decide to take French?*

The reason for this question was to see whether the demand for French was due to the World War.

To this question one man answered in the negative, one thought that he would "probably not", one "preferred German" and the other 47 voted overwhelmingly "yes". Some added phrases like "absolutely", "certainly", "most assuredly", "you bet, only four years instead of three", "yes, begin with French instead of wasting time on Latin".

Question 4. *If you took it again would you want:*

a) More or less practice in French conversation?
b) More or less reading of modern newspaper French?
c) More or less reading of classic drama?
d) More or less reading of modern plays?
e) More or less scientific or commercial French?
f) More or less formal grammar?
g) More or less formal composition?
h) More or less information (in English) about France, the country and the French people?
i) Other suggestions.

The replies to this question brought out the defects of the Clinton French course as seen by the graduates. 49 declared enthusiastically for *more* practice in French conversation, only one wanted less talking, 42 voted for *more* reading of modern newspaper French, and 5 wanted less of it. The classics are evidently in disfavor, for only 5 wanted *more* reading of classic drama while 16 demanded less of it. On the contrary 30 expressed a desire for *more* reading of modern plays, 9 for less of it. 29 seems to be quite a considerable contigent favoring *more* reading of scientific or commercial French although as many as 5 voted against it. The advocates of formal grammar are dealt a knockout blow by the vote of 34 against it with only 10 in favor. On the subject of formal composition, opinion is fairly evenly divided, 25 favoring *more* of it, versus 23 favoring less of it. 30 want *more* and 10 *less* information (in English) about the French people and their country. On all these subjects there are four or five neutrals.

Under the head of "other suggestions" one proposal was for "as much French atmosphere as possible", another wanted French "made more alive", another proposed "a different teacher for each period", another suggested "smaller classes, more oral work", one man proposed "more history of France in French, more government and politics", one graduate wanted "classes conducted entirely in French", and another desired "more memory work, selected French poetry and songs of the people". The reigning tendency of the suggestions is toward informal conversation and away from formal grammar. One man (now a High School teacher of History) pertinently asks, "Don't people read and speak English (and French too), without a knowledge of grammar?" And a prominent business-man testifies that "at two years of age my baby spent two months in France. At the end of that time she understood practically everything said to her in French. Certainly more than a high school student. She knows no grammar, no gender, no verbs—but her ear had attained the necessary."

Question 5. *For college entrance should the requirement be* 0, 1, 2, 3, 4, *or more years of French?*

The great majority favored three years, the present usual requirement in colleges of the better grade; one would drop French entirely as a college requirement, and one expressed the idea that "the college has no right to dictate the high school curriculum". The most surprising fact in regard to this question is the relatively large number of 10 who favor raising the college requirement to four years.

Question 6.

a) *Should French be dropped as a High School subject?*
b) *If yes, what subject should replace it?*
c) *Or should more French be required in High School?*

No one proposed dropping French as a high school subject. 47 would retain it. If eliminated, Spanish, Italian or German were suggested as substitutes. 15 favored a requirement of more high school French, 26 stood pat, and 7 were opposed to adding more French. The idea of reserving French as a college subject seemed to be foreign to the minds of these graduates.

Question 7. *What changes would you suggest in the way French was taught at Clinton?*

a) In methods employed.
b) In aim and scope.
c) In types of teachers.
d) Otherwise.

Here the number that were satisfied and offered no changes were 13 for methods, 9 in the matter of aims and scope, 14 as far as types of teachers were concerned, and 11 otherwise. On the fence, perfectly neutral, were 14 for methods used, 16 for aim and scope, 13 for types of teachers, and 6 otherwise. Voting affirmatively in favor of changes were 9 in methods, 8 for the types of teachers employed, and 2 otherwise. As far as the suggested changes in **Methods** were concerned most of them, though stated differently, all tended toward more use of conversation and direct method in the class-room, less formalism, French as the language of the class-room, more aural and oral training.

When it came to suggested changes in **Aim and scope,** there proved to be less unanimity. Some suggestions offered were "broaden the scope", "more conversation", "more current literature", "train ear more", "teach more how to understand French literature", "improve everyday French, leaving classic and modern drama to the college", "make it more practical, for practical, everyday use", "teach French and forget the exams at the end of the term".

In the important matter of **types of teachers,** opinion was most divided. One man proposed to "eliminate the foreign-born Frenchman: he is not temperamentally adapted to teach boys of high school age". Over against this comes the proposal "As many as possible of French nativity". One man writes "get the older and more cultured type, preferably not Frenchmen"; another replies "I prefer more teachers of Latin or French origin". The great majority ask for men of personality, ability, spirit, pep, enthusiasm, sympathy, and express a preference for native Americans who have been in France.

Noteworthy is it that while there are many women teachers in the school and many of them enjoy great and deserved popularity, no one asked for women teachers.

Question No. 8. *In what was your high school preparation in French inadequate?*

a) In pronunciation; b) in reading; c) in translation; d) in speaking; e) otherwise.

Those who expressed themselves as perfectly content with what they had received in pronunciation numbered 8, in reading 24, in translation 23, in speaking 6, and in every other way 15. The neutrals, who had neither commendation nor complaint to offer, numbered 14 for pronunciation, 15 for reading, 16 for translation, 6 for speaking, and 22 otherwise. But there were some who did not hesitate to say that they did find the Clinton course in French inadequate, and indeed, 9 in the attention given to pronunciation, 10 in the time devoted to reading, 6 in the way translation was treated, 38 in the little attention paid to speaking, and 7 registered other inadequacies.

In analyzing these complaints, it seemed to be the belief that only a certain two teachers ever emphasized correct pronunciation in class and ever corrected gross errors. In the matter of reading, there was a general appeal for more reading aloud in the vernacular without bothering about accurate translation. Speaking seemed to have been generally neglected. One man found it "markedly deficient"; another said, "there was hardly any in the class"; a third remembered that when there was practice in conversation in the class it was "too grammatical, not colloquial"; a fourth contributed the thot-provoking aphorism, "bad grammar well-pronounced is better than good grammar badly pronounced".

The comments on "other complaints" were most illuminating. They well merit repetition here. "Classes too large". "Not opportunity enough to hear French". "I found it difficult to grasp the full meaning of what French people said to me when I was in France in 1917-1918". "I got no *feel* for the language, its idioms were neglected". "I studied French for six years in school and college, and when I arrived in France did not know the word for baggage-car, which word I needed most". "The emphasis on colloquial or conversational French should not be directed to make the boy say 'this is the book of my uncle's sister', but rather 'yes, the poor girl has been laid up with tonsilitis and her employer held back her pay. She thinks if she can't collect it, she'll have to go to some cheap summer hotel next summer instead of making that trip to Alaska, etc.' In other words, colloquial conversation should include the words that we use in everyday intercourse. In the class-room I never learned the French words for coat-hanger, wash-cloth, or cork-screw. Complete ignorance of French is a terrible handicap for anyone with more than a ten-year old mind".

Question No. 9. *Is there, after graduation, enough use of French, both pleasurable and practical, to justify the expenditure of the public funds?*

40 thotful men answered this question categorically "yes"; 5 just as definitely "no", and 4 tempered their answers with provisos. One proviso said, "if it is justifiable to spend public moneys on the teaching of any foreign languages in America, then it is justifiable for French". Another, a writer of considerable prominence, thinks "for intellectuals, the expense is certainly justified; for the office-man it is justifiable enough; for the average citizen of the tabloid-reading type, no. It depends on the cultural leanings of the individual". Still another public man believes "if fewer were allowed French and each got more out of it, the expense would be more justified. As it is at present, there is much waste on pupils for whom the subject means nothing".

CONCLUSIONS

1. The French Department of the DeWitt Clinton High School has always enjoyed great popularity, and for many years has been the leading language department in point of numbers, yet no less can be said of practically every French Department in all large city schools. French at DeWitt Clinton probably occupies no different position locally than French at any other city school. Therefore it should give all French teachers a sense of satisfaction to know that their work is appreciated. In spite of the carping criticisms of superiors who do not see beyond the cold columns of statistics and who cry aloud against freshman mortality, yet when evaluated by our own customers, both our wares and our business methods are found worthwhile. When 47 out of 50 experienced, (for the most part) college-trained, representative men of mature minds find that French has been of practi-

cal use to them, that it has enriched their lives, and that, in the light of their present knowledge, had they to choose their course over again, they would again choose French, every French teacher who reads these words can join with the French teachers of Clinton in taking heart, in renewing his faith, in entering his classroom with head up, convinced that his work is really worth while.

2. The community, too, can gain a measure of contentment from the mature decision of 40 thinking men to the effect that in providing French instruction in high schools, public funds are not being wasted.

3. When it comes to the criticism of the Clinton course of study in French, the strictures may well be applicable to the other large city high schools, for Clinton follows the same city and state syllabi as do they. Clinton gives State Regents' examinations and college entrance examinations, and her French pupils have a high measure of success on both. She prepares her pupils for college, and Columbia, City College, N. Y. U., Princeton, Cornell, give glad greeting to her graduates in French.

The glaring criticism of the lack of conversational practice was more deserved ten years ago than now. Changes in syllabus requirements, readjustment of the work, better equipped teachers, the advent of the Direct and Yersin methods, emphasis on phonetics, new-type oral and aural tests, dictations, changes in State Regents' and College Board examinations, all have tended to swing a heavier emphasis on conversational practice in the classroom. Some of these gentlemen, were they to enter their old French classrooms today, would be hard put to it to understand the fluent flow of the vernacular. Yet it is also no doubt true that the old bugaboo of formal grammatical drill would still jump up to greet them.

The ripened ideas of these wise practical men must give us pause, and the thought suggests itself, and is here thrown out for the thotful consideration of all who care to ponder over it, whether it would not be a wise and worthwile proposition to build a course of study that for three terms would emphasize the spoken word, that would be devoted to learning simple phrases, that would give oral and aural training, every opportunity to hear talk and to talk, that would give a minimum of grammar, practically no paradigms, few grammar rules, that would offer plenty of memory work, jingles, poems, fables, songs, stories, anecdotes, dialogues, where there would be much discussion of the habits and life of the French people, where little scenes would be learned and stories dramatized in the classroom. In such a class the teacher must have a fairly free hand, and competition between teachers would be encouraged. There would be no written "homework" in the sense of verb-paradigms and sentences to test the agreement of the past participle. A pupil would not learn "je vais, tu vas, il va, etc." but would learn that when he wants to express the idea "I am going" he must say, "je vais".

Can you see the pupils rushing joyously to such a class? Is there anything more pathetic than to see the bubbling enthusiasm of our entering youngsters the first few days in French eager to learn to say the simple phrases of everyday life in that new strange tongue, gradually stifled, asphyxiated and killed under a nauseous gas of rules, paradigms and tense-forms? Can you see the joy on the face and feel the happiness in the heart of the teacher of a class of the kind suggested? No more precious home hours wasted on a fruitless search for misplaced accents and incorrect endings. Even the principals and superintendents would welcome such a course, for freshman mortality wuld wane. Everyone would pass.

"And after that?" you ask? The answer comes that in the fourth term you differentiate your course. On the basis of your conversational background, and with a large vocabulary already known and used, you develop your course in grammar. All the rules for the position of words in a sentence, for the agreement of past participles, for the use of the subjunctive, all the other basic rules of elementary grammar can be taught in one frankly and defiinitely grammatical term. Under this new plan, the third year would then be devoted to copious reading, with emphasis on aural comprehension and oral discussion, together with a fuller treatment of syntax and irregular verbs in conscious preparation for Regents' and College Board examinations, for we can not forget that the most immediate and present need of a language for every pupil is to get into college. The fourth year would emphasize appreciation of literature and history. No doubt our fourth year classes would be far larger in size, for the interest of the pupils would be keener.

If this questionnaire is to be anything more than a waste of effort and of many people's valuable time, it must bear fruit in a change of our methods of presentation of our subject. In Dr. Tildsley's remarkably inspiring article on "Better Teaching in the High Schools" (Bulletin of High Points, for October 1927) the French teachers run a poor sixth in point of popularity in a popularity contest conducted in English classes. Who knows? Perhaps a course in French developed along the lines suggested here may put all French teachers first in the van of "vitalized", "super-maximum", "creative" teachers.

De Witt Clinton High School
New York City.

FRENCH CLASS-TEXTS

PUBLISHED IN THE UNITED STATES [1]

By ALEXANDER GREEN

A FEW years ago the Modern Language Association of America did me the honor of inviting me to deliver a paper on the publication of books that have a scholarly rather than a mercantile value, books that are both the products of serious research and the tools essential for the prosecution of adequate graduate studies. The present invitation extended to me to discuss the status of French texts published to serve lower grades of instruction, I consider not only an equal honor, of which I am keenly sensible, but a more difficult and, at the same time, more important task; for it touches the very fundamentals of our foreign language study and the welfare of a much larger number of students, for whom the crucial distinction between solid gain and utter waste often revolves about the right selection of the textbooks to be studied.

From time to time we hear a good deal about the wastes and losses that confront us in the field of Modern Language instruction. Sometimes they are blamed on the personality of the teachers; at other times on one of the half dozen methods of instruction current in our schools. More often the charge is leveled at the choice of books, and, by inference, at the publishers who issue these books. And this charge is most frequently raised in connection with the reading texts that form the center of language instruction after the student has more or less mastered the fundamentals of the foreign language.

We learn from the mass of contradictory statements that the publishers turn out reading texts in a haphazard and unscientific fashion; that they do not publish a sufficient number of texts to

1). Paper read on April 21, 1927 before the *Cinquième Congrès de Langue et Littérature Française.*

suit the aims, let us say, of French teaching; that, on the other hand, they are overcrowding the field with a multiplicity of reading texts and doing their best to create a confusion of minds. These charges would be serious matters if they were actually true and did not, rather, disclose an interesting bit of telltale information about such teachers as have contracted the habit of criticism. For my part, with your indulgence, I feel as did an old doctor when he was called in to examine a *nouveau-riche* patient who had, as is so often the case, overeaten. "Doctor," asked the patient, his voice trembling with apprehension, "Doctor, do you think that the trouble is in the appendix?" "The appendix?... The appendix?" replied the doctor. "No, I don't think so; it is more likely to be in the table of contents."

There is indeed an apparent congestion in the field of reading texts. Their number is steadily on the increase; but who shall say that this is an unwholesome condition? Twenty-seven years ago *The Report of the Committee of Twelve* laid down the principle that the preferences of teachers with respect to reading texts and the needs of the classes are so divergent that the only safe course is to leave a large latitude of choice. These words are as apt to-day as when first enunciated, the only difference being that teachers to-day have an immeasurably larger latitude of choice in regard to both the quantity and the quality of the texts published. More and better editions of texts then available have since been issued. Richer veins of literature have since been tapped. Broader fields have been laid under contribution. The table to which the *nouveau-riche* is invited is more ample; the fare is more abundant and more tempting. There is an embarrassment of good things to meet the eye. We are in the midst of the seven years of plenty. Should we then revert to the seven lean years just because an apparent embarrassment of dishes gives some of our less cautious, less discriminating friends a case of acute indigestion?

Let us now alight on the other horn of our dilemna? It is stated by some that not enough texts are published to satisfy the aims of French instruction. A word as to these aims: Aside from the goodly number of our students whose ultimate object in the French course is to pass the examinations that, like accusing milestones, mark the various stages of their discomfort, we find a larger body of boys and girls who wish to attain a speaking or writing knowledge of French. But their number is limited and, for them, the special social situation in which the proper motivation and the proper types of assimilative experience are present, is as good as lacking. There thus remains the reading knowledge as an outstanding objective, and, for the large majority of our students, this is all that is essential, or even desirable. For them this knowledge is the special contribution of the French course to a general education. By means of this knowledge they will be able to read books, periodicals, and newspapers, and enjoy the treasures of French literature. By means of their reading course in school, they will secure a more immediate contact with the life and thoughts and manners of the French people... In all this I am rehearsing platitudes. What I now wish to add to the discussion in the way of concrete deduction, is the warning that the justness of the appreciation thus to be gained, the scope of the cultural values thus to be acquired will vary in direct proportion to the kind and character of the books that are held up before our students as models wherefrom to learn and means whereby to pass judgment.

Now, what is the actual state of affairs? I may be in error as to exact historical details, but I imagine that when the Committee of Twelve sat down to formulate their recommendations, they chose the shortest road and the most pragmatic manner in dealing with the reading text situation. There was a definite number of annotated texts at hand in 1900, and the Committee cut the Gordian knot by classifying these texts according to their respective degrees of difficulty, and thus produced the celebrated Reading List. In the opinion of many qualified men, this procedure was the wisest that could have been followed at that time. Objections were raised in some quarters to specific details of the Reading List; in other places to the Reading List itself, if it were to be rigidly applied. But on the whole the List, in those formative years of Modern Language instruction, was highly beneficial. A certain amount of authority simply had to be exercised, in order to consolidate the gains of previous years, place the Modern Languages on a more solid basis, and provide for a policy of future development. The astounding thing however is that our Modern Language instruction, in the matter of text selection, has never since been quite able to emancipate itself from the well-intentioned dictates of the Committee of Twelve.

Some of the books they recommended have fallen by the wayside. Their very mention sounds strange to us today. Who ever uses nowadays Foa's *Contes biographiques* and *Le petit Robinson de Paris?* Thierry's *Récits des Temps mérovingiens,* or *Mignet's* historical writings? On the other hand, we meet with titles of books that should evoke responsive memories,—About's *Le Roi des Montagnes,* Bruno's *Le Tour de la France,* Daudet's short stories and novels, Erckmann-Chatrian's novels, Labiche and Martin's *Le Voyage de M. Perrichon* and *La Poudre aux Yeux,* Malot's *Sans Famille,* Mairet's *La Tâche du Petit Pierre,* Mérimée's *Colomba,* the novels of Jules Verne, Augier and Sandeau's *Le Gendre de M. Poirier,* La Brète's *Mon Oncle et mon Curé,* Loti's *Pêcheur d'Islande,* Dumas' novels, Hugo's *La Chute,* and others. You may say that Hugo never wrote a work by the title of *La Chute.* That merely goes to prove that an extract from *Les Misérables* under that title was in existence in 1900 and that the Committee promptly impressed it into its service. Which again corroborates in a small way my suspicion of how the Reading List actually originated.

Ten years after, another Committee of the Modern Language Association met to revise this List. There had been an increase of new available texts in the meantime. The List was not, however, revised, but rather increased; and the Committee ended its labors by setting up another but shorter Reading List for each year of secondary instruction. We now see such additional titles emerging as Compayré's *Yvan Gall,* Laboulaye's *Contes Bleus,* Halévy's *L'Abbé Constantin,* Lavisse's *Histoire de France,* Bazin's *Les Oberlé* and Hugo's *Les Misérables.* This took place in 1910. The fact that the reading recommendations of the College Entrance Board for the present year still correspond with this seventeen-year-old List, practically title by title and grade by grade, is a striking testimony to the attitude of reverence which we, Modern Language teachers, observe toward the canons of tradition.

Lest one be inclined to feel that this characterization of teachers is too sweeping, let me add without delay that there is a suspicious similarity between the recommendations of the College Entrance Board and what we might call the "semi-classics" most widely read in our secondary grades of instruction. Perhaps there is even a causal relation. The statistical material collected by Professor John Van Horne from the year 1913 on bears ample witness to this interesting circumstance. In the High Schools, it is in the second, and still more in the third years, that literary texts are the rule. The ones most widely read stand out so clearly that they hardly need comment. The following ten literary texts in the order given seem to lead in the second year: *Perrichon, La Poudre aux Yeux, Colomba, Sans Famille, L'Abbé Constantin,* Lavisse's *Histoire de France,* Bruno's *Le Tour de la France, Madame Thérèse,* Daudet's short stories, Mairet's *La Tâche du Petit Pierre.* In the third year, the leaders are *Colomba,* Daudet's short stories, *Les Oberlé, Pêcheur d'Islande, Mlle de la Seiglière, Perrichon, Les Misérables, La Mare au Diable, Tartarin de Tarascon* and *La Tulipe Noire.* As for the fourth year, we have *Pêcheur d'Islande, Mlle de la Seiglière, Eugénie Grandet, Le Cid, Le Bourgeois Gentilhomme, Les Misérables, Hernani, Quatre-Vingt-Treize, Cyrano,* and *Colomba.* On the whole, classical texts are poorly represented even in fourth-year French.

In Colleges, where the first two years may safely be taken as constituting secondary school instruction, we likewise have *Perrichon* as a perennial first favorite. Then follow, in the first year, such texts as Lavisse's *Histoire de France, L'Abbé Constantin, Madame Thérèse, La Poudre aux Yeux,* Daudet's short stories, *La Mare au Diable, La Chute,* and *Mon Oncle et mon Curé.*

In the second year the preponderance seems to be given to *Les Oberlé,* Maupassant's short stories, *Tartarin de Tarascon, La Mare au Diable, Colomba, Le Gendre de M. Poirier, Le Livre de mon Ami, Les Misérables, Eugénie Grandet, Le Roi des Montagnes.*

Admittedly such an enumeration is an unfair gauge of the practices that are prevalent in the entire field. It touches only upon the high spots. Many scores of additional titles are being read thruout the United States. But the fact remains that French instruction in this country, taken as a whole, has had its traditional favorites. It is also clear that, while these favorites may vary among themselves in relative degrees of popularity, taken as a class they never fail to recur year after year and to outweigh the other aspirants to similar high placement. What is the result? These titles receive an undue share of attention from publishers and are perhaps in turn urged by them, all the more strongly, as safe, sane, and staple articles of consumption. *Perrichon, Colomba* and the short stories of Daudet and Maupassant have up to date, each of them no less than ten separate editions, and the *Abbé, Sans Famille,* and *La Poudre aux Yeux* trail behind them at a not very respectful distance. And since publishers, as I have so often said, are neither philanthropists nor the beneficiaries of philanthropic gifts, this race to supply the best possible editions of the staple books continues and, as far as I can see, will continue ad infinitum, unless in time it will simply reduce itself to absurdity.

Now I, for one, am not of those who see only an unmitigated blight in the reading of these semi-classical texts of older vintage. Many of the books I have mentioned have a good *raison d'être,* namely that they appeal to the peculiar intelligence and imagination of the High School pupil and the Junior College student. Say what you will, there is real human interest in *L'Abbé Constantin;* rapid action (so well appreciated by our movie-struck youth) in Jules Verne's extravagant plots; adventure aplenty in any book of Dumas; humor in a Daudet story, and outright fun in the theater of Labiche. And every once in a while some one tells me of his amazement that many boys still enjoy the novels of Erckmann-Chatrian, tedious though they may be for us more adult readers. Perhaps if a census were taken recording the views of the students with regard to the texts that they have read, the results would in many respects correspond to the relative popularity of these books as shown both by the preferences of teachers and the returns of publishers' sales. It may be, after all, that we have reached the golden medium in regard to one criterion at least, namely catching to interest and captivating the benevolence of our students. Who can say?

But, some of you will interpose, is this the sum total of our attitude,—to furnish our boys with books that treat of adventure, strength, magnanimity, and our girls with romantic, chivalrous, and even sentimental novels and plays? Are we to sit back self-satisfied once we have succeeded in leading our youth to the fount and in prevailing upon them to drink from it? Was it not before a former session of this same Congress—or perhaps it was in his book on the United States—that Professor Lanson expressed his astonishment that *Monte-Cristo* should be thought of as an ideal book to read? "Qu'est-ce que *Monte-Cristo* peut avoir d'éducatif?" I believe he asked, and this leads us to a matter of greater importance than those heretofore touched upon.

That literature is a cultural force of the first magnitude is recognized by leaders in education. A reading course in French, if its purpose is not to be merely linguistic, should be such as to result in a reasonably rich fund of informative values. I mean not mere scraps or skeletons of information, but well-rounded and well-coordinated ideas concerning France and the French; in short, a body of knowledge that may form an adequate apperceptive mass, a beacon of light that may guide the student's literary path, illuminate his thoughts, clarify his judgment long after he has left the school world behind him. Measured by such standards, the literary texts most widely used in our schools and colleges are found sadly wanting. They contain, indeed, allusions and suggestions of an informative character, but these are merely incidental occurrences and serve at most as the pegs upon which the editor or the teacher is obliged to hang his more or less desultory explanations, if the book is to register to any extent as a means of interpreting French civilization to the student. And what is perhaps still more reprehensible, in being rushed thru a vertical course from *Sans Famille* to *M. Perrichon* or the *Cid,* and lacking a good opportunity to extend his notions along a horizontal surface, the student ends by becoming filled with a false idea of modern France and an innocent suspicion that the extinct manners and discarded standards which he has read about can be met with on any of the Paris boulevards.

It will need a wide investigation to ascertain whether or not, and in what manner, a choice of titles different from those now most widely read could in some way remedy the situation. I submit, however, that the experiment is worth the trial, and that the texts more directly concerned with modern and contemporary France—and this, after all, remains our chief emphasis in the secondary grades—have now reached such a figure that the material necessary for a trial is conveniently at hand. We have made big strides since the days of the Committee of Twelve. Look into the catalogs of the publishers and you will find,—to mention only a few—novels by Barrès, Bordeaux, Theuriet, Guillaumin, Pérochon; plays by Brieux, Becque, Hervieu, de Curel, de Flers and Caillavet; representative short stories by Bourget, Coppée, Anatole France, Anatole Le Braz, Richepin, Bergerat, Boylesve, Pierre Mille, and Barbusse. Two of the leading publishers of modern language texts in this country have even launched special series of contemporary French texts, thus evidencing their interest in things as they should or might be, and that despite the fact that Professor Van Horne's tabulations, to which reference has been made before, assign very low ratings to the popularity of contemporary works in the High Schools and in the Junior Colleges.

Now if we could only get away from the principle of so much time-to-be-spent and ground-to-be-covered, which seems to hold the secondary grades under its spell, and devote some earnest thought to the combination of cultural and literary values, we should be doing our students and the Modern Language cause in general a signal service. The College Entrance Board, in its English section, has stolen a march on us in that its specifications now include such features as the modern novel, modern short stories, contemporary verse, modern plays, and prose writings on matters of current interest. While we cannot and should not hope, because of the self-evident differences in aims and environments, to attain the high ideals that are possible in the English field, we can at least borrow the idea and modify it to suit our purposes and possibilities. Why not combine the best of the older with the best of the newer books, those that have literary excellence and definite cultural values, and in recommending them for reading, arrange the titles not only in accordance with degrees of difficulty but, and this is more essential, in accordance with the degrees of the cultural potentiality that is in them? If we followed some such orientation; if we established new focal points around which we could assemble suitable teaching material—such high point as historical and geographical knowledge, French life and manners, French thought and achievements,—and if we modified this material at regular intervals to take into account the changes that go on about us, then Modern Language teaching would not be charged with haphazard purposes and uncertain aims. The very stories of Daudet, Maupassant, Vigny, and Mérimée that are now read at random in unevenly apportioned collections would have a new meaning and a lasting message if they were reassembled, let us say, around the idea of historical information. I am sure that I am interpreting the views of the publishers who specialize in the Modern Language field, when I venture to say that they would welcome such a new dispensation as a distinct relief from the more or less hazy practice according to which teachers offer and publishers issue texts on grounds, it would seem, of individual preference, and without the feeling that such books would find a clear-cut place in Modern Language instruction or would be used by the generality of Modern Language teachers.

The path ahead of us will by no means be as clear at first as we might desire. There will be some who will question whether the choice of texts that touch more explicitly upon French civilization would be preferable to those now most widely read. There will be the difficulty of finding and agreeing upon suitable reading material, particularly in the modern field, that would lend itself to such grouping as I have mentioned. We shall also have to distinguish between the books of the hour and the books of all time, to borrow a phrase from Ruskin. We shall continually have to face the fact that French writers, at all times able raconteurs and dramatists, do not write with an eye to availability in American schools. We shall, too, for some time have with us the inertia of teachers who cling to the texts and the viewpoints that have been recommended by our elders. But, happily, not all of us are like the fabled German professor of Roman jurisprudence who, on the occasion of his twenty-fifth jubilee, was at last persuaded by his well-wishers to stop repeating the jokes which he had carefully written out at regular intervals on the margin of his lecture book. Regretfully he struck the blue pencil across these hoary anecdotes and ascended the platform to deliver his next lecture. He began to read the Roman law, read on with due dignity, then all of a sudden, paused, stroked his beard in a reminiscent way and solemnly announced: "At this point, gentlemen, in former years, I was in the habit of reading the following anecdote..." My hopes for the future are bright and optimistic,—provided only that we carry out to its logical results the implication contained in that ever-true French proverb, *Autre temps, autre mœurs,* Other days, other ways.

New York City.

VARIA

By J. F. Mason

Professor Camillo von Klenze has written a *Preliminary Bulletin* for the American Association of Teachers of German. The following quotations suggest the purpose of the American Association of Teachers of German and the spirit which has actuated its founders.

"But as the editor of Hispania has well pointed out (Vol. X, p. 189), no teacher can owe allegiance to more than one language and the teaching of any language can be improved by nothing so much as by every teacher's concentrating on the language of his or her predilection." The aim of the Association is stated as follows: "To spread the knowledge of German in this country by increasing the efficiency of the teaching of German." "Not only have important new theories arisen in the pedagogy of language but the new conditions in Germany make a review of our textbooks imperative."

The Metropolitan Chapter has appointed committees to report on questions vital to teachers of German. "One of these committees brought in a report showing the increasing importance of German to the modern American business man. The report of another committee made us acquainted with the activities of Americans of German descent in New York and vicinity and with the activities of Deutche Vereine in schools and Colleges. Still another committee is preparing an elaborate report on the treatment of music in connection with the teaching of German."

This programme of the American Association of Teachers of German should be suggestive to the other language associations.

In *Spanish, its Value and Place in American Education, a Symposium of Authoritative Opinion,* the Committee on Information of the American Association of Teachers of Spanish has brought together a large number of very interesting facts and opinions regarding the study of Spanish. Mr. W. M. Barlow, the Chairman of the committee which has had charge of the pamphlet, states in the preface that its purpose and nature are expository rather than controversial and that the Association of Teachers of Spanish asks only equality of opportunity and equality of status. After an excellent résumé of the value and influence of Spanish Literature by Professor de Onis, there follow a number of succinct and well presented articles on such subjects as Real and Potential Spanish America, Character of the Spanish Race, Fine Arts in Spain, Spanish America as a Factor in World Civilization. Many points are proved by well chosen quotations. No teacher of Spanish should be without this pamphlet which is distributed by the Office of the Secretary-Treasurer of the Association, Stanford University, California.

What the American Association of Teachers of Spanish has done for Spanish in this case should be followed by the other language associations, in order that by combined effort we may demonstrate to those educators who would put the study of modern foreign languages in the category of "études-outils" that there are definite and real objectives in the study of these languages.

The recent numbers of *Italica* contain much material of interest to teachers of Italian and teachers of modern foreign languages in general. In the May number (Vol. IV, No. 2) E. H. Wilkins writes on Books on Italian Art, while in the following number of August, G. B. Weston gives an extended list of Books on Italian Music. Following the example of *Italica* it is hoped that the *French Review* may be able to give its readers similar articles on French art and French music.

* * *

In *Hispania* (Vol. X, No. 4) L. A. Wilkins meets, in his article entitled the Chapters of the American Association of Teachers of Spanish, with some very pertinent arguments, the objections of B. Q. Morgan, editor of *The Modern Language Journal,* to the formation of the separate associations for the teachers of modern foreign languages. In the same article Mr. Wilkins calls attention to some of the difficulties encountered in keeping up the interests in some of the chapters of the A. A. T. S. All teachers of modern foreign languages should recognize the necessity of becoming a member of one of the various associations and especially young teachers who are looking forward to advancement should remember that one of the best indications of a progressive teacher is his or her activity in a professional organization such as the A. A. T. S., the A. A. T. F. or the other language associations.

* * *

The University of the State of New York has ordered a revision of the Syllabus for modern foreign languages for the secondary schools. The committee under the Chairmanship of Dr. William R. Price, State Inspector of Modern Languages, has already met for a preliminary consideration of the revision. The present Syllabus, which has been in existence for a considerable number of years, requires much change in order to bring it abreast of the recent developments in the field of modern foreign language teaching. Any programme of study should, of course, be revised with great frequency. As J. H. Newlon says in the foreword to the *Course of Study Monograph,* devoted to French, which is published by the Board of Education of Denver, Colorado, "Curriculum revision must be a continuous process. It is too much to expect that any course of study, no matter with what pains and expert guidance it may be constructed, can embody all that has been learned about the subject-matter and method in its field. The best course that can be constructed will, then, be imperfect, and as long as society is changing, and as long as the science of education is developing, adjustments and improvements will have to be made. The process of curriculum making is exceedingly complex and tedious. The requirement of time is far greater than has been generally supposed even by the profession". The Denver French syllabus is one of the most elaborate and comprehensive in America.

The Modern Foreign Language Study has published with Mac Millan two works which show results of some investigations carried on by the Study. In the *New York Experiments with the New Type Modern Language Tests,* B. D. Wood has given us an exhaustive study of the new-type test and endeavors to prove by a great amount of statistical material and numerous charts the superiority of these tests over those formerly used. The author makes some illuminating remarks concerning the teaching of modern foreign languages and every progressive teacher should read the work attentively. It is not, however, easy reading but the teacher of to-day should recognize that the art of teaching must, to a certain extent, be controlled by the science of examining. As Mr. Wood says: "However, teachers of the foreign languages are coming to recognize the importance of recent educational research for their work and are familiarizing themselves in ever-increasing numbers with the terminology which the use of statistical methods involves. To those readers who do not readily comprehend the more intricate discussions of correlations, probable errors, deviations, and the like, the following reports offer nevertheless in non-technical language a wealth of significant detail on a subject of paramount importance for the organization of modern language teaching."

In the second volume entitled *A Laboratory Study of the Reading of Modern Foreign Languages,* G. T. Buswell reaches some conclusions which will interest all teachers: "Judging from the maturity of a student's fundamental reading habits which result from two years of study of French, there is no notable difference between students who begin the study of the language in high school and students who begin at the college level. On the same basis of judgment, children who begin the language in the elementary grades fall very much below the level of maturity of the high-school and college students at the end of two years...... The method of teaching a foreign language has a striking effect upon the reading habits of students. The maturity in reading which results from two years of study is decidedly greater with students taught by a direct method than with students taught by an indirect translation method... During equal periods of time, approximately equal degrees of maturity are reached in the study of French, German, and Spanish when these languages are taught by similar methods and under similar conditions."

* * *

Since the reading of a language is generally conceded to be one of the more important objectives for its study, all teachers should read Bulletin, 1927, No. 16 of the Bureau of Education (United States Government Printing Office, Washington, 1927), in which M. V. O'Shea under the title of *The Reading of Modern Foreign Languages* studies the extent to which those who have pursued French, German, or Spanish in high school or in college or in both read these languages after graduation. While this report should be carefully examined, one should hesitate to draw hasty conclusions from the statistics. Mr. O'Shea makes the following point: "The very large proportion of our correspondents who say that they have read no material, either in the original or in translation, in any foreign language since graduation from high school or college is somewhat depressing, unless there are other benefits than reading that may be derived from the pursuit of a foreign language."

The author goes on to state that many other subjects in the curriculum present similiar difficulties when the question of definite achievement arises: "Suppose 20.000 persons who had pursued algebra, geometry, psychology, ancient history, principles of education, physics, or rhetoric should be asked to testify as to whether they had made use of any one or of all of these branches since graduation from high school or college." Mr. O'Shea makes some interesting recommendations which teachers would do well to consider. "The first principle that teachers of foreign languages should take account of is that reading and grammatical diagnosis are psychologically contrasted and antagonistic processes. Reading may be called—using popular terms—a synthetic mental process, while grammatical diagnosis is an analytical process."

* * *

Teachers who are carrying on research work or are publishing school texts will welcome the announcement that the Bibliothèque Nationale of Paris has established an "Office de documentation bibliographique" for the use of all such research workers as may be prevented from pursuing their investigations in Paris. Communications should be addressed to Madame S. Dupuy, Bibliothèque Nationale, Paris.

Cornell University, Ithaca, N. Y.

BOOK REVIEW

BOUDDHA VIVANT

Ce livre a pu décevoir ceux des admirateurs d'*Ouvert la Nuit* et de l'*Europe Galante,* qui n'aiment pas la perspective d'un Morand sociologue ou moraliste, et qui voudraient s'amuser encore à ces jeux modernes qu'il a inventés et déjà laissés à ses imitateurs.

L'auteur de *Bouddha Vivant* est le même que celui de l'*Europe Galante;* seulement, comme les aviateurs, dans cet été de 1927, il a remporté une nouvelle victoire sur le temps et l'espace.

Parti des bars et des cinémas, il s'était fait le conquérant de l'Europe; aujourd'hui, il fait en un livre le tour du monde avec le prince Jâli, fils du roi de Karastra, royaume situé entre le Siam et la Birmanie.

Bouddha Vivant déroule la fresque où se peignent: l'Asie, Londres, Paris, New-York, San Francisco et de nouveau l'Asie. Tous ces tableaux sont excellents: l'Asie est magique dans son luxe simple, primitif; dans le mystère de ses longues forêts que tranche la Bugatti du Prince. L'Angleterre, c'est celle un peu attendue des brumes, des taudis, de la faim et de la prostitution; et aussi celle des universités et des clubs religieux. New-York est d'une somptuosité et d'un luxe formidables, avec son profil saisissant, le port, Park Avenue où passent "les merveilleuses serrées dans leurs peaux de panthère". Dans toutes ces exécutions, Morand se sert du style le plus souple, le plus rapide. En rapidité et en vivacité il dépasse la perception même.

Ce tour du monde, qui procure à Paul Morand l'occasion de peintures très vives tour à tour amères ou amusantes, rappellerait l'usage que firent Montesquieu et Voltaire des visites d'Orientaux en Occident. Ce n'est pas là pourtant tout le mérite du livre.

J'en vois la beauté dans le mystère du conflit de races dont l'âme de Jâli est l'écho et qui s'exaspère chez tous les peuples où

1) Paul Morand, *Bouddha Vivant,* Grasset, Paris, 1927.

il passe. En Angleterre, la mort de Renaud d'Ecouen dont le prince avait fait son chauffeur en Asie et qui avait été sa première attirance vers l'âme occidentale, est un des endroits les plus beaux du livre. Renaud meurt devant un "Jâli en bronze, doré par la lampe, qui ne parle plus." Ce seul ami européen du prince supplie maintenant la nurse: "Faites que je reste seul, nurse... éloignez cette figure noire... ne le laissez plus rentrer, ce n'est pas mon ami. Il n'inquiète pas, il rassure, il endort... L'équateur... on étouffe..." Et devant cette agonie, Jâli vient de comprendre: "qu'un blanc, même supérieur, n'est jamais supérieur à la vie, puisqu'il croit en elle."

Chacun des pays, chacune des villes vers où se dirige le Bouddha moderne est un nouvel espoir et une nouvelle déception; nulle part il ne sera compris, nulle part sa foi ne sera la foi des Occidentaux. A New-York, où il est allé retrouver la jeune Américaine qui l'avait aimé à Paris et qui a repris dans son pays les sentiments de sa race, c'est son dernier espoir qui tombe, et Jâli part pour San Francisco où il va traîner sa misère dans les bas quartiers.

Quelques pages plus loin, nous le retrouvons au centre d'une cérémonie éblouissante. Le roi Indra est mort et Jâli monte sur le trône. La fresque se termine sur les tableaux du commencement et c'est la conclusion du livre que cette intelligence asiatique qui partout avait jugé et compris l'Occident doit se fermer à lui et vivre des traditions de ces ancêtres.

RENE TAUPIN

BIBLIOGRAPHY

SCHOOL TEXTS

ADIE, C. J. M., *The essentials of French Syntax,* Text pp. 1-54; Index, pp. 55-56. Oxford University Press, 1927. Price, $0.40.

ALANIC, Mathilde, *Le Maître du Moulin-Blanc.* Edited by C. W. Bell. Introduction, pp. 7-8; Text, pp. 9-160; Notes, pp. 161-183; Exercises, pp. 184-189; Vocabulary, pp. 190-248. D. C. Heath and Co., 1927. Price, $1.00.

ARMSTRONG, E. C., *Syntax of the French Verb,* Revised Edition, Holt and Co., 1927.

BASSETT, M. E. *La Carte de France,* a book on French geography to be used also as a composition book. Holt, 1927. Price, $1.68.

BAZIN, René. *Madame Corentine.* Edited with Introduction, Notes, Exercises, and Vocabulary. Alfred Knopf, 1927.

BRENNER, Clarence D. and GOODYEAR, Nolan A. *Eighteenth Century French Plays.* Introduction, pp. vii-xix. Texts, 15 plays, each with a brief biographical introduction, pp. 1-561. The Century Co., 1927. Price, $4.25.

BRIEUX, Eugène. *La Française.* Comédie en trois actes. Edited by Simone de la Souchère Deléry and Gladys Anne Renshaw. Introduction, pp. v-xi; Text, pp. 3-102; Notes, pp. 103-112; Exercises, pp. 113-118; Vocabulary, pp. 119-150. The Century Company, 1927. Price, $1.00.

CHARVET, Louise. *Glanes de France.* En Automne. Edited with Exercises and Vocabulary. Ginn and Co.

CHATEAUBRIAND, François-René De. *Sélections.* Introduction and Notes, by Georges Roger. Oxford Press.

ERCKMANN-CHATRIAN. *Madame Thérèse.* Introduction by George W. Rollins, pp. vi; Text, pp. 1-189; Notes, pp. 191-211; Exercises by Noëlia Dubrule, pp. 213-220; Vocabulary by the same, pp. 221-289. Ginn and Co., 1927. Price, $0.80.

FAYETTE, Madame de la. *La Princesse de Clèves.* Edited by Maurice Baudin. Notice, pp. v-x; Text, pp. 3-224; Notes, pp. 225-243. Oxford Press, 1927. Price, $1.15.

FISHER, Max and ALEX. *Des Histoires drôles pour la jeunesse.* Edited by Gino A. Ratti. Alfred Knopf, 1927. Price, $1.50.

FRANCE, Anatole. *Le Livre de mon ami.* Edited by B. F. Boyson. Contemporary French Series. Oxford Press, 1927.

HOLZWARTH AND PRICE. Intermediate French. D. C. Heath and Co., 1927, 401 pages.

HUGO, Victor. *Les Misérables.* Edited by Flora Campbell. Introduction, pp. vii-ix; Text, pp. 3-184; Notes, pp. 185-202; Exercices, pp. 203-240; Vocabulary, pp. 241-315. D. C. Heath and Co., 1927. Price, $0.88.

LABICHE et MARTIN. *Le Voyage de Monsieur Perrichon.* Edited by Léopold Cardon. Scribners Sons, 1927. Price, $0.80.

LAZARE, Jules. *Lectures Faciles.* Leçons de Choses, pp. 1-18; Anecdotes et Historiettes, pp. 19-51; Exercises de Mémoire, pp. 52-61; Questions and Exercises, pp. 63-80; Vocabulary, pp. 81-108. Ginn and Co., 1927. Price, $0.56.

LICHTENBERGER, André. *Contes de Minnie.* Edited by J. G. Anderson. With a Vocabulary. Oxford Junior French Series. Oxford Press, 1927. Price, $0.45.

LA ROCHEFOUCAULD. *Maximes.* Edited by Robert L. Cru. Introduction, pp. v-xxxi; Text, pp. 1-136; Notes, pp. 139-155. Oxford University Press, 1927. Price, $1.00.

LUCAS, St. John. *A Book of French Verse.* New and enlarged edition. Introductory Notes, pp. 1-27; Texts, pp. 29-269; Explanatory Notes, pp. 271-296; Indexes, pp. 297-302. Oxford Press, 1927.

MALET. *Histoire de France.* Edited by Paul Rice Doolin. Doubleday Page and Co., 1927.

MARGUERITE, Paul. *Gens qui Passent. Nine Tales.* Chosen and edited with Introduction, Notes and Glossary by F.. C. Green. Oxford Contemporary French Series. Oxford Press, 1927. Price, $0.50.

MÉRIMÉE, Prosper. *Colomba.* Edited by O. T. Robert, xviii-350 pages. D. C. Heath and Co., 1927. Price, $0.92.

MÉRIMÉE, Prosper. *Le Carrosse du Saint Sacrement* and **Henri GHÉON,** *La Farce de pendu dépendu.* Edited by Hélène Harvitt. Editor's Note, p. v.; Introduction, pp. ix-x; Bibliography, pp. xi-xii; Text, pp. 1-124; Biographical Note, pp. 125-128; Bibliography, p. 129; Text, pp. 132-193; Notes, pp. 195-216; Vocabulary, pp. 217-277. Oxford French Series, Oxford Press, 1927. Price, $1.35.

MOLIÈRE. *Le Misanthrope.* Edited by T. E. Oliver. With an Introduction, Notes and Vocabulary. Holt and Co., 1927. Price, $1.20.

POTTER, H. A. *Dix Contes Modernes.* Text, pp. 1-72; Notes, pp. 73-80; English Paraphrases, pp. 81-96; Vocabulary, pp. 97-136. Ginn and Co., 1927. Price, $0.60.

ROMAINS, Jules. *Knock.* Edited by Albert D. Menut and Dwight Ingersoll Chapman. 150 pages. Introductiono, Notes, Vocabulary. The Century Company, 1927. Price, $0.90.

SIXTEENTH CENTURY FRENCH ANTHOLOGY. Edited by Stephen H. Bush and Charles E. Poung. D. C. Heath and Co., 1927, 157 pages.

VAN ROOSBROECK, Gustave Léopold. *An Anthology of Modern French Poetry.* Alfred Knopf and Co., 1927.

PERIODICALS

LANCASTER, H. C. *The Origin of the Lyric Monologue in French Classical Tragedy.* Publ. Mod. Lang. Assoc. Vol. XLIII, No. 3, Sept., 1927, pp. 782-787.

VIGNERON, Robert. *Explication de textes* and its adaptation to the teaching of modern languages. Mod. Lang. Journal, Vol. XII, No. 1, Oct. 1927, pp. 19-35.

GENERAL WORKS

CHURCHMAN, Philip H., and YOUNG, Charles E. *French Literature in Outline.* 300 pp. Century Company, 1927.

HARVARD TESTS IN FRENCH VOCABULARY, Form A. Ginn and Co., 1927.

KASTNER, L. E. *French Poets of the Twentieth Century.* Dent and Co., 1927.

SCHWARTZ, H. Stanley. *Dumas Fils, Dramatist.* New York University Press, 1927.

SHANKS, LEWIS PIAGET, *Flaubert's Youth.* Johns Hopkins Press, 1927.

STEWART, HERBERT LESLIE. *France the Parisian.* Dodd Mead and Co., 1927.

FOREIGN BOOKS

ANTHOLOGIE DU XVIe SIÈCLE FRANÇAIS, par Jean Plattard. Nelson, 1927.

BALLY, Charles. *Le langage et la vie.* Le langage et la vie. Linguistique générale et stylistique. Mécanisme de l'expressivité linguistique. Langage transmis et langage acquis. L'enseignement de la langue maternelle et la formation de l'esprit. Payot, 1926, 237 pages.

BRUNEAU, Charles. *Manuel de phonétique.* Berger-Levrault. Price, 6 fr. 20.

BRUNOT, Ferdinand. *Histoire de la langue française,* Vol IX. Librairie Armand Colin, 1927.

HISTOIRE DE LA NATION FRANÇAISE. Edited by Gabriel Hanotaux. Vol. X.

HISTOIRE ÉCONOMIQUE ET FINANCIÈRE, by Germain Martin. Plon, 1927.

LANSON, Gustave. *Esquisse d'une histoire de la tragédie française.* Nouvelle édition revue et corrigée. Champion, 1927. Price, 15 francs.

MARTINON, Ph. *Comment on parle en français.* Larousse, 1927, 600 pages.

LES PROVINCES DE FRANCE ILLUSTRÉES ET LEURS DIVISIONS DÉPARTEMENTALES. Album de 48 pages en 4 couleurs, illustrées par J.-P. Pinchon. Blondel La Rougery, 7, rue Saint-Lazare, Paris, 19927. L'album cartonné, dos toile, 18 francs.

SIEGFRIED, André. *Les Etats-Unis d'aujourd'hui.* 362 pages. Colin 1927.

TARDIEU, André. *Devant l'obstacle.* Emile-Paul, 1927.

WELTER. *La France d'aujourd'hui.* Payot, 1927.

Hélène HARVITT.

THE LIBRARIAN'S CORNER

The librarian of the A. A. T. F., Professor A. L. Cru, will answer in each issue of **The French Review** *a certain number of questions from members of the Association desiring information about text books, methods and teaching material. Questions should bear the name and address of the sender and be sent to* ***The Librarian of the A. A. T. F.,*** Room 204, *Teachers College, Columbia University, New York City.*

J. A. F. S. Two Paris publishers specialize in printing excellent modern maps: A. Hatier, 8, Rue d'Assas, and Armand Colin, 103, Boulevard Saint-Michel, Paris. For your 3rd and 4th year class in High School, I recommend the following maps:

1. France politique; 2. France physique; 3. France agriculture et industrie; 4. Plan de Paris (or environs de Paris); 5. France chemins de fer; 6. Europe politique.

The maps from A. Colin are on heavy cardboard and may be obtained from the Columbia University Bookstore for $2.50 each. The maps from Hatier are either on cardboard (same price), or on paper. These paper maps may be procured for $1.00 each (plus postage) from the French Dept. Teachers College, Columbia.

All these maps are in several colors, clear, and up to date.

A. A. T. F. NEWS

The French Review *will be glad to print items of news concerning the activities of the various chapters of the Association.* ***These items should be sent to The Business Manager.***

METROPOLITAN CHAPTER, N. Y. C.,

Dec. 10, 1927, 10:30 A. M. at Hunter College.

PROGRAM

1. *Good will address* . . . . M. Gaston Tisné,
   President of the Alliance Française of N. Y.
2. *Significant trends in modern language teaching.*
   Prof. Robert H. Fife,
   Chairman of the American Committee of the Modern Language Study.
3. *Dramatic reading* . . . . Mme Jeanne Roulet-Pavey.

All members and their friends are cordially invited to attend.

13.50 per ~~M~~

PRINTED IN U. S. A.

FRENCH PRINTING & PUBLISHING CO
149 WEST 24TH STREET, NEW YOR

Vol. I JANUARY, 1928 No. 2

THE FRENCH REVIEW

Devoted to the Interests of Teachers of French

Published by the
American Association of Teachers of French

Vol. I JANUARY, 1928 No. 2

CONTENTS

TRENDS IN MODERN LANGUAGE TEACHING, *Robert Herndon Fife* 5
ITEMS FROM FRANCE, *Harry Kurz* 18
PRESENT STATUS OF THE JUNIOR YEAR ABROAD, *Walter Hullihen* 25
THE REAL PURPOSE OF PHONETIC TRANSCRIPTION, *Philip H. Churchman* 38
FRENCH ART IN NEW YORK, *Hélène Harvitt* 52
FRENCH TEACHER'S FORUM 54
VARIA 59
BOOK REVIEWS 65
BIBLIOGRAPHY 68
RECENT TEXTS 71
THE LIBRARIAN'S CORNER 81
A. A. T. F. NEWS, ... 85
THE AMERICAN ASSOCIATION OF TEACHERS OF FRENCH 86

The *French Review* is the official journal of the American Association of Teachers of French and is published four times during the year, November, January, March, May.

Office of Publication, George Washington High School, Audubon Avenue and 192nd Street, New York City.

Application made for second-class mailing privilege.

The annual dues of the American Association of Teachers of French, including subscription to the *French Review,* are $2.50. Single copies. $.50 Applications for membership should be addressed to E. A. Méras, the Secretary of the Association, Adelphi College, Brooklyn, New York.

Communications to the editors, manuscripts, etc., should be addressed to the Editor of the *French Review,* Cornell University, Ithaca, N. Y.

All correspondence concerning advertising should be forwarded to Edward O. Perry, Business Manager of the *French Review,* George Washington High School, 192nd St., New York City.

Kindly notify the Circulation Manager of any change in address.

All books, texts, publications which may interest the teacher of French will receive mention in the bibliography or critical comment, if a copy is sent to a member of the editorial staff. Literary and scholarly works should be forwarded to A. G. H. Spiers, Columbia University, New York City, while texts and other publications should be sent to Dr. Hélène Harvitt, 1309 Carroll Street, Brooklyn, N. Y.

Exchange of the *French Review* with other journals may be arranged by addressing the Editor of the *French Review,* Ithaca, N. Y.

American Association of Teachers of French

THE FRENCH REVIEW

EDITORIAL BOARD

THE

FRENCH REVIEW

VOL. I JANUARY, 1928 No. 2

TRENDS IN MODERN LANGUAGE TEACHING[1]

By ROBERT HERNDON FIFE

The present situation as regards the teaching of the modern languages, whether viewed locally, regionally or nationally, is in the melting pot. The great enthusiasm which blazed up for the study of French ten years ago, when every soldier wanted at least a few phrases for use "over there" and all the army camps sought volunteer teachers of the language, burned itself out very quickly. The net result of the World War has been for many Americans a disillusionment with European affairs and a violent reaction against any relationship with them:

What's Hecuba to him, or he to Hecuba,
That he should weep for her?

This has led to a certain reaction against the study of the European languages, especially in the North Central States, where German was once strong and where well trained teachers of French and Spanish are difficult to obtain.

It cannot be overlooked of course that there has been a great gain quantitatively in French studies throughout the secondary schools and colleges. Particularly in the North Central States and West Central States the language has invaded many sections

(1) Paper read by the Chairman of the Committee on Direction and Control of the Modern Foreign Language Study on Dec. 10, 1927, at Hunter College, before the Metropolitan Chapter of the American Association of Teachers of French.

which before the war rarely heard a French word spoken in the schools. In Cleveland, where today Professor de Sauzé has a highly organized system of French instruction that expands through all the secondary schools and is topped by a summer session for French teachers, twenty-five years ago French did not appear on the program of a single public high school. At that time students came into the Western Reserve University who, though American born, had been taught all of their school subjects in German,—geography, history and arithmetic, algebra and geometry! Spanish has not been the only profiter and profiteer from the German collapse. French also has filtered in everywhere, so that now 53% of all the modern language pupils in the country study French.

Nevertheless, the situation has not adjusted itself since the World War to the advantage of the modern languages as a group. While both Spanish and French have penetrated into many places left vacant by the German collapse, great areas of the country where German was once freely taught now lie relatively barren of modern language study. Here Latin holds the field alone. It is difficult for us here on the Eastern seabord, where the modern languages are offered on almost every school program, to realize the hold which Latin retains on the secondary schools of the country at large. The claim made by the committee of the Classical Investigation three years ago that Latin pupils exceeded the enrollments in all other foreign languages combined has been confirmed by the statistical researches of the Modern Foreign Language Study. There were, to be sure, in 1925, in the 10.887 public secondary schools tabulated by the Study, 649,496 students in the modern foreign languages, as compared with 611,680 in Latin, but this tabulation was based on reports from only 71.5% of the schools in the continental United States. The balance are for the most part smaller schools in smaller communities and these have a relatively higher percentage of Latin pupils.[2] As is well

[2] The total number of public schools reporting enrollment facts for 1925 was 13,371. Of these 2,533 reported no foreign language; 4,544 reported Latin only; and 355 or 1.83 per cent, returned schedules which were usable for the general totals, but contained defects that made a detailed tabulation impossible. For a part of the unreported schools, 2,740, totals were secured

known, the modern languages tend to be an urban subject and a subject for the larger schools, while the ratio of Latin enrollment to the total school enrollment declines as we pass from the smaller to the larger institutions and with certain modifications, as we pass from the rural communities up through the cities of increasing sizes. This is true from a national standpoint, although there are important regional modifications. In the areas where the modern languages are most extensively studied,—New England, where French is in the ascendant, and the Southwest and California, where Spanish rules,—these languages invade even the smallest schools and show a ratio to the total school enrollment that is as large in the small community as in the larger community. In the great inland areas, however, where language interest is weak, whatever modern language instruction there is, belongs prevailingly to the large schools and the large cities.

A lively interest in modern language study in this country, like international interests in general, is mainly an affair of the Northeast and the Southwest. If we pass in review the states from East to West, we find French a factor of great importance on the school programs of New England, where the enrollment includes nearly 36% of all pupils in the schools, and of the Middle Atlantic States, where it includes 22%. In these districts Spanish is relatively much less important, with about one-fifth of the French figures in New England and a fraction over one-half of these figures in the Middle Atlantic States.[3] In the Southern States French falls to 14% of the school population, Spanish

---

from the 1922 canvass by the Bureau of Education. The schools which did not report and for which no documentary figures could be obtained numbered 3,233. By a method of comparison with other schools of the same class, and similarly located, for which figures were known, it has been possible to make estimates of national totals which cannot be far wrong. These statistics, with a discussion of their validity, will be found in the *Enrollment in Modern Foreign Languages in Secondary Schools and Colleges of the United States,* prepared for the Modern Foreign Language Study by C. A. Wheeler and others. The Macmillan Company (*in press*).

[3] New York shows a little larger percentages of Spanish pupils than the other Middle Atlantic States. Of all public secondary school pupils in this State, 26% were reported in French and 14% in Spanish classes.

maintaining a ratio of one-half the French enrollment, while Latin rises to twice the figures of French. When we cross the Alleghenies and enter the Mississippi Valley, we find that not quite 8% of the pupils study French, while 21% study Latin, and Spanish rises in importance. In the states that lie between the Missouri and the Mississippi and border on the mountains in the West and the old Spanish territory in the South, modern language interest is also very slight, the total enrollments forming only 12% of the total school enrollment. Here Spanish begins to be the predominant language, including 8% of the school population as against 4% for French. When one enters the states which until 1848 were in great part under the Spanish flag, the language of the original settlers rises to 26% of the total enrollment and French sinks to an insignificant figure. Here Spanish greatly surpasses Latin also as a school subject. This is likewise true, although on not quite so large a scale, in California, where Spanish students include nearly 25% of the whole secondary school population. In the Northwest, Latin resumes its ancient supremacy from the Dakotas to the Pacific, though here Spanish still exceeds French (9% of the total school enrollment as against 7%).

To sum up, it will be seen that so far as the secondary schools are concerned, while French is the language of widest dispersion as well as that most largely sought by pupils, it is only in New England, New York, New Jersey, Maryland and Delaware, that the ratio of French enrollment rises above 15% of the total. In the vast region west of the Alleghenies and north of the Ohio, comprising nearly 60% of the whole secondary school population of the country, no one of the modern languages plays an important role, except in the old Spanish territory. Of the preparatory schools in the whole country west of the Middle Atlantic States, 55% of those which offer a foreign language teach only Latin.

In the private schools the modern languages play a more important part. The private secondary school population probably does not amount to 8% of that of the public high schools, nevertheless, it is qualitatively a very important group. Regional statistics play no significant rôle here. Taking the group as a whole

French appears on the programs of probably 35% of the pupils. Here again, however, Latin students more than outnumber all modern language enrollments combined.[4] In the colleges the percentages are considerably higher.[5] Generalizing from data obtained from 39% of the colleges and universities of the country and including more than 75% of the better institutions, it may be said with confidence that approximately 29% of all students in liberal arts colleges are to be found in French classes. The regional trend is about as we have seen it in the secondary schools, save that both the Middle Atlantic States and the Southern States surpass the New England group in enrollments in French courses. Here again, as in the schools, students of French make up about one-half of all modern language students. Spanish includes about 30% and German 18%.

A far larger percentage of college undergraduates than of secondary school pupils take the modern languages (57% as compared with 25% for all modern language enrollments combined). It is doubtful, however, whether this can be counted as a gain for the modern languages. More than one-quarter (nearly 28%) of all undergraduate French students are just beginning the language; more than half (58%) are no further than the second year. More than half will thus break off the study of the language at the point where the minimum knowledge should be set for beginning college courses. It is rather cold comfort for the

[4] The Study's figures include reports from 1,341 private secondary schools, which are about 54% of the total number listed by the Bureau of Education in 1925. The balance must include many schools without foreign language courses. The enrollment in the schools tabulated totalled about one-half of the entire school population of the private secondary schools. No account was taken of secondary courses in normal schools or of college preparatory departments.

[5] The statistics of enrollment in undergraduate courses in the modern foreign languages were gathered for the spring session or semester of 1925. Requests for information were sent to 774 institutions, of which 293 sent adequate responses. Contained in this number were 150 out of the 198 institutions which were at that time on the "accepted" list of the Association of American Universities. The full figures appear in the statistical volume of the Study's reports, *Enrollment in the Modern Foreign Languages in the Schools and Colleges of the United States*. The Macmillan Company (*in press*).

college teacher of French to remember that his colleagues in German and Spanish are much worse off. A real ray of comfort should, however, be found in the fact that in the five years between 1921 and 1925 the ratio of advanced students in college classes was steadily though slowly increasing.

Taken as a whole, the situation is not encouraging for those who would set their faith in the future of modern language study in this country on numbers. That, however, is a question which should interest the modern language teacher only in so far as it bears on organization and methods. The time is past when the modern language teacher, especially the French teacher, could look upon the growth of enrollment figures with any feeling except one of concern lest the problems arising from defective school organization and a lack of time be aggravated by an increase in registrants. From this standpoint it can arouse only a mild interest when we hear that in 1925 14% of all the secondary school pupils in the United States were studying French, nearly 10% Spanish and 1.25% German, and that in the colleges the corresponding figures were 29, 17 and 10. There will always be French student in the secondary schools and colleges, even though their number may decrease relatively. The important point is, that we should have better students and should be able to give them more adequate opportunities.

We lack many things at the present time in order to attain these results, the chief of which are standards of achievement and adequate time for instruction. With regard to the first, no one knows at present what a student of average intelligence under fair conditions of instruction should accomplish in one, two or three years of French study; how much working knowledge of vocabulary and of grammar and what capacity in reading or in understanding the spoken language and speaking it he should acquire in these periods. The teacher is therefore working almost in the dark. Beyond his own quite subjective impressions, he has as guides only College Entrance Board examinations or Regents' examinations or the tests set up by some college admission authority. All of these vary from year to year, and with the best intention in the world on the part of the persons who construct them, all are highly subjective in the selection of materials and in scoring. In the main, they still operate to a considerable extent with the traditional techniques of translation into English and translation into the foreign idiom. So far as they employ content or paragraph questions, these are used without having been tried out in practice sufficiently to determine whether they can stand the test of pupil comprehension and can develop objectivity of response, and whether the questions present such an ascending scale of difficulty as can be used to measure accomplishment at various stages of language growth. Thus two of the necessary qualities of a test, general reliability and objectivity of response and of grading, are quite lacking, and it is highly doubtful whether they are any better off as regards another, the validity of the materials use for testing.[6]

Almost all of us now know some one or another of the modern language tests, standardized or partly standardized, which have been put before the public. The Modern Foreign Language Study and the Canadian Committee on Modern Languages have devoted a great deal of time and money to the development of some of these tools of measurement and have worked out norms which are fairly reliable for a large number of pupils.[7] It is possible to measure objectively with these the performance of students for each of the eight semesters against the performance of a very large number of other students who have studied French for a corresponding period and thus to determine whether the achievement of our students in vocabulary, in grammar and in reading with comprehension ranks above or below the national standard for these capacities. It is possible also, with the help of the composition scale, to rate the written compositions of pupils

[6] Cf. Professor Ben D. Wood's noteworthy analysis of the characteristics of old-type and new-type modern language tests in *New York Experiments with New Type Modern Language Tests.* "Publications of the American and Canadian Committees on Modern Languages", Vol. I, The Macmillan Co., 1927, *passim.*

[7] The American Council Alpha and Beta Tests in French, German, Italian and Spanish. Published, with Directions for Administration and Composition Scales by the World Book Co., Yonkers-on-Hudson. Also the Van Wagenen-Hubman-Patterson German Reading Scales, published by the Public School Publishing Company, Bloomington, Ill.

with an objectivity which to those who train themselves in its use for the first time seems actually uncanny. Nobody contends that these instruments are perfect. There will probably always be arguments for or against the "plus-minus" technique or the "paragraph" technique or the "multiple-choice" technique, etc. The main point is that these experiments, and such tests as those issued by the Columbia College Bureau of Collegiate Educational Research, [8] at least present a beginning and have a claim to further experimentation and improvement. Many teachers do not understand this type of tests at all and their suspicion and dislike bear a direct ratio to this lack of understanding. Let us see what it can accomplish.

First of all, it substitutes an instrument which can be objectively administered for one that is highly subjective. Second, it enables us to make a comparison with published norms for a great group of schools and colleges and thus check the progress of our own pupils from semester to semester and from year to year. Third, it brings to light errors in classification, since a simple statistical series of our students will show how far the better ones in the upper quarter of a class overlap the lower quarter of the class or semester above.[9] Fourth, it is of high clinical value, in that it enables us to check the particular defects of our students, such as weaknesses in vocabulary, grammar, reading for comprehension and free composition, and after thus diagnosing the particular evil, to suggest a remedy. Much is said of the pedagogical value of examinations. Their true pedagogical value lies, not in taking an examination, as we do the College Entrance Board Examinations, and using it as a model to coach our classes, but in making the achievement of pupils an accurate index of capacity in each field and using the results to strengthen weaknesses. Finally, such a test keeps our eyes open constantly for the objectives of our teaching.

[8] Published for French, German and Spanish by the World Book Co., Yonkers-on-Hudson.

[9] Note the appaling cases of bad classification in the New York Junior High Schools, shown by Wood, *op. cit.*, p. 9 ff., especially p. 19 with the accompanying charts.

When we shall have found devices for testing other capacities, such as mass tests of aural understanding, of pronunciation and of oral free composition or speaking the foreign language and of translation, we shall have for the first time an adequate set of instruments which will reveal any weaknesses in the student's equipment. The discovery or invention of techniques for this purpose is as yet scarcely under way and every teacher of French is invited to experiment and make suggestions. [10]

Nobody expects the millennium to come to French teaching through the administration of tests. It is perfectly clear that there will always be a great inequality in student achievement and that the more accurate the tool of measurement, the more widely our pupils will be differentiated. The lowest quarter of the class will always remain the lowest quarter and will always offer administrative difficulties. But the achievement test is also a prognosis test. No principal or administrator can altogether neglect its findings. We have as yet no reliable prognosis tests for language study except the ordinary intelligence tests. [11] However, when once the language pupil gets under way, the standardized test will at least demonstrate his progress or lack of progress, and the facts upon which the elimination of the linguistic moron depends will be more plainly written than ever before.

No tests will ever be satisfactory however, so long as we have to depend altogether on subjective ideas and on tradition for the materials that go into our courses. A test may select samples here and there from the vocabulary of the text-books found in our syllabus, but no one knows whether the words of the texts or the

[10] A fully equipped battery for the modern languages should include different tests, each of which should be provided in alternative forms, fully equalized in all respects. Such an equipment can hardly be looked for; nor is it necessary since it is probable that a high correlation exists between achievement in certain capacities, such as aural and oral use of the foreign language. Cf. V. A. C. Henmon, *Achievement Tests in the Modern Foreign Languages*. Prepared for the American and Canadian Committees on Modern Languages. The Macmillan Co., (*in press*).

[11] Various experiments in the field have been undertaken under the sponsorship of the Modern Foreign Language Study and the Canadian Committee on Modern Languages. The results, as yet quite tentative, will be published in the spring of 1928.

grammars are the words the student is going to find useful for reading, speaking or writing after he gets away from our syllabus. No one knows whether the grammatical phenomena that we make the basis for our courses are the ones which the student will need in his practical use of the language or whether the habits of the foreign language and the psychology of the learner require that these grammatical facts should be presented in the sequence in which we now present them and test them. We might be inclined to believe that the use of certain modern language texts in school and college and the employment of certain idioms in our grammars were the result of the operation of the law of the survival of the fittest did we not have before our eyes the monstrous workings of tradition in Latin syntax recently exposed by Byrne. This fetichism is, to be sure, not so bad in the modern languages, where it has a constant corrective in the spoken language, but the mass of modern reading material makes a selection so much the more difficult.

All this points to the necessity for an objective study of the basic habits of language. There is no other way to discover these than by going to usage itself. We must determine what words, what idioms, what grammatical phenomena are those which the Frenchman finds most necessary to express his ideas. It is for this reason that Professor Henmon organized his *French Word Book,* [12] based on a count of 400,000 running words in many categories of speech, leading to the arrangement of 4,000 words in a sequence of descending frequency. This undertaking is now being continued with three times the original material. [13] Buchanan has published a *Spanish Word Book* [14] built on similar principles, and Morgan has in press a *German Word Book* of a similar character. [15] Hence also the frequency studies of idiom which have

[12] Bulletin of the University of Wisconsin, Department of Education, 1924.

[13] By A. Coleman and George Vander Beke. To be published by the American and Canadian Committees in the spring of 1928.

[14] M. A. Buchanan, *A Graded Spanish Word Book.* "Publications of the American and Canadian Committees on Modern Languages." University of Toronto Press, 1927.

[15] B. Q. Morgan, *A German Frequency Word Book,* based on *Kaeding's Häufigkeitswörterbuch.* "Publications of the American and Canadian Committees on Modern Languages." The Macmillan Co., (*in press*).

been undertaken, and those of syntax, a far more difficult proceeding, which we hope may eventually be carried out. The resulting arrangements of words and idiomatic phrases will be, of course, but raw material and it will be necessary to re-study it and modify it in the light of the experience of teachers and the objectives of instruction, but these word and form studies will at least lay the bases upon which to build.

All of this hangs together with the second great difficulty which we have to face, the lack of sufficient time. The modern languages are now in great part compressed into a very brief period in an overcrowded curriculum. The penalty which we pay in America for free secondary schooling to all classes and for our whole social attitude toward education results in the crowding of the modern language course into a period so short that a foreign teacher would regard the course as futile. The situation is, however, pressing and we have to face it as it is. Out of 359,219 students of French in the public secondary schools in the continental United States, in 1925 nearly 88% are found in the first two years of study. In other words, of all the French pupils, only 11% study it in the third year, and less than 1.5% in the fourth year. In New England the figures are slightly better: 14% and 2%. In the Middle Atlantic States they are slightly higher than the national mean. In the private schools the number of pupils in the third and fourth year of study is a little larger: 15,5% of the total in the third year and 5% in the fourth year. This abbreviation of foreign language study applies to Latin as well, although not so acutely in the fourth year: the national percentages for Latin are: 9% in the third and 4% in the fourth year. It seems a disease of our secondary schools which is incurable.

In order to meet the situation squarely both in school and college, we must first re-study our objectives and endeavor to bring our methods to bear upon them as directly as possible. Heretofore we have borrowed our procedures from the European schools without asking whether our objectives, the purposes for which we study the foreign languages, are the same as theirs. It is hardly necessary to refer again to the great disparity between the conditions surrounding modern language study in our secondary schools and colleges and those prevailing in France and Germany. They are, in the main, as little to be compared as a Rotary Club convention with a session of the French Academy. We lack, among other things, selected pupils; we lack the economic motivation for success, the cultural background, the international orientation; not to mention the carefully trained teachers, the traditionally standardized school curriculum and the powerfully centralized school authority. In place of these we have unending numbers, great economic resources, energy and optimism which have already overcome many difficulties, a sense of responsibility for our problems and a readiness of to experiment. Already American students have made one great contribution to secondary education, the application of quantitative methods of measurement.

This is not the place to discuss the bearing of our national situation on the objectives of modern language study. It is enough to say that whatever may be the cultural and social values of the modern languages for the American man or woman after graduation, they involve first of all the ability to *read* the foreign language with ease and understanding. It is manifestly our duty to exert ourselves to the utmost to extend the period of preparation for capable students, and it is of course evident that the better we succeed in attaining definite capacities in the first two years, the greater will be the number of capable students who continue the study of the language for three or four years.

Can a reading knowledge of French be acquired in two years? Undoubtedly with large groups of mentally handicapped students and with the present tools of instruction the answer must be in the negative. New conditions and new tools must be created. Leaving aside any discussion of the preparation of the teacher, the first of these conditions is the elimination from our classes of those who are mentally unfit for foreign language study. Until we shall have adequate prognosis tests, intelligence tests and a progressive use of standardized language tests must suffice. Secondly, the classification of students on a basis of achievement measured by standardized tests, so as to give a better chance to those who are capable of real accomplishment in the language. Third, a syllabus developed from a scientific investigation of the fundamental bases of usage in the fields of vocabulary, idiom and syntax. Fourth, experimentation with reading courses, which shall employ minima of grammar and of aural and oral practice in a judicious manner, to the end that the desired goal, reading with ease and comprehension, may be realized as early as possible. For this, wide experiments with reading courses are necessary. We do not yet know what part aural and oral practice play in learning to read a language. Our experience as teachers and our subjective impressions lead us to believe that it does play an important part. This also should be followed up by experimentation over a series of years.

The most important thing is that we should be willing to experiment with our objectives and not continue to burn incense before this or that idol of modern language method. It is only an article of my faith, yet I should be "altogether as those that have no hope" were it taken from me, that for a mentally capable student the shortest road to one capacity in the modern language is at the same time the shortest road to others. If this is true and we seek first diligently the most important objective, reading with comprehension, we shall find that all the other things worth having "shall be added unto us."

Columbia University.

ITEMS FROM FRANCE

By Harry Kurz

Strasbourg is busy with the return of her children to school. Shops here wear very much the same air of a resumption of scholarly activities. Like the leit-motif in a musical piece, school supplies are a predominant note in window displays. I have never seen before so thoroughly presented to me the intimate connection between study and business. It would take a parent to sense it more deeply—and a parent, alas! I am not.

The great lycée which adjoins and abuts the magnificent cathedral is polishing its windows and dusting its floors. Notices are flourshing on bulletin boards. Local papers print the solemn announcements of the opening of sessions signed by the mayor of the city. I append here one of these notices, interesting because it mentions the penalties involved in not sending children to school.

La rentrée des classes dans les écoles primaires élémentaires aura lieu le lundi, 26 septembre 1927, à 8 heures du matin.

Les parents des enfants qui atteindront l'âge de 6 ans avant le 1er janvier 1928, sont invités à faire inscrire ceux-ci pour la rentrée à l'école primaire du quartier où ils sont domiciliés, à moins qu'ils n'entendent faire donner à leurs enfants un enseignement équivalent, soit dans la famille, soit dans une école, suivant le programme de l'école élémentaire.

Dans toutes les écoles primaires, les fournitures scolaires (livres, cahiers), seront gratuitement mises à la disposition des élèves. Les élèves auront l'occasion d'obtenir le certificat d'études, après quoi ils pourront entrer aux Ecoles primaires supérieures, Ecoles pratiques, etc.

Conformément à l'article 4 de l'ordonnance sur l'enseignement du 18 avril 1871, les parents et tout représentant légal d'un enfant qui ne l'obligeront pas à fréquenter l'école, seront passibles des peines suivantes: l'avertissement officiel, une amende qui pourra s'élever jusqu'à 10 francs, la privation équivalente des secours du bureau de bienfaisance, et, au cas de récidive habituelle, l'emprisonnement pouvant durer jusqu'à huit jours.

Teachers of French in America, as well as teachers of other foreign languages, will be interested in the problem that faces their colleagues in Alsace and Lorraine. Although of a transitional nature, it is acute at present, and forces the classes in language into new channels of experiment that must prove of service elsewhere.

There is no doubt that at present Strasbourg is bi-lingual; but the surprising thing is that the French government intends that it remain so. M. Pfister, the rector of the University of this city, issued a circular recently in which he advanced the teaching of German in primary school to the middle of the second year instead of the third. This lengthening of the time given to German is encouraged by M. Poincaré, head of the cabinet, and is indeed a proof of far-sighted liberalism. This method of treating the regained provinces stands out in striking contrast with the procedure in 1871, when assimilation became a matter of sudden and brutal regulation. The French government has in these nine years of rule wisely never attempted to suppress the Germanic dialect, which I hear on all sides spoken by the adults, even in positions maintained by the government. Two generations have lived under German control and here are evident needs and conditions that have to be gently met.

The question of bilingualism has been shifted from the political to the pedagogic. In that phrase I have indicated the solution of the French government. All the little Alsatians will naturally learn to speak French. Yet they must not be embarrassed by ignorance of German, a language absolutely necessary here in social and business relationship. The problem is delicate—not any too easy to handle, requiring infiinite tact and mutual good will from both elements of the local population. One can appreciate the wisdom of the French governement in placing the matter in the hands of teachers, and preventing politicians from making issues where the only way that is fair is this benign procedure of an enlightened democracy.

In time, German will become the primary *foreign* language

taught in Alsatian schools, and French the first and native medium of communication. All with whom I have talked agree that French should and must be the preponderant language. But with such a deliberately planned bilingualism, new problems of language teaching will come up largely colored by local conditions. We are very far here from the iron heel of fifty years ago. Formalism, dogmatism,—isms in general, are to be abandoned. One might say each valley will have its own pedagogic system in foreign language, adapted by its teachers to its conditions and needs.

It remains to be seen if two such languages as French and German can be intensively assimilated by young children. Such is the plan at present. There is a fundamental principle which guides the government in this unusual procedure in a reconquered province. It is recognized that Alsace has always been a frontier region where Latin and Teuton traditions have endlessly mingled. Instead of stamping one of these out, is it not a wiser guarantee for the future to make this place an experimental station where these two civilizations may learn to harmonize successfully? There is something attractive in this idea of a progressive alliance between two such mentalities as the French and German. Each has something to gain from the other.

There is one more topic that might be mentioned here related to the teaching of language. With a practical sense that adequately sees the local problems, the needs of adults are being considered and met. Thc accompanying notice shows how the pacific infiltration of French is going on. I am informed that the classes are large. I want to add that on every hand, except with station porters, I have been understood and answered in almost perfect French. Some of the pronunciation is Germanic, but that is the only indication that in many cases French is a language acquired since the war. The notice follows:

Cours d'adultes de langue française

Les cours de français recommenceront le lundi 3 octobre. Tous les anciens cours seront réouverts. Nous prions les élèves de se présenter aux mêmes écoles, salles et heures.

Les inscriptions de nouveaux élèves seront faites au Bureau pédagogique, 15, rue Brûlée, au 2e étage, chambre 10, tous les jours de 9 à 12 et de 15 à 18 heures, le samedi après-midi excepté.

On s'inscrit aussi à l'école Schœpflin, entrée dans la cour, au rez-de-chaussée à droite, le lundi 26 septembre, le soir à 20 heures.

La cotisation trimestrielle de 4 fr. 50 doit être versée le jour de l'inscription.

Liste des cours existants

1. Cours élémentaires, moyens, supérieurs, dans toutes les écoles de la ville et des faubourgs;
2. Cours de perfectionnement de grammaire et d'orthographe (pour les personnes qui parlent le français couramment);
3. Cours de préparation à l'examen du Certificat d'études post-scolaires françaises;
4. Cours de sténographie française et de correspondance;
5. Cours de conversation française;
6. Cours de lectures d'auteurs choisis et de littérature.

M. Herriot, Minister of Public Instruction, has just appointed a committee of eleven to codify laws and rules relating to the educational system of France. The result of their labor, when published, will make an important reference book, harmonizing and bringing up to date a mass of regulations dating from the Second Empire. The Ministry of Public Instruction is situated at the Rue de Grenelle and Rue Bellechasse.

The registration at the University of Paris for the last school year, 1926-27, is us follows:

Total number of registrants	25,123
French students	19,386
Foreign students	5,737

These registrants were divided as follows among the five faculties of the University:

Law	9,265 (8,387 men, 878 women)
Medecine	5,464 (4,567 men, 897 women)
Science	3,891 (3,216 men, 675 women)
Letters	5,301 (2,740 men, 2,561 women)
Pharmacy	1,107 (697 men, 410 women)

The new figures for 1927-8 are not complete yet but your correspondent learns that they are not notably different from those above. A walk along the Boul. Mich. would lead to the conclusion that the foreigners were in greater number than ever. A visit to the Café de la Rotonde would only confirm this impression.

The battle of the classics is on. In France, as once in America, Greek is now on the defensive and Latin will in time be forced to fight for its present position. By his decree of Aug. 8, 1926, M. Edouard Herriot made Greek elective instead of obligatory in the "section classique" of the lycée from the "classe de quatrième". Feeling is running very high against this change. It is well expressed by M. Boivin, a teacher at the lycée Lakanal in Paris, who is seeking election to the Conseil Supérieur de l'Instruction Publique: Here is his platform:

A l'heure actuelle, votre délégué ne saurait être que le défenseur désespéré, ardent s'il le faut jusqu'à la brutalité, des études classiques. Certes nous ne sommes affligés d'aucun misonéisme, nous n'aimons les études classiques ni contre les sciences auxquelles elles préparent si bien, ni contre les langues modernes avec lesquelles elles peuvent si facilement s'harmoniser. Mais précisément à cause de l'importance de ces études comme préparation à la vie moderne, nous ne voulons pas qu'on les réduise par degrés à n'être plus qu'une spécialité érudite et subalterne. Votre délégué devra, d'accord avec celui des agrégés de grammaire, batailler sans cesse pour restaurer l'unité de l'enseignement littéraire, pour sauver le grec sans lequel les humanités sont découronnées et mutilées, pour amener au plus tôt la fin de la néfaste expérience qui, sous le nom d'amalgame, est en train de ruiner non seulement notre enseignement particulier, mais l'enseignement secondaire tout entier.

The amalgamation referred to is due also to ministerial decree. Where before classes were homogeneous, composed of students from the same year and from the same section, Greek, Latin, or Modern, according to the languages studied, now students with different preparations and backgrounds from various sections are sent into one class, "moderne B^4" with "classique A^3", etc. This system highly complicated has not yet received a fair trial but has certainly aroused a great deal of hostility. It is reminiscent somewhat of the organization of the high school in the United States. Formerly a teacher taught several subjects and kept one class intact. Now he teaches a specialty and students are grouped into classes accordingly. He teaches less to more students. That seems to sum up the direction in which French instruction, like ours, is moving.

The situation of French in German high schools

The German press has for some time been clamoring for a "rationalisation" of the teaching in the high schools. In Prussia there exist at present 37 different types of secondary schools. Besides the complexity of organization and control that this involves from the governmental point of view, there is a serious disadvantage for the boy or girl who moves to another neighborhood and finds himself for a while inadjustable. This difficulty is especially felt in the matter ot foreign language. Although English and French are taught in almost all of the aforementioned 37 categories of secondary schools, some begin with French as the principal language, others with English. This gives a variety of foreign language preparation in the early years which we in the United States accept as inevitable, owing to our lack of centralization of control.

The Prussian ministry of public instruction has been asked, however, to remedy this chaotic condition by a definite scheme of language study to be applied to all schools of secondary instruction. This involves the momentous decision as to whether English or French is to become the first language. An expert from Berlin, appointed to examine the question, whose name has not come to me, though I have seen an abstract of his report, recommends English as the principal language, largely on the ground that it will be the world language of the future.

The minister of public instruction Herr Becker, is nevertheless quite likely to decide on French as the more important of the two for German school boys. Here is a translation of his opinion recently publicly expressed: "According to my view the popular sentiment in favor of English results from a mistake which attributes greater importance to the point of view of salesmanship than to that of culture. Naturally a man who is properly trained ought to know both languages; but he should begin with French, which is harder to learn. Whoever learns only one foreign language should prefer French for the simple reason of culture; without French there is no true understanding of our language and of our history; without French we cannot even understand the letters written by our grand-parents, we shut ourselves off from even a glimpse of our own evolution as a cultured people and make scientific historical training completely impossible."

With French the first foreign language in Prussia, Bavaria and Saxony would be the only German principalities left that still yield to English a major importance.

Knox College.

PRESENT STATUS

OF THE

"JUNIOR YEAR ABROAD"[1]

By WALTER HULLIHEN

Four years ago this month, in November 1923, I made a report to this Association on an educational experiment the University of Delaware was just launching: that of sending selected students to France for the Junior year with the intention of giving full credit for the year toward the baccalaureate degree in Arts and Science to those who should complete successfully the program of work outlined for them there.

Today I have been asked to attempt to give you a report upon the present status of the "Junior year in Europe" for American undergraduates, which was being tried out that year for the first time by a group of students sent out to pursue a definite program of work approved by an American college faculty and under the guidance of a member of that faculty.

I must ask your pardon if in making such a report I seem to my hearers to confine myself too largely to the activities of the institution with which I am connected, for, while a wide-spread interest in the Junior year in Europe has been aroused among colleges generally during the past four years, as far as I know the University of Delaware and Smith College are the only colleges that are sending organized, supervised groups to Europe (in both of these cases to France) for Junior year study.

Historical Review

In 1922 Delaware sent a member of its faculty to France for a year's study of educational conditions there in relation to Amer-

(1) Paper written by president Hullihen, Chairman of the Committee on Foreign Study of the University of Delaware, to be delivered before the annual meeting of the Association of State Universities held at Chicago in November, 1927.

ican undergraduate instruction. In 1923, upon the basis of extended and detailed reports received from him and carefully studied by the Faculty, the first group, composed of seven Delaware Juniors and one Senior, was permitted to go to France under his supervision to inaugurate this rather interesting educational experiment. In 1924, 1925, 1926, 1927 other Delaware groups followed, those of the last three years being largely composed of students from other colleges and universities. In 1925 Smith College sent a group of more than thirty of its own students to France under the supervision of a member of its Modern Language staff, and even larger groups have gone from that college in 1926 and 1927.

The plan followed by Smith is described in the Smith College catalogs of 1926 and 1927. The Delaware Plan is described in bulletins issued by the Delaware Committee on Foreign Study in 1923, 1924, 1925, and 1926. These bulletins were presented as reports on the undertaking to the Board of Trustees of the University and were printed in sufficient numbers to permit copies to be sent to college officials who it was thought would be interested and to be used in answering detailed inquiries on this subject which came to the Committee from all parts of the country in such numbers as to make it difficult to answer them in any other way.

The only other agencies that have concerned themselves directly with the idea of undergraduate foreign study are the Institute of International Education, the American Council on Education, and the so-called Marks Committee of New York.

In the early months of 1924, Mr. Marcus M. Marks, of New York, gathered together a group of men to discuss the subject of undergraduate study and travel in foreign lands. The original members of this committee, besides Mr. Marks, were Senator T. Coleman du Pont, Mr. Felix Warburg, Dr. C. A. Mann and Dr. David Robertson, of the American Council, Dr. S. P. Duggan, of the Institute of International Education, President Frederick B. Robinson of C. C. N. Y., and the writer. This committee planned to broaden the program of undergraduate foreign study, which had been tried only in France, to include other European countries, and, out of funds contributed by members of the Committee and other generous donors, decided to advertise the idea of undergraduate foreign study by offering six or seven scholarships of $1000 each to be competed for by students from any of the accredited colleges in the country, the American Council on Education agreeing to inform colleges of the plan and to lay down the conditions under which the scholarships would be awarded. No restriction was imposed as to the country in which the scholarships were to be used. Dr. Robertson, in the Educational Record of April 1926 gave an extended account of the scholarship winners of the first year, 1925: three went to England; one to Spain; one to Germany; and two to France; all of them went alone and independently of any American supervision except the advice and guidance received from Dr. Robertson who made arrangements for them by correspondence with the foreign universities in which they desired to study.

In 1926 all seven of these scholarship winners elected to study in France. Six of them were admitted to the Delaware Group and one, a student of Smith College, was a member of the Smith Unit. In 1927 six scholarships were awarded. One student went to Berlin, one to Spain, one to Scotland, and three to France.

It is to be hoped that these generous scholarships will be continued. Some of those most interested in undergraduate study abroad consider them the best method for bringing the subject to the attention of students and faculties throughout the country. The writer of this report, however, while a member of the Committee and thoroughly appreciative of the value of the scholarships for the purpose named, has some doubts about the policy of encouraging American college juniors to go to foreign lands and there attempt to orient themselves and, unsupervised and unguided, to select courses suited to their intellectual maturity and previous training in educational systems so different from ours.

In 1927 the American Council on Education turned the administration of these scholarships over to the Institute of International Education, now a constituent part of the Council. Application for information about them should therefore be made to the Institute of International Education, 2 West 45th Street, New York.

Supervised Groups

It was stated above that Delaware and Smith are the only colleges that have sent out organized groups for Junior year study in France, but that fact does not at all measure the extent of the interest of American colleges in this subject. In the Delaware group of 1925 six different colleges were represented; in 1926 nineteen colleges; in 1927 (the group now in France) twenty-five colleges. In all, 40 different colleges during the past three years have had, or now have, one or more students taking the Junior year in France, and quite as many more have had the matter under serious consideration. Practically all colleges that have sent students with the Delaware group have agreed to give credit for the year abroad in event of successful completion of the work described in the bulletins issued by the Delaware Committee on Foreign Study. A few have reserved the right to examine the student upon return to this country with a view to giving the faculty an opportunity to judge for themselves whether or not the work abroad and the examinations given there represent the extent and quality of progress they expect a student to make in the Junior year. This was done this Fall, for example, in the case of a single student from the University of Minnesota (one of the national scholarship winners) a member of the Delaware group last year, with entirely satisfactory results. In no case of which the Delaware Committee on Foreign Study has knowledge have the results been such as to occasion any serious question of the acceptability of the work abroad for Junior year credit.

The extent of approval that has been given to the work which is being done under the supervision of the Foreign Study Committees of the Delaware and Smith groups, which are taking substantially the same courses, is to a certain degree indicated by the number of institutions that have been represented in the Delaware groups of the past three years with the approval of the faculties concerned. They are the following: Amherst, Boston University, Brown University, Colgate, Colorado College, Columbia University, Cornell University, Dartmouth, Delaware, Dickinson, University of Florida, Hamilton, Hood, Mt. Holyoke, University of Iowa, University of Indiana, Kenyon, Knox, Lafayette, Miami, University of Minnesota, University of Montana, College of the City of New York, New York University, New Jersey College for Women, Olivet, University of Pennsylvania, University of Pittsburg, Principia Junior, Randolph-Macon College for Women, Rutgers, Sacred Heart, Syracuse, Vassar, Wellesley, Western College for Women, Western Reserve, Westminster, Wheaton, Williams.

Some of these institutions in permitting their students to spend the Junior year abroad have doubtless been animated by the same pioneer spirit which prompted Delaware and Smith in sending out their first groups, considering it in a certain sense an educational experiment, and many of those who sent students to France for the first time last year have not yet been able to appraise very confidently the effect upon the student or the value of the year to him. Even the students themselves in some cases feel that they are still too close to the experience to evaluate it well.

Nevertheless it seemed necessary in attempting to make this a report on the present status of the undergraduate foreign study plan to secure the present opinions of the students who have been members of the Delaware groups that have gone abroad during the past three or four years and of teachers or administrative officers of the colleges from which they came. A letter was accordingly sent out to students and college officers asking for a perfectly frank expression of opinion as to the value of the Junior year in France and inviting candid comment and criticism.

Opinions of Returning Students

The answers received show a surprising degree of unanimity of approval. Only a few of them have any criticisms to offer and nearly all of these have to do with minor matters of internal organization and involve no suggestion of change in the general plan or of dissatisfaction with it. In not a single reply—a fact which was quite a surprise to our Committee—is there any indication that college officer or student was disappointed in the results secured.

A few typical letters from students have already been published in Delaware Foreign Study bulletins which those more recently received seem only to supplement and corroborate. Almost without exception they are highly enthusiastic about the educational values of the year abroad. Nor can their judgments be lightly discounted even by those of us who have devoted many more years than they to evaluating educational programs. It is they who have had the experience and in most cases they are students who have been selected as being mature and gifted young people, representing the very best element in the colleges from which they come, considered by their teachers qualified to profit by study abroad and consequently, I think, competent to judge of its value to themselves at least.

All of them seem to have experienced and to have prized, in addition to the purely academic progress made, a consciousness of release from a stereotyped and restricted point of view in education, a broadening of interests and outlook, contact with an atmosphere of cultural and aesthetic ideals quite new, very stimulating, and different from anything which they had previously known. Some report that, while they had to work harder and for longer hours than ever before in their lives on their subjects of study, and made proprortionately greater progress in them, they consider the incidental and less ponderable advantages of their year abroad as perhaps the most valuable part of the experience. Not a few mention a changed attitude on their part toward scholarship, new ideals of study, gained from the greater seriousness of purpose of French students and from the higher esteen in which scholarship and learning are held in France; a thought which recurs with striking frequency in letters from widely separated persons. Many naturally confine their discussion to the subjects of study, the graduate school methods of instruction, the necessity for individual initiative, the greater insistence in France upon form of expression than prevails here, and the difficulties these things present to the American student. All, of course, mention as undoubtedly greatest among the values secured the knowledge they have gained of France, the French people, and their contributions to civilization, and the degree of mastery of the French language attained in the year of foreign residence so much of which is devoted to purely language study.

The criticisms and suggestions in letters from students are summarized below:

The question is raised whether the discipline of the Foreign Study organization is not more strict than necessary.

Whether it is necessary for American girls to conform so closely to the French conventions in the matter of chaperonage, etc., etc.

Whether it would not be better to permit students to handle their own money for payment of board, theaters, trips, and other such expenses.

It is suggested that more frequent and intimate social contacts with French students, such as we have among students in a American college, would be desirable, if this could be arranged.

Lack of opportunity for exercise in the form of sports is deplored.

The difference in the standards of comfort in French homes as compared with American is put down as a serious draw-back for those who cannot afford to board in the more expensive places.

The granting of only one college year's credit for eleven months of intensive study is commented upon adversely.

Opinions of College Officers

From college officers, deans, and teachers, the replies received have, of course, been much more conservative than those from the students. In many cases deans and teachers have had little opportunity to make careful inquiry about the one, two, or three students they may have had abroad, and a highly commendable prudence prevents them from jumping to too definite conclusions on the basis of experience with so limited a number of students. None, however, have any serious criticism of the plan to offer and it is noticeable that the most commendatory letters are from those who have had the best opportunity to examine the program of work and to note the results secured by their students.

From Dean Bernard, of Smith College, the report on the Smith Unit is of especial value and importance since Smith has had its own organization and has had a much larger number of its own students take the Junior year in France than any other American college:

"..... The results are very satisfactory. Not only have the students a better command of the French language and a thorough knowledge of French culture, but their minds have developed more than had been expected. As far as it can be determined the Faculty here find them more mature and interested in their work. From outside the College good reports have been received on the value of this experiment. Six of the students back from France stood out in an examination for the teaching of French in New York State, four of them receiving 95%, one 90%. Another student who had spent the junior year in France received, in July 1927, the first prize of the national competition for the best translation of Briand's speech. The students themselves think the Junior Year in France is the most valuable experience in their college career and that it has broadened their outlook on life. It is characteristic that most of the students of the first group, who graduated in June 1927, are now engaged in more advanced studies, combining these with their jobs. Two students doing advanced work at Radcliffe have been especially commented upon by their professors."

From colleges which have had students in the Delaware Group:

From President Pierce, Kenyon College:

"I can assure you of the hearty and unanimous approval on the part of our faculty of the foreign study plan."

From Professor Florence D. White, Vassar College:

"I have had the pleasure of seeing members of your group several times. I have met all the preceptors and have had every opportunity to study the work of the year from various points of view and I believe the plan to be a very sound one and cannot sufficiently express my admiration of the way in which the organization is conducted."

From Professor Mary V. Young, Mt. Holyoke College:

"We are delighted with the work of our students who were in France last year. I spent ten days with them in Nancy and was more than satisfied with everything. I am strongly in favor of the policy of giving this privilege *only* to superior students."

From Dean Filler of Dickinson College:

"... I do not want to close this letter without stating that it is the opinion of our faculty that this plan for carefully selected students has very great promise."

From Dean Howes, of Williams College:

"Professor Grimm is very much impressed with S's knowledge of the French literature, his fluency in the use of the language, and his accurate understanding of it, which is, of course, largely the result of his year's serious work in France. While one must not draw inferences from a single case, we were a priori convinced and our judgment is now confirmed that, in the case of exceptional students at least, such a year as is offered under this plan is an extremely valuable year."

From Dean Turner, of New York University:

"... I am very favorably impressed as regards the general cultural advantages to be derived by especially endowed students from study abroad. I have had a number of conversations with Mr. S. and, although I understand he was not sufficiently prepared in French to take full advantage of his studies, I can see that he has made a vast improvement.

From another point of view, namely that of intensive training on a particular line of subject matter, I am not convinced that foreign study of this character is helpful. I believe it scatters the energies and prevents the continuous concentration required for high attainments in a special field.

It is my judgment that a year of such training affords the student an equipment he could attain in no other way, but diminishing returns, I think, would set in after the lapse of the first year."

From Professor J. F. Mason, Cornell University:

"... I was astonished at the remarkable progress these two students had made... My former skepticism regarding the Delaware Plan was entirely dissipated by its success with these two students. I am especially interested in it from the point of view of the preparation of teachers. France requires residence in the foreign country before the teacher is allowed to teach a given foreign language. We should in America make the same requirement. The Junior year in France offers the only solution possible for the large majority of prospective teachers of French."

From Professor Margaret Fraser, Randolph Macon Woman's College:

"... We are all delighted with the improvement and progress made by our girls who were abroad last year with your Foreign Study Group. I have ben enthusiastic from the beginning about the Foreign Study Plan and feel that I can hardly praise too highly the whole programme as now organized and carried out."

From Professor Francis B. Barton, University of Minnesota:

"... In the case of an exceptionally well prepared student like Mr. J. the plan has certainly worked out excellently. I am sure that Mr. J. obtained more from this experience in France than he could possibly have obtained from a junior year in Minnesota."

From Professor Horatio Smith, Brown University:

"... My appraisal of the results in F's case convinces me that for certain students who are especially equipped, this junior year in Paris is invaluable... I am heartily in favor of the enterprise and sincerely hope it may be continued in the same way."

The judgments of the Delaware Committee on Foreign Study have been given in several bulletins issued by that Committee. To quote from the last of these:

"The Foreign Study Committee itself in reviewing the results of the four years is glad to be able to express the opinion that these results have been satisfactory to a gratifying degree both to the Faculty and to the students concerned.

"At the same time the Committee desires to avoid conveying the impression that foreign study of the sort herein described should be made available for *all* students who desire to join a foreign study group. It is convinced from the experience of those who have been members of the groups under its charge that only very carefully selected students of high intellectual gifts, mature character, and industrious habits should be permitted to spend an undergraduate year abroad; that the average student would have little or no chance to succeed and ought not to be permitted to go.

The Committee, therefore, desires to call attention to, and to emphasize, the following as the outstanding conclusions drawn from its experience:

(a) That capable supervision by members of the Faculty is indispensable; that there should be at least one faculty adviser to every eighteen or twenty students.

(b) That not less than three months of preliminary training in France is necessary.

(c) That the student, having a foreign language as well as his subjects of study to master, must be prepared to do harder and more continuous work than is required in the average year in the undergraduate American college.

(d) That the methods of instruction and consequently the necessary methods of study in France are quite different from ours and demand a high degree of intellectual initiative and concentration of effort.

(e) That the year abroad would probably result in disastrous failure for any but a very carefully selected group."

Communications from many other colleges and individuals might be added here, if time and space permitted. It may suffice, however, to say that the opinions quoted above reflect with at least a fair degree of accuracy the tenor of all the replies received to the letter of inquiry. Apart from the question of "concentration" raised in Dean Turner's letter, most of the adverse criticism, implied and expressed, could, I think, be summarized under two heads, as follows:

(1) Regret is expressed that the number of courses available for American undergraduates is so limited.

(2) Many faculty members feel that they are insufficiently informed about the nature, content, and scope of the courses taken in Paris.

As to (1), the number of courses available for American college Juniors, it is unquestionably true that this number is very limited as compared with what is available in an American university. In fact the courses investigated by the Delaware Committee and recommended by them to American undergraduates are confined to the fields of Modern Languages, especially the French language and literature, History, Philosophy, Economics, the History of Art, and a few special courses in other departments, and no student is advised to take the year in France unless he is willing to devote a large amount of time to mastery of spoken and written French and can find in the departments enumerated a year's work that will fit into the course he is taking in the American college.

To meet the very real difficulty referred to in (2) and to provide the desired information as to the content and scope of the courses most commonly taken by our American students in France, the University of Delaware has this year sent to France a second member of its teaching staff, who is especially qualified for such a task, to attend a number of these courses and to prepare full and careful synopses of them covering an entire semester's work. These synopses will be multigraphed or printed and made available for members of college faculties interested in the foreign study idea who would like to have more detailed information than could heretofore be obtained. It is hoped that such an account of several typical courses in different fields of study will give an adequate conception of the character and scope of the courses in general. These synopses cannot be ready for distribution, however, before the end of March since they are to cover courses taken by our students this year in Paris from November 1, when the regular session opens, till about February 20, when the first semester examinations begin.

Definiteness of Objective

The problem of correlation of the work in France with that of the American college is, of course, not a simple one, and where "concentration" or "majors" is greatly stressed in the college's program for the baccalaureate degree this problem becomes more difficult. At the same time it is worthy of note that the year's work of most of our students in France has a coherence and definiteness of objective which is entirely lacking in many a student's year in an American college. It's purpose, like that of the famous Meiklejohn experiment at Wisconsin, is to "study a civilization other than our own" as intensively as is possible in one year, with a view to securing the benefits that come from the ability to compare our nation and our institutions with another nation, another people, and other institutions. The student pursues a course definitely designed to acquaint him with the history, the literature, the drama, the art, the government, and the customs of a great and ancient people. He is guided in his studies by the scholars best able to interpret that people and he supplements this with first-hand observations resulting from his social contacts with those around him, at the same time gaining a mastery of a foreign tongue and securing the benefits of courses of instruction which apart from their interrelationship would be counted individually as desirable "credits" for the degree in the largely unmotivated and often haphazard course of our American college.

In conclusion, it may be said that the plan for a supervised Junior year in France, in so far as it has gone, has been in many ways highly successful. It seems to have won the approval of a large proportion of those persons in the educational world who have investigated carefully the program that is being carried out; and a considerable number of our leading colleges and universities have confirmed that approval by vote of the faculty.

This report has been prepared in the hope that it may again bring the subject with which it is concerned to the attention of the Universities of this Association in such a way as to encourage a wider participation in the program it describes. May I in closing again assure you that the University of Delaware will count it a privilege to give any information it possesses on this subject to any who desire it, the generous subsidy it has received from Mr. P. S. du Pont having been granted not only to make possible the initial experiment but also to provide for reporting the results of it to other institutions of learning.

University of Delaware.

THE REAL PURPOSE

OF

PHONETIC TRANSCRIPTION[1]

A very brief experience in teaching pronunciation would soon convince an observing person that there are two separate and distinct problems or difficulties to be met. The problem that used to get all the attention in the older days was the orthographic one; how do we pronounce *an, ei,* etc.? These questions were glibly answered in "English equivalents", and the battle was held to be won.

More recently the science of phonetics has come to the fore, with its more exact standard of statement, its distrust of "English equivalents," and its more scientific basis of explanation (physiological and phonetic.) With "phonetics" there has come to be associated a convenient system of representing sounds called "phonetic spelling". For instance, when it was found that there are in French 16 vowel sounds, it at once became clear that the five vowel letters of the traditional alphabet were inadequate; and, since digraphs and other inconsistencies are undesirable in an accurate alphabet, it became necessary either to standardize the use of accents and other diacritics or to invent new symbols. Then, as their conceptions have become more complicated or more minute, phoneticians have adopted even further modifications of the 37 simple phonetic signs that suffice to represent the ordinary French sounds with reasonable accuracy.

But phonetic spelling is not merely the tool of the scientific phonetician. In fact it is not even strictly essential to work in phonetics, but may be said to find its greater justification rather as an elucidation of purely orthographic difficulties than as an instrument for the representation of phonetic niceties. And so,

1). An article that repeats some things that have been said elsewhere, but attempts a new coordination and development of ideas. The arguments are formulated as if for persons wholly ignorant of phonetics and of French, but are of course not addressed to such persons only, nor even chiefly.

however useful to phonetics, however closely associated historically with that science, and however and whenever it may have arisen, the value of phonetic spelling to the practical student of pronunciation is as a substitute for a bad orthography and not as a help in learning or picturing new sounds. Phonetic spelling helps us to decide how a word ought to be pronounced, because it employs no silent letters, uses each symbol always for the same sound, and indicates the same sound always by the same symbol; thus it would spell *debt* and *lamb* in English as "det" and "lam"; a *bow* (of salutation) would be "bau" [1] and a *bow* (for the arrow) would be "bo". But it offers no help in making new sounds, nor other assistance of a purely "phonetic" nature. Phonetic spelling is phonetic in being a consistent key to sounds that one is mastering by some other process, and not in conveying any idea of the nature of these sounds.

Let us then remember that the two problems of (1) making sounds, and (2) understanding what sounds are called for by a given spelling, are absolutely distinct. For a *perfect* pronunciation, the first problem is probably more important than the second, though both must be met; for a *good* pronunciation the reverse is certainly true, after a few basic phonetic facts have been learned. Also let us not forget that, regardless of its association with phonetics, phonetic spelling is of practical importance to the student of French chiefly in the way of untangling the spelling; this has little to do with real phonetics.

But the two things have become associated in the popular mind. Classes using the accurate analysis of sound which we call "phonetics" and the accurate representation of the various sounds called "phonetic spelling" might easily believe themselves, and be believed by others, to identify the two processes. This is natural, but not accurate, for "phonetics", being simply the accurate and methodical study of speech sounds, is independent of any and all systems of symbols. Furthermore, it is helpless to cure defects of pronunciation which are due merely to bad spellings (such as *monsieur, doigt, parlent,* pronounced "mesyeu", "dwa", "parl") and which disappear when once such words are phonetically spelled; and, on the other hand, it often busies itself with difficulties

1). *au* = "ah + oo", as in *sauerkraut.*

of pronunciation for which the quite adequate traditional spelling, or the most perfect phonetic substitute, brings no relief,—*été, rural, lire, parle, patte, car.*

In other words, the phonetician's chief interest lies in obtaining a correct *description of sounds* along acoustic and physiological lines, and in getting his pupil to reproduce them accurately. For many sounds the conventional letter may be, and in fact often is, used, without any advance toward a good pronunciation, for instance *r, l, p, t, b, d;* orthographic simplicity does not affect the great difficulties experienced in defining and teaching these sounds. There are, in fact, finer differences between certain of these sounds roughly common to French and English (*p, b, t, d*) that phonetic spelling does not ordinarily attempt to represent. On the other hand, some words would be relatively easy to pronounce if their spelling were not so misleading, and, as we shall see below, phonetic spelling is often of the greatest use in untangling their pronunciation; but in these the student of mere phonetics (*i, e.,* problems of sound) has very little interest, since there is relatively little difficulty in making the necessary sounds when once it is made clear just what sounds one ought to aim at. Such a word, for instance, is the French *doigt,* pronounced "dwa", and quite easy to pronounce when the misleading spelling is out of the way. *Rural,* on the other hand contains no orthographic difficulties that can be helped by a different spelling, but is full of phonetic difficulties.

"Phonetics", then, is not primarily the basis for the belief in the value of phonetic spelling in foreign language study (that is of an accurate system of understandable signs aiming to indicate to the eye the exact pronunciation of the words of a language), any more than it is the reason for the presence of the "key to pronunciation" in a dictionary in our own language, whose author, however innocent of phonetic science, can help us with our pronunciation of difficult words if only he has a good ear and uses his symbols consistently. It does not take a phonetic specialist, for instance, to tell us how to produce the sounds in *ark* and *arch,* but there are many who welcome the transcription or "key" in the dictionary telling which of these syllables should begin the words *architect* and *architrave.*

So "phonetic transcription" turns out to be simply a practical method of indicating to the eye the departures of the common orthography from common sense,—using a system of symbols that happens to be useful to the phonetician also, but which would have its value if the science of phonetics did not exist. Such phonetic writing ignores the problem of the production of difficult sounds—which it is powerless to solve—and concentrates its attention upon untangling the spelling of words which, whether their sounds themselves be easy or difficult, are bothersome because misleadingly represented in the traditional spelling. A spelling of this kind, when it differs conspicuously from the traditional spelling—as, for instance, when it substitutes "dwa" for *doigt*—does so in order to correct false views of pronunciation which the inherited spelling might and does create; it aims to tell us what sounds we should try to make, without indicating whether those sounds are easy or difficult. Phonetics interests itself in sounds alone, and especially in teaching us how to make the more difficult ones. Those who desire to pronounce conspicuously well need to cultivate both processes.

A few illustrations should make clear just what "phonetic spelling" aims at, and how useful it is in its field. Some of us may have heard Frenchmen struggle to pronounce the *b* of "doubt" and "debt", or turn "shepherd" into "sheferd". What was the trouble? Are the sounds difficult to conceive or to make? Is the problem one of phonetics? Not in the least. It is the standard spelling which misleads every foreigner—as well as many a native child—when he first tries to pronounce such words. If, now, by the side of the illogical form which we must learn to spell in order to be "correct", we carried in our mind's eye a true picture of the word as it is pronounced, such mistakes would be impossible. On the top of the London busses one reads this injunction: "In wet weather refix cover over seat", a wise plea, easily understood by those whose life has been spent threading the mazes of English spelling. But how about the foreigner? How long will it take him to remember that *e* in "wet" and *ea* in "weather" are pronounced alike, whereas the *ea* in "seat" has a different sound from *ea* in "weather", but like the *e* in "refix", and yet different from the *e* in "wet"? or that *o-v-e-r* is one thing when standing alone, and a different thing when preceded by *c*? Through a long hardening process, we who speak English as a native tongue have lost the power to appreciate these absurdities, but our foreign friends feel them keenly and are baffled by them; if we should supply these foreign friends with some such key as this to that confusing medley of spellings, "In wet weth'r reefiks kuv'r ov'r seet", should we not be immediately justified by evidence that we had smoothed the road leading to a prompt attainment of a better pronunciation?

To be sure, there seems to exist among those who have not experimented with phonetic spelling a very natural opinion that it will create "incorrect" habits of spelling. But it is asserted, upon the authority of those who have so experimented, that no such thing takes place. It would appear that the use of phonetic spelling makes many of the departures from reason so conspicuous that we remember them even more easily;[1] but, incidentally, is it worse to risk bungling our writing than our speech?

The foregoing presentation of English in phonetic spelling for foreign learners was a mere illustration, and perhaps even such theoretic contemplation of altered spelling looms as sacrilege before eyes accustomed to traditional forms. But even those who might dislike such temporary changes in the spelling of our own language—though for a worthy pedagogical purpose—even these may be open to persuasion that the attainment of a correct pronunciation of some *foreign* languages would be rendered easier *for us* by a phonetic spelling.

Let us examine the possibilities in French. *Souhaite* looks like an easy word, and probably most of those who pronounce it "soo-

1). See an interesting pamphlet published by the Simplified Spelling Society (20 Southampton St., Bloomsbury Square, London, W. C. 1.), called *The Best Method of Teaching Children to Read and Write; a Report of an Experiment Conducted in Sixteen Schools*: "Contrary to expectation, the transition from the phonetic to the ordinary spelling is attended by no difficulty, and indeed, children who pass from the former to the latter acquire something like proficiency in the ordinary spelling sooner than children do who are familiar with no other" (p. 4). See also, in *Miscelanea Phonetica* (to commemorate the 25th year of *Le Maître phonétique*), an article by Robert Jackson on "Phonetics and Phonetic Texts in the Teaching of Reading" (p. 33), with the same report.

ate", or even "soo-hate", fancy that they are pronouncing it quite properly. In fact many such people would resent the suggestion of a different pronunciation as the vain imaginings of phonetic cranks who are intolerably fussy, even when not wholly astray. Indeed, such a word is a good illustration of the inaccuracies common among people intolerant of phonetics and phonetic spelling, but unaware how far their own pronunciation is from being real French. It has been my own observation, by the way, that something like a majority of those who have really mastered the pronunciation of French (outside of that small class who have combined unusual imitative capacities with extraordinary opportunities), that a majority of these appreciate the value both of phonetics and of phonetic spelling, and have utilized both to some extent in their own efforts and in their teaching. At any rate careful attention to the pronunciation of any Frenchman saying *souhaite* will show that he really says something like our word "sweat", instead of the monstrous "soo-ate" produced by English speaking people. If we had written the word "swet"[1] from the start, "soo-ate" would never have been heard.

Here, too, are groups of words pronounced exactly alike but spelled in all sorts of different ways, puzzling to the conscientious learner, who may feel that he ought to find a different pronunciation for each different spelling. *Aller, allez, allé, allai* have but one pronunciation, similar to the English "allay"; phonetic spelling writes them all "alé".[2] *Sans, sens, sent, sang, cent* are identical in

1) [swɛt] in the alphabet of the International Phonetic Association. Since, next to consistency, common acceptance as a conventional medium of written communication is what, in the last analysis, conditions the usefulness of any alphabet, many who do not think the I. P. A. ideal for the phonetic spelling of French accept it as it is, though not blind to its defects, —e. g., such spellings as [tu] and [pje], which indicate something wholly different from the French words *tu* and *je*. It is to be hoped that the time may come when a phonetic system shall be in common use for the *teaching* of French that may not aspire to be international and shall never conflict with the standard spelling. In the meantime, with all its faults, the I. P. A. is a most efficient tool. See H. V. Groves (*Modern Languages* VII 3-4): "Can Phonetics be Taught Without Symbols?", an article which states frankly the defects of the I. P. A. and in fact advances some arguments at variance with the views expressed in this paper.

2). I. P. A. [ale].

sound; phonetic spelling *makes* them all "sã", using the sign "*ã*" to represent a nazalised "ah", a spelling which has the great advantage of getting rid of an *m* and an *n* which ought never to be heard but often are. *Rompt,* with a perfectly useless *p* and *t,* is pronounced exactly like *rond,* with a useless *d;* the *on* in *rond* being identical with the *om* in *rompt,* phonetically both are "rõ" ("õ" being nazalised "aw" or "oh"). *Donne, donnes, donnent* again are identical; we may write them all "dɔn", in which "ɔ" represents a sound similar to o in "for". *Elle* is identical with *aile;* we may write them both "èl".[1]

On the other hand, some words that look very much alike are totally different in sound. Thus, by the side of *aile* ("èl") we have *ail* and *aille,* which sound like the English "eye" and may be written "ay".[2]

So, by the side of *donne* ("dɔn") we have the quite different *don,* with a nasal vowel and no *n*-sound, which is written "dõ". *Excellent* is pronounced with two syllables when a verb (èksèl)[3], and three when an adjective (èksèlã).[4]

Other irregularities and inconsistencies also disappear in phonetic spelling. Thus, in the phonetic spelling of *doigt,* the silent *g* and *t* are ignored, and the misleading *oi* is written as pronounced; and so *doigt* becomes "dwa". The inconsistency between *mot* with silent *t* and *dot* with *t* sounded disappears when we write the words "mô" and "dɔt". Even a complicated expression like *Champs Elysées* will be simplified for us by the transcription "shãzélizé"[5], "*ã*" being used for the nazalised "ah" and the other symbols having an obvious French or English value.

Help comes also in many familiar groups and phrases. Thus we realize the difference between *la petite* ("laptit")[6] in which the first *e* normally disappears, and *une petite* ("unpetit")[7] in which

1). I. P. A. [ɛl].
2). I. P. A. [a:j].
3). I. P. A. [ɛksɛl].
4). I. P. A. [ɛksɛlã].
5). I. P. A. [ʃãzelize].
6). [laptit].
7). [ynpətit].

this *e* must be retained. "Samfrèdlapèn"[1] is what the French really say (and expect us to say) for the phrase which their books print as *ça me ferait de la peine*. And "âksèbô"[2] gives a correct image of a common phrase very deceptively represented for speech by the spelling "ah, que c'est beau". *Là-dessus* is not often conceived of as "latsu"[3], and yet this is what the French usually say.

In all this, it will be observed, there is not an iota of "phonetics", if by that term we mean struggling to conquer very difficult sounds or to establish minute distinctions. These transcriptions merely take the first and essential step toward honestly recognizing the facts along broad lines, namely toward deciding what sounds we shall try to make in producing certain French words and phrases; and this is a conception which must certainly be obtained by some means or other before we can even begin to pronounce acceptably. For this purpose "phonetic spelling" of some sort—conscious or unconscious, systematic or haphazard—is the only intelligent means conceivable.

All the foregoing discussion presupposes certain simple agreements. It assumes that something more than mere reading knowledge is aimed at, and therefore posits a definite interest in pronunciation, not necessarily the exaggerated emphasis of extremists, but an interest arising from the conviction that oral-aural work is of importance in almost any course and that accuracy is commendable everywhere. Granting these assumptions and conditions the case for phonetic spelling seems secure.

Having come to an understanding about the nature and the usefulness of phonetic spelling, we may next consider the manner of its application and its place in the best approach to the general problem of teaching pronunciation. This is important, lest our argument be distorted into anything like advocacy of an extreme or fanatical attitude.

First of all comes psychological preparation, which includes, on the part of teacher and class, an understanding of the function and value of phonetic spelling, a willingness to use a few

1). [samfrɛdlapɛn].
2). [ɑksɛbo].
3). [latsy].

strange symbols in spite of ancient prejudices, and finally a little patience in becoming accustomed to these new symbols.

It should be agreed by this time that our work in pronunciation will never be quite clear until we have insisted that our students shall appreciate this difference between two distinct sets of difficulties,—the *phonetic* (having to do with unfamiliar sounds), and the *orthographic* (having to do with matters of spelling). Serious students who have the time to do things thoroughly should of course busy themselves with both problems, whereas a few hasty classes with reading alone in view may ignore pronunciation almost entirely. But there may be found a perfectly respectable intermediate sort of students of French who would say, if they understood the whole situation, that, while they do wish to pronounce *decently,* they are not intent upon perfection in the production of French *l* or "close *e*"or other sounds so difficult of attainment; they simply wish to avoid the more common blunders for which the strange spelling is chiefly responsible. For instance, they do not wish to be caught saying "eye-yea" for *ayez,* "vale" for *vaille,* "eye" for *aile,* "el" for *aille,* or "met" for *mets.* Keeping in mind this important subdivision of the problem of pronunciation into its two major difficulties of sound production and of orthography, we may formulate two possible attacks on pronunciation called (1) the Phonetic Approach and (2) the Orthographic Approach, recommending the former to those interested in the niceties of pronunciation and having plenty of time at their disposal, and the second to average students with only a moderately good pronunciation as their goal, and a limited amount of time in which to attain it. But in reality, no serious student can afford wholly to ignore the study either of sound or of spelling; the most hasty smatterer in orthography must learn about the more important peculiarities of French sounds; and the serious student of phonetics must also undertake a serious study of orthography, unless his mere phonetic skill is to be neutralized by blundering when he has to read actual French letter combinations. It is better, then, to speak rather of the phonetic and the orthographic *emphasis,* since the word *approach* may prove misleading.

For the *orthographic emphasis* the preliminary period of drill on mere sounds will be brief; but it is vitally important and it should come at the very beginning of the course; most of the later pronunciation work, however, will be devoted simply to making sure that any reasonable combination of letters shall be pronounced as intended. Students in this class would not display great interest in "The Phonetic Emphasis"; not learning the language orally, but rather making generous use of the printed page (in the traditional spelling), they will seek, above all, usable definitions of the ordinary pronunciation of the various groups of letters. The point to be stressed is that this is the group for whom phonetic spelling is of the greatest value, for it is an unrivalled antidote to the ordinary blunders which, misled by the present spelling situation, they keep making, and is thus really a great time-saver in the end. It should be taught early.

For the *phonetic emphasis* the preliminary sound drill will last longer and in fact be continued indefinitely until every sound is actually mastered; but problems of spelling will ultimately receive as much attention by this group as by the orthographers, since phonetic perfection without practical application to French words is useless.

The more specific class-room problem of where and how to apply instruction in sound and especially when and how to introduce phonetic spelling comes up finally for consideration. Shall we give our pronunciation all at the beginning or string it out through many months? When shall we discuss the sounds? When shall we use phonetic symbols? And when the standard orthography? Shall we stand for a rigorously exclusive use of phonetic spelling at the start?—and if so for how long?—or for occasional transcription?—or for the phonetic reader?

Unless we are content to eliminate the spoken word altogether from our French courses and to limit ourselves, for instance, to hastily acquiring a mere reading knowledge (a procedure not wholly inconceivable or reprehensible), we shall have to treat oral-aural work seriously from the start; therefore it would be altogether reasonable to get this proper start by a period of exclusively phonetic instruction at the outset of the course (using a phonetic notation and no standard spelling.)[1]

1). For French, that is to say. The use of phonetic spelling in other languages is a different problem.

This is the extreme, concentrated form of instruction using phonetic spelling, but it is not a fad of extremists. Incidentally it can be used with others than beginners,—wherever the need for a pronunciation house-cleaning is in order.

According to a wise provision in the British program of French courses for young children it is now a common practice in the best schools for one whole term (about one third of a year) to be devoted to the study of the language in phonetic texts, followed by a little consideration of the transition to the standard spelling. This should be imitated in all of our own classes for young American children. For our somewhat older high school pupils, the same plan could easily be followed, though the amount of time devoted to phonetic texts could be reduced to a month or two, unless pronunciation were assumed to be of primary importance, in which case more time could be spent on phonetic texts. Even for college beginners a similar preliminary phonetic period of from two weeks to a month is quite as desirable and workable. It will be understood of course that this preliminary phonetic period means a period in which the language is studied through phonetic texts and not a time of exclusive devotion to phonetics or even pronunciation.

To appreciate more clearly the merits of a program of instruction in which the danger of bad pronunciation is diminished by substituting phonetic texts for the misleading standard spelling during the early weeks of the course, one has but to recall to mind the tremendous importance of first impressions in any sphere of life. Let your first impression of a strange city reverse the points of the compass and you may have to spend weeks getting your bearings; let your first idea of the sounds or the constructions of a new language be faulty and you will be struggling against the stream forever; but get your first impressions correct and you will be instinctively right ever thereafter. With correct phonetic impressions at the outset, reinforced by a spelling that will fix them, correct habits will be favored from the start and accurate oral-aural work will be thereafter more likely. This is said with no intention of arguing for conversation courses, but simply because oral-aural work should be accurate if utilized at all.

This rigorous and consistent use of purely phonetic texts in at least the early weeks or months of instruction is the best way to give phonetic spelling a chance to send down deep roots for fixed habits of correct pronunciation. For the young—for all, in fact, who have a reasonable amount of time for French—this is by far the best plan during at least a very brief period at the outset. Aural-oral work is not only an end in itself; it is a form of language experience that is sure to react helpfully upon reading; if aural-oral exercises are to be used, the words must be caught by the ear and pronounced properly, and the traditional spelling is often a hindrance rather than a help to distinctions of sound either by the ear or the vocal organs.

As an introduction to the familiar use of phonetic symbols and for training the ear in nice appreciation of distinctions in sound, the "identification exercise" cannot be too highly recommended. For this exercise one places on the blackboard where everyone can see it a table containing a complete set of phonetic symbols by the side of each of which is a number which will be used to label the various sounds or symbols beyond possibility of confusion. (It is assumed, of course, that by this time the students know the sounds for which the various symbols or numbers stand; if not, some brief description should be at hand). The teacher now pronounces a word and directs the class to identify the successive sounds by the numbers; as this is being done he writes on the board the corresponding symbol and possibly the identifying number,—and lo! the word has been phonetically written. The teacher here does all the phonetic transcribing himself as the successive sounds are identified, and in this process not only demonstrates to the class the utility of the phonetic alphabet but also strengthens their use of it in other exercises.

A specific program for the use of phonetics and phonetic spelling in the early weeks of a French course, might read somewhat as follows (the first three steps not being necessarily sharply separated):

1. The opening lessons to be devoted exclusively to a description of the 36 or 37 French sounds, with some drill. Some teachers believe that not even phonetic symbols should be used at first, lest we encourage the pernicious habit of trusting too much to the eye. Various devices are in order for the use of the student's

outside time during this period, which will be short for those leaning toward the orthographic emphasis, longer for others.

2. Introduction of the phonetic alphabet, the "identification exercise" being a help in associating sound and symbol, as well as in training the ear.

3. A period devoted exclusively to phonetic texts should follow. These texts should not concentrate attention upon the problem of pronunciation alone, but combine with pronunciation the study of the language itself.

4. Explanation of the relation of sounds to standard spelling. This is the chief business of the orthographic emphasis, but will need serious attention from all. Here again the continued use of phonetic texts or occasional transcriptions will be of great value.

5. We are now ready for the lesson book in the standard spelling.

So much for the exclusive use of phonetic forms at the outset of the course. At the opposite extreme comes the mildest form of the application of phonetic spelling, the method that we may call *occasional transcription,* a curative device running parallel to other work rather than a scheme of orientation at the outset. Almost any satisfactory teaching of pronunciation nowadays assumes something of phonetics, in connection with which phonetic symbols may well be used as tools, whether one follow the strictly phonetic path or not. Assuming such a foundation, it is the teacher's next problem to convince his class of the value of placing occasional phonetic transcriptions of words by the side of the standard forms which they are regularly using, and here he must be tactful. He may begin with "identification exercises" similar to those described above; the particular utility of these for those who are learning French in the standard spelling will be that they will be required to *identify sounds really heard,* and not sounds guessed at (often incorrectly) with the aid (or the hindrance) of the remembered spelling of familiar words. Very unusual words or even nonsense forms will compel students to use the ear and not the visual memory. Other simple graded exercises will follow, leading to independent transcription by the class. Occasional written tests of ability to transcribe important words (*monsieur, vaille, mets*) are useful.

The use of a phonetic reader as a corrective of the standard spelling is a third possibility, lying midway between the exclusive use of phonetic texts and the corrective use of occasional transcriptions. Phonetic readers abound; some of these, by placing the standard text by the side of the phonetic form, constantly remind the student of the relation between standard orthography and sound.

For "occasional transcription" no separate text will be needed. For an exclusively phonetic preliminary period a very few phonetic texts have been recently published, and several well-known "Grammars" or "Courses" provide phonetic treatment of the earlier lessons. In any case it is not difficult to find a book combining the functions of the phonetic primer and the elementary language lesson-book, thus meeting the criticism that a preliminary phonetic period gives too much time exclusively to pronunciation and requires the purchase of a superfluous text.

PHILIP H. CHURCHMAN.

FRENCH ART IN NEW YORK

This autumn the teacher of French interested in contemporary French art has had unusual opportunities for becoming acquainted with the work of the most prominent artists of to-day. The Reinhardt galleries opened their season with a splendid exhibition of paintings by contemporary French artists of recognized merit such as Matisse, Vlaminck, Derain, Utrillo, Pascin, Dufy and others—all excellent examples of their art. Earlier in the season there was held in one of the leading galleries an exhibition of French primitives. The De Hauck galleries (in the Seligman Galleries building) have held two exhibitions of contemporary French art, the first, of the best known artists such as the names found above, and the second of younger men several of whom are already known in this country, others whose paintings are shown for the first time. The Brummer Galleries have had on exhibition sculpture by Despiau and the Valentine Gallery of modern art has exhibited water-colors and drawings by Dunoyer de Segonzac. The Wildenstein galleries have held an exhibition of drawings by Picasso and Durand-Ruel has shown small paintings by Renoir. Surely there is no lack of material in New York for the study of French art.

The International Exhibition of the Carnegie Institute of Pittsburgh, where a still-life by Matisse won first prize, and where many French paintings were shown, is now being held (Jan.-Feb.) at the Brooklyn Museum of Art.

An exhibition of paintings by Cézanne for the benefit of the French Hospital, is being held at the Wildenstein Galleries.

The department stores are all purchasing work by the leading French craftsmen in furniture, glass, textiles and all applied arts. On the shelves of these stores one can see glassware from the hand of Lalique, textiles by Rodier, pottery from the studios of Primavera (the department of decorative art of the store le Printemps), etc. At Wanamakers' *Venturus,* a salon of French decorative art, one can see examples of the best work of contemporary French craftsmen; Wanamakers have also held this fall an exhibition of the French painters of Northern Africa.

French teachers may not know that the Metropolitan Museum of Art has a permanent exhibition of contemporary French decorative art, most of the examples having been acquired from the Exposition des Arts décoratifs in Paris (of 1925) and that the New York Public Library has a permanent exhibition of contemporary French book-binding. The façade of the building of the Cheney silk company is an example of the excellent work of one of the leading French craftsmen in bronze, Edgar Brandt.

Teachers who have students interested in art can easily stimulate their interest in both French and their vocation by directing them to the art galleries of the city. A glance at the art news in the papers will reveal the rich material to be found in New York for all who want to become familiar with French art, and that knowledge can be acquired gratis, for in nearly every case admission to the galleries is free.

Hélène HARVITT.

Lord and Taylor's is going to hold an educational exhibition of French decorative art at the end of February.

THE FRENCH TEACHER'S FORUM

DAILY FREE PERIOD

The Forum is open to discussion of all matters vitally affecting the various aspects of the French teacher's duties. We therefore take pleasure in publishing the following communication upon the Daily Free Period.

My dear Sir,

The curriculum in Modern Languages has steadily improved in the past few years, certain conditions for the control of admission into Modern Language classes are fast obtaining recognition and requirements for Licenses to teach a Modern Foreign Language are on the upward path.

Unfortunately, there still exist, however, too many and too great differences in the conditions under which Teachers of Modern Foreign Languages work.

Strangely, not the least of the evils directly affecting the teaching of Modern Foreign Languages has received thus far little enough attention from administrators and the public. We mean the matter of the Daily Program of the Modern Language Teacher. There still exist schools that require six and seven consecutive periods of not less than forty minutes per period of continuous attention on the part of the teacher to routine duty. Such a continuous session, broken only by a brief lunch period of perhaps half an hour reacts unfavorably upon the efficiency of the teacher and directly affects in a negative, if not in a positively harmful way, the pupil, who in the last analysis, is the innocent victim of every adverse condition that may be about him.

Schools with a six and seven period day program do not require every period to be spent by the teacher in teaching, perhaps, but every period is frequently utilized to the limit in sponsorship, clerical, disciplinary, Study Hall or other school activities (no wonder class after class is found steeped in drowsy inertia when supervisors visit them!)

For instance, the following is typical.

Teacher	Per. I	Per. II	Per. III	Per. IV	Per. V	Per. VI
A	S. H.	Span.	Span.	Span.	Span.	Span.
B	German	French	French	French	S. H.	German
C	French	French	French	French	French	S. H.

This schedule displays six periods for the day—each period at least forty minutes long. No Lunch Period is indicated, probably because the Session is regarded as a "Continuous Session", nor does the "Club Period", so-called, appear on the schedule; an additional "Club Period" likewise of not less than forty minutes (thus actually a seven period day). During the

"Club Period" the teacher has definite duties of one kind or another frequently the supervision of a Reporting Room of more than a score of pupils for each one of whom the teacher is sponsor in matters of attendance, tardiness, general discipline and scholarship. Where Study Hall is listed, it frequently means a Study Hall seating one hundred pupils.

Suffice it to say that no teacher of any subject can carry year in and year out such a program without paying the price of an inevitably weakened efficiency. Teachers realize, furthermore, that the day is not done, when the dismissal bell rings, but does the public realize this last detail so thoroughly? Certain it is, that any teacher who maintains a wholesome and well balanced interest in the pupil and the school does so, *in spite of* and never *because* of the strain that such a program entails. In the long run, is not such an arrangement poor economy of energy and money—is it not a case of quantity expected from the teacher rather than quality?

And too, because all teachers may not immediatly be granted a Daily Free Period as a permanent part of their program, is that any argument in favor of witholding it from Teachers of Modern Languages?

Many of the newer and generally reputed to be the best schools in the country are granting more and more at least one Daily Free Period to the teacher, regardless of the subject taught. Teachers of English have practically had it for years. Why?

Teachers of Modern Foreign Languages, are not ashamed, but on the contrary, are proud to approve and to work for the permanent incorporation into their schedules of at least one Daily Free Period.

Sincerely Yours, *A Teacher.*

In connection with the subject of the above letter, the Editor has been requested to insert in *The French Review* the following:

Extract from the Minutes of the French Round Table (Modern Language Section, S. E. District, N. Y. States—Hotel McAlpin, N. Y. City, Nov. 18, 1927.)

It was moved, seconded and unanimously carried that

1. This body reiterate its expression of interest in this matter of a Daily Free Period for Modern Foreign Language Teachers, originally considered by it three (3) years ago.

2. This body places itself upon record as favoring and desiring a Daily Free Period to be made a permanent part of the daily schedule of all Modern Foreign Language Teachers.

3. This body extends its congratulations to all Teachers of all subjects whose programs do already grant to them a Daily Free Period.

4. A copy of these resolutions be sent to
   - (a) The French Review.
   - (b) The Modern Language Journal.
   - (c) The N. Y. State Education.

(Signed) Gertrude Raftery, *Secretary.*

THE FORUM RESOLUTION

This resolution, as proposed in our last issue, has aroused such interest that we shall continue to print a certain number of comments upon the same resolution in our next number. Readers are again reminded that comments must not exceed 200 *words in length, that they should bear the name and address of the sender (we shall print initials only, if so requested) and be sent to "The French Review Forum",* 306 *Hamilton Hall, Columbia University.*

The French Teacher's Forum resolved that students in High School are not sufficiently advanced to read with profit the French classics of the seventeenth century. Well they should.

What they need to know of French grammar and irregular verbs is not in itself an inexhaustible subject and after three years of it, they should be introduced to the study of classical literature. They are criticized for being immature, unable to grasp the significance of a philosophical abstraction and generally lacking in background. Why not supply them with it, appeal to thinking rather than mechanism and try the more to obtain the less.

At sixteen or seventeen years of age, High School students read Shakespeare. It does not mean they understand all there is in Hamlet or Macbeth. But it provides their memory with splendid material and awakens their literary sense if they are susceptible of any. Corneille, Molière and Racine likewise offer plenty of first class material which, if handled properly, will interest them and prepare them for what College French is supposed to be. The "vers alexandrin" and the peculiar language of the classical dramas are not serious obstacles, and if their human appeal is emphasized, students cannot fail to take great pleasure in them. Speaking from experience I got very interesting comments from the students who read Andromaque and roarings from the class when we studied Le Misanthrope.

ANTOINETTE N. HOFFHERR.

Your resolution is dead right. Has the hour come at last when the task of the school teacher may be simplified to the point of being humanly possible? High School students are not incapable of enjoying the classics; but they cannot appreciate them fully and they should be occupied with other things in their French classes. What little time they have should be devoted to acquiring a thorough grounding in the French of today. Having acquired this, they can take up 17th century authors later—at College or in their own private reading. To study Corneille, Molière and Racine in the early years of French disturbs a foundation that is, alas!, none too secure.

A. R. F.

I feel I must protest against the sentiments expressed in the resolution published in the first number of *The French Review,* namely, 'that students in our high schools are not sufficientl advanced to read with profit the French classics of the seventeenth century such as Corneille, Racine and Molière.'

I shall always be very grateful to my teachers in high school who made me read Vergil, Cicero, and Homer. Since I studied Greek in a high school in America, you can easily see that I am *déjà d'un certain âge* and perhaps somewhat old fashioned. I greatly prefer the Aeneid and the Iliad to some of the fabricated texts which the so-called up-to-date teachers of Latin are trying to introduce. Even now when I read little Latin and no Greek, I realize more than ever how much I owe to the fact that I very early became acquainted with the Vergilian gentleness, the sonorous Ciceronian periods, and that marvelous poetic simplicity of the Homeric poems. You may smile and question how much appreciation a young high school girl may have of such master-pieces and yet, however inadequate my preparation and immaturity was to appreciate fully what I read, I still did obtain something very tangible from my study.

So in my own teaching of French I have always endeavored to have my pupils, who do three years of French with me, take away with them the remembrance of at least one master-piece. *Le Bourgeois Gentilhomme* always pleases, as do some of the other comedies of Molière; *Le Cid* has aroused even the young generation of to-day to admire its fine moral quality, so that *beau comme le Cid* was not necessarily a meaningless term; even *Phèdre* became interesting when the more sophisticated wished to place the phrase, *Vénus à sa proie attachée,* which Carl Van Vechten so frequently quoted in one of his earlier novels. It requires more enthusiasm on the part of the teacher, more ingenuity to draw parallels between the life of the age of the Roi-Soleil and that of this age, a little boldness to point out that the young girls of to-day are lineal descendants of the affected ladies of Molière. Yet how fully repaid I have been when a pupil in after years has mentioned to me the pleasure he had in being introduced by me to Mascarille or Monsieur Jourdain. How I should blush for shame if I had never allowed my students to receive any more elevated view of the genius of the French beyond what they might find in *Le Voyage de M. Perrichon, la Tulipe Noire, Colomba,* etc. Corsican bandits, monomaniacs, silly and finicky old gentlemen are not more characteristic of France than America. The universality of the characters of the literature of the seventeenth century places them in world literature, with which every one should have some acquaintance.

Furthermore, how do you explain the remarkable success of Walter Hampden's revival of *Cyrano de Bergerac?* Certainly here is a play which would seem to require such an intimate knowledge of life and manners in the seventeenth century that one can hardly explain its popularity on Broadway to-day. How many persons have said to me, 'I should like to study French only to read *Cyrano* in the original', and many a student has remarked to me that he felt amply repaid for all his drudgery in French grammar, since he had read in the original Rostand's great play.

After all one very legitimate objective in the study of French is the reading of a small amount of the best in French literature and especially that period of French Literature which is generally conceded to be her best.

I realize all too well how much easier it is to cater to the tastes of my pupils by reading wild, lurid tales or popular modern fliction of a very ephemeral character. How many texts are being edited to-day which will and should be entirely forgotten to-morrow. In pleading for a small space for the French classics in our high schools I must seem to some of my younger colleagues somewhat out of date, perhaps even a précieuse. I accept the accusation ***mais, monsieur, on peut être précieuse, même aujourd'hui, sans être ridicule.***

An 'old' teacher of French.

There are two valid reasons why neither Corneille nor Racine can be taught successfully in the high-schools. First, there is a wide-spread feeling that verse is much more difficult than prose. The students share this attitude with their elders; they seem to feel that poetry can be only hard, never interesting. The fact that the vocabulary and style of these classics is in reality far simpler than that of most prose writers does not offset this prejudice. The second reason is fundamental, since it involves appreciation of the ideational content of French classical tragedy. How is it possible to interest students in an antiquity of which they know next to nothing through the medium of a foreign tongue which they read with difficulty? To teach these authors effectively makes demands upon both teacher and student which neither is at present prepared to meet.

Molière's comedies in verse are generally more difficult to read than either Corneille or Racine, and should certainly not be attempted in the high-school. But his best prose comedies can be read with ease and infinite pleasure and profit by third and fourth year students. Under these circumstances it seems unpardonable to omit the greatest name of French literature from the required reading-list of the high-schools.

ALBERT D. MENUT.

VARIA

By J. F. Mason

According to the National Sabbatic Leave Association, the leave of absence plan has now spread to some 200 cities. Teachers of French will be much interested in this, because no group can ask for sabbatic leave with greater justice than the teachers of French, who find here in America so little opportunity to speak French and hear it spoken. In this respect teachers of other modern foreign languages are in a somewhat better situation. For the teacher of French, however, residence in France for a more or less extended period becomes imperative, and nothing can replace the knowledge and comprehension of both the language and the people which may be gained by personal contact with the French in their own country.

* * *

School administrators recognize more and more the wisdom of expending public funds to enable teachers to continue their preparation for their professional work. A conscientious teacher of French, for example, has never, in spite of any advanced degrees, completed his or her training. Many school systems make provision for assisting teachers who desire to attend the summer sessions at universities which offer special courses in methods or advanced courses in the subjects taught in secondary schools. In some cases a school board has presented a teacher of French with the necessary sum to spend a summer in France.

In this connection one may recall the suggestion which Mr. John D. Rockefeller made at Brown University last year, that college students pay in full for their instruction. Provided that the gifted student may rely upon scholarships in case of need, no one can question the advantage to be derived from such an innovation. The time and expense involved in the preparation of a teacher of French amounts to much more than in the case of teachers of most subjects generally taught in high schools and colleges. School boards should manifest some willingness to share the financial burden which rests upon the teacher of French who wishes to neglect no part of his or her preparation for effective teaching. Teachers of other modern foreign languages, who find themselves in more or less the same situation, should join with us in insisting that school authorities assume the financial responsibility for properly preparing teachers of subjects, such as the modern foreign languages, which require not only a certain native linguistic ability, but also special opportunities.

* * *

Some of the best students in French in college trace their interest in the subject to an enthusiastic teacher in their preparatory school. The colleges owe a debt of gratitude to such teachers, because no one questions Renan's famous dictum, 'l'essentiel dans l'éducation, ce n'est pas la doctrine enseignée, c'est l'éveil.' These high school teachers always follow closely the career of their former pupils and manifest a very justifiable pride, when they continue successfully their study of French in college. After reading President Hullihen's interesting article in this issue of *The French Review,* they should encourage their better pupils to consider the possibility of taking advantage of this Junior Year in France plan, which offers so many possibilities to students, not only for the continuation of their studies in French, but for residence in France under the most favorable conditions.

* * *

Under the caption of 'The Modern Foreign Languages in American Education' in School and Society, Nov. 12, 1927, Mr. Henry G. Doyle calls attention to the importance of the modern foreign languages in our curricula. After some timely quotations from *the Teaching of Modern Foreign Languages* by H. G. Atkins and H. L. Hutton, and *High School and Class Management* by H. A. Hollister, Mr. Doyle makes the following very admirable suggestions for placing our teaching of modern foreign languages on a firmer basis:

"If we are to meet the challenge of contemporary civilization, we must have—among other things—more teaching of modern foreign languages; and—this is just as vital—we must have more effective teaching of them. We must begin the study of foreign languages earlier and continue it longer. We must insist that the pupil obtain more than a smattering of one language before he turns to another. We must increase the time allotted to foreign languages; for, as President William Mather Lewis has pointed out, it is hardly fair to speak of "three years of French" when one means too often merely three school years of 26 weeks each, in a class meeting at most five times a week but more generally only three, and with periods of 35 to 40 minutes—minus the time devoted to discipline, school bookkeeping, and visitors! We must reduce the size of these classes, realizing that it is almost hopeless to attempt to teach a foreign language in classes of more than thirty pupils except under the most unusual circumstances. Last but not least, we must have better prepared teachers. We must pay them better salaries if we expect them to study and travel abroad; we must give them leaves on part-pay if we expect them to make their subjects alive and interesting in the way that only those who have enjoyed foreign travel can do. We must protect the properly trained American teacher of foreign languages against the somewhat widespread belief that any "native" can teach his own language to American boys and girls, and we must protect the efficient "native" teacher who *can* teach from the competition of his fellows who have merely drifted into such teaching—the all-too-common itinerant "foreign language professors" for whom school administrators—and some parents—have such a superstitious regard."

The Twenty-Seventh Annual Report of the Secretary of the College Entrance Examination Board contains a number of items of interest to teachers of French. All teachers who have implicit confidence in the work as it is carried on will note with satisfaction that the activities of the Board more than doubled during the past decade. The Board examinations in French have done much to raise the standard of instruction in French and to standardize it thruout the country.

The following statistics taken from the report may have some interest:

Total number of candidates who took examinations in the four modern foreign languages.

French.		
Cp.2.	Two-Year	4893
B.	Third Year	1416
Cp.3.	Three-Year	4391
Cp.4.	Four-Year	622
German		
Cp.2.	Two-Year	815
B.	Third Year	120
Cp.3.	Three-Year	133
Cp.4.	Four-Year	24
Italian		
Cp.2.	Two-Year	44
B.	Third Year	4
Cp.3.	Three-Year	8
Cp.4.	Four-Year	6
Spanish		
Cp.2.	Two-Year	752
B.	Third Year	77
Cp.3.	Three-Year	171
Cp.4.	Four-Year	18

Subjects elected by New Plan Candidates in 1927:

English	2820
Mathematics	2257
French	2143
Latin	2032
History	956
Chemistry	646
Physics	448
Spanish	130
German	94
Biology	53
Greek	46
Italian	6
Botany	5
Physical Geography	4
Zoology	1
Total	11641

The report includes a General Report on the Scholastic Aptitude Test from which the following paragraph is taken:

"The scholastic aptitude test was given to the class entering a college for men at which all members of the Freshman class took the same course of study. Disregarding entirely all cases eliminated from college during the year, the correlation between first year college grades and the scholastic aptitude test was .598 (262 cases). Since all students had taken the same courses, it was considered worth while to correlate the results of the scholastic aptitude test with marks in the various courses. This was done with the following results:

Correlation with marks in English	.70
Correlation with marks in Mathematics	.52
Correlation with marks in Surveying	.44
Correlation with marks in French	.36

It would be interesting to study from several different angles the correlation in regard to French.

While all teachers of French recognize how much they owe the College Entrance Examination Board for what it has accomplished in the past, they are very hopeful that the Board may very soon see fit to change somewhat the nature of the examinations in French so that teachers may be encouraged to teach French not as a dead, but a living language. No examination in modern foreign languages which fails to test the ability of the candidate to speak the language and understand it when spoken will ever satisfy the progressive teacher of French.

No institution in America could bring about such a momentous reform in the teaching of modern foreign languages as the College Entrance Examination Board, were it to revise its examinations so as to include an oral and aural test. Up to the present time the Board has uttered a *non possumus* when confronted with the difficulties inherent in standardizing an oral test in a large number of examination centers, but, having solved so many complex problems in the past, it will undoubtedly find a solution to this one.

The Regents Examinations of the State of New York have made an important step forward in this direction with the recently introduced aural tests. The beneficial influence of these tests in forcing the teachers to pay more attention to the spoken languages is already being noticed.

* * *

Teachers frequently request information regarding study in France. The Institute of International Education published in 1926 a *Handbook for American Students in France* by Dr. Horatio S. Krans, which in some 160 pages gives all the necessary information for an American Student in France. The Institute of International Education, 2 West 45th Street, New York City, will supply copies of this handbook for the nominal sum of twenty-five cents.

J. F. Mason.

BOOK REVIEWS

FROM ARIEL TO DIZZY

It is a far cry from Shelley to Disraeli, yet this holds no terror for André Maurois, who, in his latest biography*, offers us an engaging picture of a great statesman and, in general, an alert account of the times he lived in. Disraeli's career, under the pen of his French biographer, assumes the swift, brilliant character of fiction; his figure, at once romantic and real, emerges with extraordinary clarity. Within the limits he ascribed to himself, with the aim he had in view, M. Maurois may be said to have succeeded fully.

These limits and this aim prove to be M. Maurois' strength and his weakness. Here, as with all the biographies in this particular series or of this particular sort, is an outline of a life rather than a life, a *précis* of a period rather than that period. What is gained in color frequently proves a loss in depth; when the author, in a few, rapid, luminous strokes intensifies the physical reality of his personage, the reader is apt to miss the background from which this personage is sprung, and in relation to which he should properly be viewed. Thus, for example, while M. Maurois gives us a splendid verbal comparison of the characters of Gladstone and Disraeli—a prose-passage of acuity, balance and polish to be placed beside Hazzlitt's amazing picture of Rabelais, Swift and Voltaire—still, Gladstone but rarely appears of his true stature. Moreover, when he does, we invariably perceive that M. Maurois was not deaf to the tremendous conflict between the Titans of the century, but that he deliberately muffled it in order to remain within the bounds he had set for himself.

What a career it was and what grist for M. Maurois' mill! The curious, sensitive, conceited little Jew, who learned to box in secret and won his fight against his bullying schoolfellow; the potential newspaper magnate, ruined at twenty; the rage in letters, the successful novelist almost in spite of himself, at twenty-one. Then his 'grand tour', via Malta, where the officers found him 'a boastful little Hebrew', to Turkey, where, in his rôle of neo-Byron, he was adored, and to Palestine, the remote and glamorous cradle of his race. Next his theatrical bids for parliamentary election, his apparent recklessness over the shrewd, practical, persevering plans he had laid; the fiasco of his maiden speech, his *revanche*, his rise seemingly meteoric but in reality so patiently graduated. And the man's friends: Caroline Norton, Lady Blessington, D'Orsay, most of all his wife, the dull Mrs. Lewis, to whom he always remained so exaggeratedly good. A prince, too, later to be an Emperor Disraeli was to visit at the Tuileries; a king, Louis-Philippe, 'who spoke English with an American accent', until the day when Disraeli, breaking down every obstacle of prejudice and animus by flattery and patience, was to sit on the right hand of that queen he made Empress of India... And, finally, the ministry with its trials and triumphs, and the apotheosis of the Congress of Berlin. Here, indeed, M. Maurois finds perfect material for his bright, straightforward utterance, for his clarity in portraiture, for his exquisite sensitivity and his beautifully easy sense of sentimental values. And here we leave Disraeli, after his sovereign's reward (*"C'était vrai d'ailleurs qu'il aimait la Reine!"*) and the admiration of Europe (*"Les traditions de l'Angleterre ne sont pas tout à fait mortes : elles survivent dans les esprits d'une femme et d'un vieil homme d'Etat"*), under the light, unconsciously ironic burden of a verse of the Psalms and a crown of primroses, "his favorite flowers"!

Columbia University. JACQUES LE CLERCQ.

LE PRIX GONCOURT

Par une majorité de six voix, contre trois accordées à M. Chamson et une à M. Wild, l'Académie Goncourt vient de couronner un écrivain inconnu jusqu'ici non seulement du public, mais encore de la plupart des professionnels. Pour son coup d'essai, M. Maurice Bedel a fait un coup de maître. Il n'a même manqué que de bien peu le "coup double", puisque le jury du Prix Théophraste Renaudot, au moment de le proclamer vainqueur, a changé sa décision en apprenant le résultat du Goncourt. La gloire naissante du jeune écrivain n'a pas besoin de lauriers supplémentaires.

Deux jurys, proclamant simultanément *Jérôme, 60 Degrés de Latitude Nord* le meilleur livre de l'année, voilà un compliment peu ordinaire. Avec un pareil patronage, l'ouvrage ne peut manquer d'obtenir du public une faveur qu'il mérite amplement.

M. Maurice Bedel, né à Paris en 1884, est un Parisien d'une vieille famille parisienne. Il est médecin, comme Duhamel qui fut son camarade de classe et qui l'a précédé au prix Goncourt. (A ce propos je me permets de signaler un intéressant sujet de thèse aux aspirants Ph. D. — *De l'influence de la médecine sur la production littéraire française contemporaine* — les exemples ne font pas défaut!) Il est également peintre. Il est encore entomologiste. Le lauréat du prix Goncourt a débuté dans les lettres en publiant, comme de juste, quelques poèmes dans des revues à tirage restreint. Au lycée, il nous le dit lui-même, il était toujours le dernier en narration française. N'est-ce pas tout à fait conforme à la tradition?

"*Jérôme, 60 Degrés de Latitude Nord*" est un roman moderne, léger, dans le goût du jour. Celui qui en commence la lecture ne le lâchera pas facilement avant d'en avoir tourné la dernière page. Le sujet: l'Amour, naturellement. M. Maurice Bedel est arrivé à en tirer quelque chose de nouveau, ce dont on ne saurait assez le féliciter. Il nous raconte les aventures amoureuses d'un Français en Norvège. Son héros est le Français "type", tel que le conçoivent tous les étrangers et en particulier mes amis américains. C'est le Français romantique, latin, homme du Midi. L'héroïne, c'est la jeune fille du Nord, telle que se la figurent tous les Français. C'est l'Anglo-Saxonne aux cheveux très blonds, aux yeux très bleus, au teint blanc et rose. Que peut-il résulter de la rencontre de ces deux personnages, si ce n'est le coup de foudre? Bien entendu, c'est le Latin qui s'enflamme le premier... et comment! Chez la Norvégienne, le sentiment amoureux ne s'éveillera que plus tard. Il se développera petit à petit, insensiblement, et le lecteur s'en apercevra avant que la jeune fille s'en rende compte elle-même.

Hélas! pourquoi faut-il qu'une si belle histoire finisse aussi mal? Jérôme aime comme un idéaliste exalté, selon la plus pure tradition romantique. Dans sa fiancée il aime surtout l'Amour, les petits rendez-vous secrets (quand il lui est si facile de la voir au grand jour), les billets doux glissés en cachette (ce qui est parfaitement inutile puisqu'il peut lui parler tous les jours), les tendres soupirs au clair de lune par de belles nuits d'hiver (quand la neige est si belle pour faire du ski et qu'il serait si bête de ne pas en profiter). Il s'obstine à vouloir se faire deviner, il est symboliste, il suggère.

Uni ne comprend pas grand chose à cette puérile comédie. Elle a bien, tout d'abord, un vague soupçon, mais, comme rien de tangible ne vient confirmer ses suppositions, elle croira bien vite qu'elle s'est trompée. Pour qu'elle sache à quoi s'en tenir, il faudra la déclaration qui ne vient pas vite et n'a pas lieu sans efforts.

Il ne suffit pas toujours d'être d'accord, de s'aimer et de se le dire, les choses seraient trop simples ainsi et il n'y aurait pas de roman possible. La conception scandinave de l'amour est bien différente de celle des Latins, et voilà la catastrophe. Les idées des deux jeunes gens, leurs mœurs, leurs habitudes ne concordent pas précisément. Elles s'opposent, elles se combattent; dans la bagarre, l'amour n'est plus qu'un impondérable: il s'évanouit et tout est fini. Quelqu'un a jadis défini la pudeur en disant que ce n'était qu'une question de climat. Je ne sais plus quel est l'auteur de cet aphorisme, mais il n'avait certainement jamais voyagé en Norvège.

Il faut féliciter l'auteur de son impartialité dans la présentation de ses personnages. Personne ne pourra l'accuser d'avoir voulu rendre son héros sympathique aux dépens de "l'étrangère". Au lecteur de se faire une opinion. M. Bedel lui offre deux théories, toutes deux soutenues par des arguments solides et convaincants, il ne peut y avoir qu'une question de préférence personnelle, un choix à faire. Dans la religion de l'Amour, il n'y a qu'un seul et unique Dieu, mais de nombreuses sectes, et chacun l'adore à sa façon.

L'ouvrage est écrit d'une façon très agréable, légère et variée. L'intérêt ne languit pas. Il y a suffisamment d'action pour contenter les jeunes gens modernes, des descriptions charmantes pour satisfaire les dilettantes, des analyses psychologiques selon la mode actuelle. L'auteur voit ses personnages comme le peintre qu'il est, il les dissèque avec l'instrument délicat et pointu dont se servent les entomologistes et son héros aime comme un poète. M. Maurice Bedel, peintre, entomologiste et poète, a bien profité de ses études, et, s'il concourrait aujourd'hui, il ne serait plus le dernier en narration française.

F. G. Hoffherr.

BIBLIOGRAPHY

TEXT BOOKS

BOND, Otto F., *Terre de France; Premières lectures.* University of Chicago Junior College Series of French, 1928. Price, $1.50.

CAMERLYNCK, Mme et G. H. *Au pays de France.* Allyn and Bacon, 1927, viii-300 pp.

DELPIT, L. *Representative contemporary French lyrics* (1855-1925). Ginn and Co., 1927, xxv-385 pp. Price, $1.20.

GROSJEAN, W. H. *French Verb Book.* A complete treatise on the conjugation of Verbs with Drills, Exercises and Verbal Idioms. I-176 pp. Thomas Nelson & Sons, 1927.

GROSJEAN, W. H. *L'Europe en Zigzag.* Thomas Nelson & Sons, 1927, I-232 pp.

LABICHE ET MARTIN. *Le Voyage de M. Perrichon.* Edited by R. W. Haller. Globe Book Company, 1927, vx-188 pp.

LÉVI, M. *Reading, Writing and Speaking French.* Henry Holt, 1927, xv-344 pp. Price, $1.40.

MOLIÈRE. *La Critique de l'Ecole des Femmes et l'Impromptu de Versailles.* Note by A. Tilley. Cambridge Plain Texts, Cambridge University Press, 1927. Price, $0.50.

PROUST, M. *Selections from.* Edited by Papen-Payne. Oxford Press, 1927, 104 pp. Price, $0.50.

ROE, F. C. *La France Laborieuse.* Thomas Nelson & Sons, 1927, xx-176 pp.

WOODBRIDGE, Benjamin M. *La Semeuse.* University of Chicago Junior College Series of French, 1928. Price, $1.50.

GENERAL

ASHTON, H. *A Preface to Molière.* Longmans, Green, 1927, xi-177 pp. Price, $2.25.

GRANT, Elliot M. *French Poetry and Modern Industry.* 1830-1870. Harvard Studies in Romance Languages. Harvard University Press, 1927. Price, $2.50.

JONES, Howard Mumford. *America and French Culture.* University of North Carolina Publications, 1927. Price, $4.50.

NITZE AND DARGAN. *A History of French Literature.* From the earliest times to the present. Revised edition. Henry Holt, 1927, xi-818 pp. Price, $4.00.

PEDAGOGICAL BOOKS AND ARTICLES

BLAKEY, Ruth. *Use of Prognosis Tests in Modern Languages.* The School Review. University of Chicago, Vol. XXXV, No. 9, Nov. 1927, pp. 692-698.

BUCHANAN, Milton. *A Modern Language Study in Canada.* Educational Record, Vol. VIII, No. 4, pp. 266-276.

BUSWELL, G. T. *A Laboratory Study of the Reading of Modern Foreign Languages.* Macmillan, 1927, 100 pp.

FIFE, Robert H. *The Modern Foreign Language Study in the United States.* Educational Record, Vol. VIII, No. 4, pp. 251-265.

LIMPER, Louis. *The Effect of having studied a Foreign Language in High School on the ability of College Freshmen to use English correctly.* The School Review, Vol. XXXV, No. 9, Nov. 1927, pp. 676-681.

ONIS, F. de. *The Coordination of the Study of French with that of the other Romance Languages.* The Romanic Review, Vol. XVIII, No. 4 Oct.-Dec., 1927, pp. 297-305.

O'SHEA, M. V. *The Reading of Modern Foreign Languages.* Bulletin No. 16, 1927, of the U. S. Bureau of Education, 78 pp.

PLAN *d'une Expérience d'étude consciente de la prononciation française.* Cercle de Recherches sur l'enseignement du français. Etudes Françaises, 13e Cahier, 1927.

THARP, J .P. *Sectioning classes in Romance Languages.* Modern Language Journal, Vol. XII, No. 2, Nov. 1927, pp. 95-114.

PERIODICALS

KRUTCH, Joseph Wood. *Paul Valéry and the Intellectual Critics.* The Nation, Oct. 12, 1927, p. 377.

LEWISOHN, Ludwig. *French Literature of to-day.* The Nation, Nov. 23, 1927.

FOREIGN PUBLICATIONS

BILLY, André. *La littérature française contemporaine.* Poésie, roman, idées. Colin, 1927.

BONNEVON, Ch. *Les Ecrivains français modernes de la France depuis le Premier Empire. Fayard,* 1927.

GENÉVRIER, P. *Précis de phonétique comparée française et anglaise.* Didier, 1927, 379 pp.

LALOU, René. *Vers une alchimie lyrique.* Saine-Beuve, Baudelaire, etc. Les Arts et le Livre, 1927, 268 pp.

PRADEZ, El. *Dictionnaire des gallicismes les plus usités.* Expliqués brièvement, illustrés par des exemples et accompagnés de leurs équivalents anglais et allemands. Payot, 1927.

SOUDAY, Paul. *Marcel Proust, André Gide, Paul Valéry.* Kra, 1927, 100 pp.

RECENT TEXTS

BRIEUX, Eugène. *La Française.* Edited with Introduction, Notes, Exercises and Vocabulary by Simone de la Souchère Deléry and Gladys Anne Renshaw. Century Co., 1927, xiii-150 pages.

La Française is a very appropriate play for reading with American students for it gives an excellent characterisation of the French woman and of the French in general, and also, through the medium of an American and a Franco-American affords an opportunity for drawing comparisons between the traits of both France and the United States. The student can only benefit by the study of the play, for it will help dispel many wrong notions concerning the French. The editors of the book deserve credit for their happy choice.

The Introduction gives sufficient information for the average student. It is a pity that the difficult words in the Introduction are not defined in the Vocabulary. Had they been defined the Introduction would have been still more valuable. On the whole the Vocabulary is very good. One criticism of a general nature: it would be better to include in the vocabulary words which are defined in the Notes, especially those defined in French, such as p. 35, *basculer;* p. 85, *mévente,* etc.

The following words are omitted from the Vocabulary: p. 32, *club d'études,* neither word is in the Vocabulary; p. 35, *bon,* which is defined under *marché* but not given separately; p. 43, *camp* is given under *ficher le camp* but not separately; p. 53, *prendre au tragique,* not to be found under *prendre* and *tragique* is not in the vocabulary; p. 83, *grosseur* is omitted; *indigné* also; p. 94, *plein* is omitted though we find the word in the expression *en pleine paix; or* on the same page is omitted; p. 101, *inférieur* is omitted and occurs with a meaning different from its English cognate. It would help the student if idiomatic expressions were listed under more than the key-word: example, *pris soin* defined under *prendre,* and *soin* is not in the vocabulary; this kind of omission occurs frequently, as on p. 9, *faire sa cour* is defined under *faire* and *cour* is not in the vocabulary; p. 34, *cheminée à manteau* is defined under *cheminée* and *manteau* is not in the vocabulary, etc. On p. 13, *faire une blague* should be given as an expression; p. 14, *ne te fais pas d'illusions;* p. 18, *si j'en juge;* p. 15, *faire la leçon* is listed neither under *faire* nor under *leçon;* p. 18, *à main* needs definition; on the same page, *faites donc;* p. 25, *ne les paraît pas* needs translation; p. 28, *je n'en sais rien;* p. 35, *tour à pointes,* —it would have been safer to include *pointe* in the vocabulary; p. 47, *de loin;* p. 62, *faire du tort* should be under *tort* just as *avoir tort* is listed; p. 65, *donner du mal* is not found as an expression either under *donner* nor under *mal;* p. 74, *qu'y a-t-il pour votre service* should be defined; p. 82, *à la fois;* on the same page, *à la réflexion;* p. 96, *à vous dire vrai; que vous étiez au courant*: *être au courant* is translated by "to be aware", which does not quite fit in here.

There are a few single words which need better translation: p. 5, *genoux* could be translated by "lap"; p. 29, *s'était tapi* is not exactly "squat, crouch"; p. 30, *vous remuer* is more than "move"; p. 44, *mes prévisions se sont réalisées* means rather "have come true"—the word is translated "to make real" and the reflexive form is not given, and on p. 94 we read: *et on ne les réalise pas,* speaking of *idées,* which is also not translated by the definition in the vocabulary, see also p. 12; p. 94 *tourbillon* is a "whirlwind" not a "whirl"; p. 84, *donner* means to "yield", to "bring".

A few constructions might have been commented upon in the Notes, as for instance, p. 10, *pas possible,* the omission of the pronoun and the negative *ne;* the same page, the omission of the article in *Moi, j'ai idée;* p. 12, *on t'enverrait en face, au musée, salle des antiquités*—omission of the preposition before *salle;* p. 22, *A Maria qu'elle a sonnée* (true enough, the verb is translated in the Vocabulary by "ring for"); p. 25, *ne les paraît pas;* p. 46, *tu la boudes—bouder* is translated by "pout, be sulky"—account for *la.* The Notes are quite complete and are in French except where translation is necessary. There the phrase stands in English. Very few misprints have been found: p. 78 "d'nt" ought to be written "don't", also p. 109 (I suppose that is how the French edition prints it); p. 90, read "candidat" instead of "candidate"; p. 106, read "héroïne" instead of "héroine".

The Exercises are good and not too long. In the Vocabulary it might have been advisable to indicate the aspirate H by some diacritical mark. Some popular expressions which occur in the Vocabulary should be marked so.

H. H.

LABICHE ET MARTIN. *Le Voyage de Monsieur Perrichon.* Edition scolaire moderne avec notes, exercices d'assimilation, et vocabulaire par Léopold Cardon. Scribners, 1927, xiv-158 pages. Price, 80 cents.

Teachers who are familiar with M. Cardon's *Première et Seconde Année Moderne* will understand what the editor means by the word "moderne" which we find in the title. His method also needs no explanation for he has alread applied it to several of his books. In his *But de cette édition scolaire* M. Cardon expresses his thanks for certain corrections made in his English. It is a pity that his French was not touched up too, for many of his sentences are quite unintelligible and often in the directions given to students they are far from clear: p. 1, "comme premier livre de lecture des auteurs, aux élèves normalement préparés à entreprendre la lecture des auteurs; les scènes de cette comédie, en vue des exercices d'assimilation qui y sont basés, ont été réparties en seize leçons ou assignements; les exercices proposés visent à l'assimilation de formes, expressions et idiotismes courants, pouvant se travailler en abordant la lecture des auteurs;" p. VI we read: "en (b), il doit faire en bon anglais la version des phrases de (a)—exercice témoin, de compréhension, de jugement, vite discuté oralement au début de la prochaine classe, avant d'en faire l'exercice". These are just examples out of many. On p. 68, "Après correction rapide en commun, au début de la prochaine classe, de votre version écrite en *b*," etc. Or on p. 89, " le correspondant anglais de cette exclamation dépend du contexte"; p. 98, "pour quoi faire ce carnet?"; p. 107, "Conjuguez aux principaux temps"; p. 109, "Faites ce qui est dit"; etc., etc.

A few words are missing in the vocabulary though in some cases they are defined in the Notes: p. 3, *auteur;* p. 7, *avancé,* where the meaning given to the infinitive in the vocabulary does not fit; p. 9, *action;* p. 30, *ferré;* p. 32, *agir,* "to act" is not found though *s'agir de* is given; p. 10, *attention* in the expression "faites donc attention"; p. 60, *tapissier* and *étoffes* are omitted; p. 80, *malheureuse;* p. 85, *obligé* as a noun. The following expressions and words are insufficiently or incorrectly translated: p. 1, *faire pitié* should be given under *faire* or *pitié;* p. 2, *à la main* should be under *main;* p. 5, *chariot* is not a truck; p. 7, *se donner rendez-vous* should be given as an expression; p. 10, *faites donc attention;* p. 10 *prenez votre tour;* p. 21, *ça ne lui a pas réussi* cannot be correctly translated by the meaning given to *réussir* in the vocabulary; p. 22, *monter à cheval;* p. 23, *fort* means "loud" or "hard"; *à mon tour* needs definition; p. 24, *décocher* is incorrectly translated; p. 47, *droits* is "duty" (customs); p. 59, *de deux choses l'une* needs translation; p. 60, *je vais au fait* cannot be correctly translated by the meaning found under *fait;* p. 62, *chercher* means to "think, cast about"; p. 71, *conduire* is to "drive"; *écrit en toutes lettres* either needs a note or should find a place in the vocabulary; p. 59, *leçon* is not in the vocabulary still we have the expression *donner une leçon;* p. 83, *je vous en prie;* p. 84, *vous n'y pensez pas* should be translated in the Notes; p. 140, we read *Chamouny* or *Chamounix*—the second form is incorrect, the correct one being *Chamonix;* p. 142, nowhere in the text does *coulisse* mean "groove; nor does *crisper* occur with the meaning of "shrivel" (the word is applied to the hands).

The fact that certain words resemble the English forms is responsible for the omission of *ruiner,* p. 11; *mérite,* p. 26; *comédie,* 35; *angle,* p. 42, etc.

There are several mistakes in the phonetic transcription: p. 133, *ah!* should be represented by *a; première* is *prəmjɛ:r; là* should be *l*a and not l*a; enregistrer* is *ãrəʒistre* and not *ãʒistre;* p. 134, again a for *a; permets* is not *pɛrmɛt;* p. 135, *préfet* is not *prefɛt;* p. 135, again wrong *a;* p. 136, *messieurs* is not *mɛsjø,* etc.

Among the misprints are: p. vii, "elle supplie *a*" for *à;* p. 15, *marchpied* for *marchepied;* p. 18, *regarde* should read *regardé;* p. 59, *d'honneur* should read *l'honneur;* p. 65, *il a du* should be *dû;* p. 68, *reuvoient* should be *renvoient;* p. 85, *pasée* should be *passée;* p. 99, *je ne pars tout de suite, pas* is omitted; p. 102, *justifiez* en is *justifiez-en;* p. 106, *il ne semble* is *il me semble;* p. 146, *gallanterie* should read *galanterie;* p. 149, no gender is given for *maman;* p. 152, *prink* should read *prick;* p. 154, *rembouser* is *rembourser,* etc., etc.

When a new edition of a well-known text appears one expects a little more accuracy than is to be found in the present volume.

H. H.

CONTES DRAMATIQUES. Hills & Dondo. Heath & Co. 1927.

Text books are produced with such rapidity nowadays that one is apt to approach the latest arrivals with more or less wariness. The more so when one realizes that the ideal in text books is so difficult to attain. Of course one must admit, trite as the remark may be, that no text book is absolutely bad with a good teacher—also is the reverse true. Before reading this text of *Contes Dramatiques,* I read carefully the foreword. The reader is to expect then, stories "that will appeal to college students as well as to beginners in the High School"... "the students even in the Junior High Schools should be able to read the book without the use of a grammar." It seems to me that college students of to-day would find the stories rather dull in subject matter and long drawn out in treatment. They probably would be able to read the text rapidly and without any great effort early in their first term of French. I do not think it wise to coddle college students to this extent. As for high school students, perhaps those in a first term class who are very young and who have had no other foreign language might enjoy the book. But my experience as a teacher makes even this to be doubted. On the other hand, *Contes Dramatiques* would probably prove a good text for junior high school pupils.

The choice of material is on the whole good. Most of the stories are little legends and folk-stories adapted simply. These are sure to interest very young pupils. The Contes seem to be graded as to difficulties in French construction—the first few are told in the present tense, but gradually, the present perfect, the past descriptive, the future, and conditional are introducd. The imperative with and without object pronouns is used affirmatively and negatively. The past absolute of the indicative as well as the tenses of the subjunctive seem to be entirely lacking—a merit in a text for beginners. The various grammatical constructions, too, find their way slowly into the text. The vocabulary seems adequate. Verbs are arranged there in such a way that they can be referred to intelligently and with no loss of time. But has the future tense or at least the first person singular of the future of orthographical changing verbs been omitted intentionally? There are enough exercises, and some are good. Those are poor which I think are meant to be drill on verbs, for example—C page 144, C page 145, D page 155, D page 160 and the others of the same type. Would the drill not be more valuable if the verb were to be supplied rather than the object and the exercise modified with that in view? As for the questions based on the text, they are probably meant to help the pupil more than the teacher, and as such are a needed exercise. Of course, all these exercises could be supplemented by a resourceful teacher and should be considered as suggestions rather than mandatory.

What probably would make *Contes Dramatiques* a successful text for Junior high school pupils is the fact that they are arranged very well for dramatization. Directions for the setting are so adequate that pupils might act them as a pupil project entirely without help from the teacher. The gay little songs, the words of which are given in the book, would be an added attraction. I think *Contes Dramatiques* will appeal to the teacher who wants to make her text book work interesting, and to the young pupils who must be interested always.

Ethel Leffert.

George Washington High School.

Mérimée. *Colomba.* Edited by O. T. Robert. D. C. Heath and Co., 1927.

Mérimée's Colomba has enjoyed such a lasting popularity among the teachers of French that the need of a new edition of this novel was strongly felt. Professor O. T. Robert of Smith college has just given us an excellent new edition of it. The book itself is too well known to insist on its literary, almost classical qualities, but what we wish to emphasize is the propaedeutic value of the text itself. Indeed the style and the syntax of the text are very simple, the sentences are in pure French and it has been established with such care by Prof. O. T. Robert that students find in it a most excellent model to go by.

The notes and glossary have been entirely and most carefully rewritten. Their aim is not so much to give complete information about a special point but to help to a clear understanding of the text itself. The meaning of a word in the vocabulary is therefore the one required by the context.

But the most important features of this edition are the introduction and the exercises.

The introduction takes into account the most recent researches on the real character of Colomba by a scholar of Corsican origin Lorenzi Bradi, a distant relative of whom was involved in one of the feuds. The results of his researches were published in 1921 in *La Revue Française* and later in a book under the title of *La vraie Colomba*. Prof. Robert's very clear and comprehensive summary throws much light on the personality of Colomba while adding interest through a clearer understanding of her.

In the exercises Prof. Robert follows his well known inductive and intensive method. To understand thoroughly a sentence, to realize the relational value of its elements and then to be able to use in sentences of similar patterns their understood relations, such is the far reaching pedagogical aim of Prof. Robert's method. It is high time that one should understand in education the mistake made in dealing with words, or elements of any sort as if they were entities, things in themselves. We shall have taught something to our students when they will understand, for instance, the system of time relations involved in the use of tenses. They will not only have improved their French, by a better grasping of the mechanism of a correct sentence, but they will also have a mind better trained to take up any other study, for what is science if not a system of relations to be understood or discovered? We are therefore very grateful to Prof. Robert for having carried out in his exercises this very intelligent method in agreement with the newest views on pedagogy and psychology. If we may express a regret, may we say that the text is somewhat long, so that this intensive method could not be carried out with quite the same detailed accuracy shown in *Le trésor du Vieux Seigneur* (1).

May we end with the wish that more and more teachers of French by using Prof. Robert's books and method, will wake up to the fact that, properly taught, the French language is a wonderful training in reasoning.

MARTHE STURM.
Assistant Professor of French, Smith College.

Jules ROMAINS. *Knock, ou le triomphe de la médecine.* Edited with Notes and a Vocabulary by A. D. Menut and D. I. Chapman. The Century Company, 1927, xxiii-109 pages.

The Century Company and the editors of this charming play, a satire in Molieresque vein on the modern methods of practicing medicine, are to be congratulated on introducing it to the American student. Those who have not had the good fortune of seeing it played in Paris (the reviewer is one of the many who have attended the production more than a half a dozen times!) will be glad of this opportunity of interpreting the play to their students. The Introduction gives a very adequate study of Jules Romains' place in contemporary literature. It is a pity that the editors did not mention the name of Louis Jouvet, Director of the *Théâtre des Champs Elysées,* who created the rôle of *M. le Trouhadec,* of *Knock* and of other characters in the plays of Romains. To the bibliographical list of critical studies may be added the book by Crémieux, "XXe Siècle", Librairie Gallimard, 1924, which contains a study of Romains.

The misprints in the book are few: p.xix, read *sociologique;* ap of "appeared" is in wrong fount; p. 12, *le* problème; p. 38, *les* and not *des* doigts; les *choses;* p. 42, *plusieurs;* p. 46, *lèvre;* p. 57, *rayons* and a comma after "X"; p. 77, *appelation* is not in alphabetical order; p. 86, *effacer;* p. 92, *isolement;* p. 94, *mécanique;* p. 100, *produire* appears twice.

(1) Certain matters were overlooked in the proof reading. On page 195 *comprend* and *comprenait* are to be substituted for *parle* and *parlait,* and in the vocabulary the word *Raphael* reference to which is made in the note on the *Transfiguration* has been omitted. This kind of thing very often happens in a first printing and does not materially detract from the value of the book.

A general mistake is non-listing of expressions and prepositional phrases which need explanation or definition: p. 10, *il se fait des illusions;* p. 13, *à la face du monde;* p. 19, *allée et venue;* p. 20, *au bon moment, où en est le docteur, que non;* p. 23, *c'est à savoir;* p. 25, *pour ne pas le nommer;* p. 29, *à nous deux;* p. 30, *coup de foudre* is not listed under *coup* nor *foudre;* p. 34, *poser en principe, par occasion;* p. 31, *d'humeur à;* p. 36, *ça se peut bien;* p. 33, *semaine et dimanche;* p. 38, *du jour au lendemain;* p. 38, *pour le plaisir qu'elles donnent* could be commented on in the Notes; p. 41 *en pleine hausse, plein* is not in the vocabulary; p. 42, *courir les aventures;* p. 47, *je n'ai rien;* p. 51, *ils ne sont pas si à plaindre;* p. 54, *toute faite;* p. 58, *en mains;* p. 60, *à bras tendu; je fais de la médecine*; p. 61, *ma présence ne pesait pas lourd;* p. 62, *tôt ou tard;* p. 63, *on fait du chemin;* p. 67, *par jeu,* etc. Sometimes expressions are to be found under the less important word of the expression.

The following words are omitted from the vocabulary: p. 7, *le regard;* p. 15, *procéder;* p. 15, *mort* (noun); p. 39, do students know what an *alpenstock* is?; p. 41, *plein;* the word *théâtre* is not in the vocabulary because it is the same as the English word, but on p. 6 it means *stage.*

Among inaccuracies in translation and incorrect definition we find the following; p. 3, *rapporter* means *join;* p. 5, *d'arrière* should be given under *arrière* with the meaning *back; les premiers temps* should be defined by "in the beginning"; p. 5, *tenez* means "listen"; p. 6, *s'offrir* inadequately translated by "offer"; p. 7, *voilà que* should be translated; *rhumatismes* means "attacks of rheumatism" and not "cases"; p. 7, *valait la peine* should be under *valoir* or *peine;* p. 8, *gardez-vous* means "keep away from"; *cherche* means "thinks" or "casts about for"; *humeurs* needs explanation; p. 9, *venir trouver; soigner* means "treat"; p. 12, *bachelier ès-lettres* should have fuller explanation in the Notes: it is not enough to say "a student becomes successively *bachelier, licencié, agrégé, docteur.* How?; p. 13, *se fichent* should be marked in the vocabulary as "pop."; p. 17, *commerce* means "trade"; *affaires* means "business"; *commune,* which is not in the vocabulary, needs explanation, also *canton;* p. 19, *style* is not merely "style" (not in the vocabulary); *tout en* should be translated;

gâcher is not exactly to "spoil" but rather to "bungle", to "fail in accomplishment"; p. 20, *où en est* should be under *être;* p. 21, translate *installation;* p. 24, *autant vaudrait* should be defined under *valoir; étranger à* should also be defined; *ivresse* is not "intoxication"; p. 25, *bien placé* needs defining; p. 30, *matière* is "material"; *se trahir,* to "reveal itself"; p. 31, *déjà* is not "already" but "to begin with"; p. 38, *rapporter* is to "yield", "bring in"; p. 37, translate *ah, là, là; c'est une désolation;* p. 40, *sabler* is to "quaff", "drain"; p. 41, *quatre sous* should be explained; *avoir* means "wealth"; p. 42, *sagement* is "obediently"; p. 44, *suivant* is "according to" p. 47, *reins* means "kidneys" and not "loins, reins"; p. 49, *monter,* to "take up" or "carry up"; *patronne,* the gender of both the masculine and the feminine form should be indicated in the vocabulary as in the case of *boulanger, boulangère;* p. 50, *loger* is to "stay" or "stop"; *à tout hasard* is incorrectly translated as "by mere chance"—here it means "at all events, at any cost"; p. 51, *monde* is "people"; p. 52, *se payer* is not to *"afford"* but rather to "treat oneself to", "allow oneself"; p. 53, *intéressé* means "interested through selfish motives";p. 54, *protecteur* is incorrectly translated by "protector, protecting"—it means "patronizing"; p. 57, *échelon* means "grade" or "degree"; p. 58, *trancher* needs better definition; p. 61, *confesser* is inadequately translated; p. 65, *largement* means "amply"; p. 66, *caser,* "find room for"; p. 67, *s'ébaucher,* means rather to "become outlined in one's mind"; *comporte,* p. 68, means to "entail, necessitate", etc.

With the vocabulary revised in a new edition this volume should enjoy great popularity.

H. H.

THE LIBRARIAN'S CORNER

*The librarian of the A. A. T. F., Professor A. L. Cru, will answer in each issue of **The French Review** a certain number of questions from members of the Association desiring information about text books, methods and teaching material. Questions should bear the name and address of the sender and be sent to **The Librarian of the A. A. T. F.**, Room* 204, *Teachers College, Columbia University, New York City.*

The Librairian, Professor Albert L. Cru, announces that he has completed arrangements with a number of publishers in France for the establishment of a circulating library of works of interest to teachers of French. Thru the kindness of the publishers, the Librairian will be able to lend these to members of the A. A. T. F. *The French Review* will publish later a list of such books. It is hoped that with the growth of our Association we may be able to place at the disposal of our members not only books but lantern slides, cinema films, made in France with the titles in French, phonographic records of French music, good reproductions of French art.

PLAYS FOR THE FRENCH CLUB,

Selected in order of difficulty.

Madame BELLIER (Marie Klecker): *Théâtre du jeune âge, Comédies enfantines et saynètes*: Albin Michel, éditeur, Paris

Four volumes, illustrated; the last, composed of dramatised fairy tales; for all grades up to and including Junior High School. Among the plays there is a wide possibility of choice and a liberal offering of colorful stage settings; plots are extremely simple, French easy, and none of the plays will need cutting.

Hills and Dondo: *Contes dramatiques;* D. C. Heath and Co. Twenty five contes in very simple French, very cleverly told in form to be dramatized; stage setting are given for each story; tales selected from this collection would add life and interest to a French Club program, and would demand very little previous preparation.

Théâtre pour la Jeunesse: Brentano, New York. Volume I. Eight one act plays, all short. La Duchesse couturière, La Somnambule, Ma Bonne, L'Idole, are the only which would appeal to High School or College Clubs; the others are too childish. The stage setting and costumes are modern and easily obtainable; plays are full of comedy and action; mostly for girls.

Théâtre pour la Jeunesse: Brentano, New York. Volume II. These plays are all for girls; the best are Nos. 1, 3, 4, 5 and 7. No. 3 is an almost literal adaptation of the philosopher's scene from "Le Mariage forcé" of Molière; all the plays have plenty of action and can be staged very simply and are in easy French.

Mayor, Paul: *Les deux moulins.* Fetisch frères, Lausanne. A very pretty little comedy in three short acts, with choruses that give a very pleasant effect; these, however, can be cut out. Very effective and not too difficult stage setting.

François: *Fifteen French plays*: Allyn & Bacon, New York. Fifteen plays graded according to length and difficulty. The longer ones offer a choice for open meetings. All are comedies with action and humor.

Dupré, Marguerite: *Drames et Comédies*: American Book Co. Barbe Bleue, Les Amies du Petit Chaperon Rouge, Treize à table, Pauvre Sylvie, La Belle et la Bête, La Princesse Emeraude. Well adapted for Junior High Schools or private schools; not difficult to stage or act; simple French.

Dupré, Marguerite: *Une Chaumière et un Cœur*: Comedy in one act to be found in "La France Pittoresque", by M. Dupré; Scribner's Sons, New York.

A very pleasant costume play; requires only one stage setting and is easy to act. The peasant costumes can be made at school, and the court costumes obtained without difficulty. The play has action, movement and plenty of charm; it would be very effective and would not require much, if any, cutting.

De Sauzé, E. B.: *Sept Comédies Modernes*: Henry Holt & Co. The best collection of short comedies for French Club presentation. All of them short, funny, full of action and in easy French; each one is preceded by a stage plan; costumes modern and staging simple; all of them are one act plays.

France, Anatole: *La Comédie de celui qui épousa une femme* *muette.* Very clever and funny, to be played in 17th century costumes and setting.

Moineaux, Jules: *Les Deux Sourds*: One act, 17 scenes. D. C. Heath & Co. or Henry Holt (in De Sauzé's "Sept Comédies Modernes).

An extremely amusing comedy full of action; not a difficult vocabulary, easy stage setting, modern costumes. Just the thing for a Cercle Français.

Bernard, Tristan: *L'Anglais tel qu'on le parle.* G. E. Stechert, New York. One short act and should need no cutting; a lively modern play easy to act and extremely amusing. This comedy requires however a clever actor in the title role of Eugène, the interpreter.

Labiche et Martin: *Le Voyage de Monsieur Perrichon et autres Comédies*: Nelson Edition. This edition contains, besides Perrichon: "Les Vivacités du Capitaine Tic", "La Poudre aux Yeux", and "Un Chapeau de paille d'Italie", three of the best comedies of Labiche.

"Le Voyage de Monsieur Perrichon" has been used a great deal for school production; one of the most popular French plays of the 19th century easy to cut and adapt for French Club production. The three other plays in this volume are very amusing, easy to cut, if needed; no long speeches, easy French. For High Schools or Colleges.

Labiche et Delacour: *La Cagnotte*: D. C. Heath & Co. Comedy in 5 acts in prose, which will need cutting, but this is not difficult; extremely funny and full of movement; about 16 characters (several can be omitted in the cutting); simple stage setting and modern costumes.

Sardou, Victorien: *Les Pattes de Mouche*: D. C. Heath & Co. A comedy full of action, not too difficult to produce if abridged; well adapted to College Clubs; modern costumes and scenery.

Meilhac et Halevy: *L'Eté de la Saint Martin*: Allyn & Bacon, New York.

Very pretty and effective play in one act. Will not require any special talent or stage setting.

Banville, Théodore: *Gringoire*: Allyn & Bacon, in the same volume as l'*Eté de la Saint Martin.*

A beautiful one act play which needs skillful acting and careful coaching. As the action is in the time of Louis XI, it requires a more difficult stage setting. However, it could be played before a dark velvet drop. This comedy should be given only before an audience understanding French easily, else all its beauty will be lost.

Pailleron, Edouard: *Le Monde où l'on s'ennuie*: D. C. Heath One of the best plays of the 19th century, witty, skillful and brilliant. To be given only by the best amateur actors, under special coaching.

Molière: *Théâtre choisi.*

Scenes from the following comedies can be used very satisfactorily by French Clubs. Abridged versions of the plays make very amusing and instructive programs. Costumes can be made or rented.

Les Précieuses Ridicules.

Le Médecin Malgré lui.

Le Bourgeois Gentilhomme.

Le Malade Imaginaire.

ALBERT L. CRU.

A. A. T. F. NEWS

Nearly three hundred persons attended a meeting of the Metropolitan Chapter of the A. A. T. F. held at Hunter College, New York, on December 10th. Owing to the regretted absence of the president, Professor Downer, his place was taken by Professor Spiers.

The program was typical of the aims and attitude of the Association. As welcome evidence of the cooperation of other societies in allied fields of activity, M. Gaston Tisné brought to the Association a word of greeting from the Alliance Française of New York, of which he is the president, and then developed further the subject which he had already touched upon in recent letters to the press: the opportunities and shortcomings of the teacher of French in the United States.

M. Tisné was followed by Professor Fife, head of the Department of German in Columbia University. Professor Fife, who is chairman of the American Committee of the Foreign Language Study, spoke of certain phases of the Study's work which are of particular significance to teachers of French. His address, printed in full in the present issue of *The French Review,* aroused much interest in the various reports which members of the speaker's large corps of investigators are about to publish. The Chapter received with much pleasure Professor Fife's graceful commendation of the activity aroused among our teachers by the founding of the A. A. T. F.

The meeting closed with a French reading by Mme Roulet-Pavey. Having selected one of the gems of modern French literature, Maupassant's "Mlle Perle", Mme Roulet-Pavey gave to this beautiful story new life through the charm of her delicate and very human interpretation.

A. G. H. S.

THE AMERICAN ASSOCIATION

OF

TEACHERS OF FRENCH

Last spring nine Chapters of the A. A. T. F. were organized outside of the Metropolitan District in the State of New York. During the past autumn large and enthusiastic meetings were held by all of these Chapters and the officers of each Chapter are as follows:

Westchester Chapter

President: Glenn M. Kelly, White Plains High School.
Vice-President: Miss Caroline Burgevin, Portchester.
Secretary: Miss Edna Palmer, Mount Vernon High School.
Treasurer: Miss Anita Piatti, White Plains High School.

Hudson Valley Chapter

President: Miss Charlotte Loeb, State College, Albany.
Secretary: Glenn M. Davis, Albany High School.
Director: Professor Florence D. White, Vassar College, Poughkeepsie.

Western New York Chapter

President: Miss Alice M. Finn, Niagara Falls High School.
First Vice-President: Mr. Felix Casassa, Hutchinson High School, Buffalo.
Second Vice-President: Miss Lucretia Terry, Bennet High School, Buffalo.
Third Vice-President: Mr. George Schneider, Technical High School, Buffalo.
Secretary: Miss Edna Carmody, Masten Park High School, Buffalo.
Treasurer: Mr. Francis Sweet, South Park High School, Buffalo.
Director: Professor J. P. Rice, University of Buffalo.

Utica Chapter

President: Miss Zoe Ward, Utica Free Academy.

First Vice-President: Mrs. M. C. Parkhurst, Peterboro High School.
Second Vice-President: Frances Dossert, Oneida High School.
Third Vice-President: Genevieve Wright, Munnsville High School.
Secretary: Mary Sullivan, Ilion High School.
Treasurer: Mr. Ralph Johnson, Oriskany Falls High School.
Director: Professor F. M. Jones, Colgate University.

St. Lawrence Chapter

President: Mrs. Beatrice Wheater, Chateaugay High School.
First Vice-President: Miss Anna Sparks, Old Forge High School.
Second Vice-President: Miss Ethel Hogan, Watertown High School.
Third Vice-President: Sister St. Ives de Blois, Tupper Lake.
Secretary: Miss Teresa Owens, Malone High School.
Treasurer: Mr. Harold P. Hayden, Antwerp High School.
Director: Professor S. Plaisance, St. Lawrence University.

Fingerlake Chapter

President: Harriet Kellogg, 1417 W. Water St., Elmira, N. Y.
First Vice-President: Marie I. Henderson, Hartwick Seminary, New York.
Second Vice-President: Nellie B. Rogers, 59 Oak St., Binghamton, New York.
Third Vice-President: Marie Landon, 124 Main St., Penn Yan, New York.
Director: E. Margaret Grimes, Elmira College, Elmira, N. Y.
Secretary: M. Louise Henderson, 18 Ferguson Av., Port Jervis, New York.
Treasurer: Ruth L. Miller, 218 University Av., Ithaca, N. Y.

Long Island Chapter

President: Ada C. Smith, Huntington, New York.
Director: Mary Louise Smith, Freeport, New York.
Secretary: Doris Benson, Lawrence, New York.
Treasurer: Julie Franchi, Bay Shore, New York.
Vice-Presidents:

Alice E. Koch, Smithtown Branch, New York.
E. Lillian Ranquist, Freeport, New York.
Helen E. Corkey, Amityville, New York.

Rochester Chapter

President: Mrs. Jane D. Dunham, East High School, Rochester.
Director: Dr. C. H. Holzwarth, Monroe High School, Rochester.
Secretary: Miss Florence Broxholm, Washington Junior High School, Rochester.
Treasurer: Louis Meinhardt, West High School, Rochester.
Vice-Presidents:
Miss Elfrieda Hill, University of Rochester.
Verne Edgcumbe, West High School, Rochester.
Miss Madeline Marshall, Spencerport High School, Spencerport, N. Y.

Central New York Chapter

President: William Schaffrath, Central High School, Syracuse, New York.
Secretary: Mr. G. H. Daniels, North High School, Syracuse, New York.
Treasurer: Mr. David M. Dougherty, The Manlius School, Manlius, New York.
Directors:
Professor L. W. Crawford, Syracuse University, Syracuse, New York.
Professor A. D. Menut, Syracuse University, Syracuse, N. Y.
First Vice-President: Professor Jean Gerard, Syracuse University, Syracuse, N. Y.
Second Vice-President: Miss Isabella M. Lanigan, Central High School, Syracuse, N. Y.
Third Vice-President: Miss Margaret Le Roy, Oswego High School, Oswego, N. Y.

President Charles A. Downer announces the appointment to the Editorial Board of *The French Review* of Professor L. J. A. Mercier of Harvard University. Mr. Mercier is President of the Modern Language Association of New England, author of 'Junior French', and very well-known to all teachers of French.

The New S. S. Ile de France

PRINTED IN U. S. A.
FRENCH PRINTING & PUBLISHING CO., 149 W. 24TH STREET, N. Y. C.

Vol. I MARCH, 1928 No. 3

THE FRENCH REVIEW

Devoted to the Interests of Teachers of French

Published by the
American Association of Teachers of French

Vol. I MARCH, 1928 No. 3

CONTENTS

CERTAIN OF OUR PROBLEMS, *Charles C. Clark* 7
ENSEIGNONS DES MOTS... ET DES IDÉES, *Marcel Moraud* .. 15
FOREIGN LITERATURE IN THE CLASS-ROOM, *Albert J. Menut* 22
FOREIGN STUDY FELLOWSHIP OPPORTUNITIES, *Archie M. Palmer* 29
PRONUNCIATION ANALYSIS, *Florence M. Baker* 37
MA VISITE A ANDREW D. WHITE, *Fernand Baldensperger* 44
VARIA 47
BOOK REVIEWS 52
RECENT TEXTS 55
BIBLIOGRAPHY 71
THE LIBRARIAN'S CORNER 73
FRENCH TEACHER'S FORUM 77
THE AMERICAN ASSOCIATION OF TEACHERS OF FRENCH 79

The *French Review* is the official journal of the American Association of Teachers of French and is published four times during the year, November, January, March, May.

Office of Publication, George Washington High School, Audubon Avenue and 192nd Street, New York City.

Application made for second-class mailing privilege.

The annual dues of the American Association of Teachers of French, including subscription to the *French Review,* are $2.50. Single copies. $.50 Applications for membership should be addressed to E. A. Méras, the Secretary of the Association, Adelphi College, Brooklyn, New York.

Communications to the editors, manuscripts, etc., should be addressed to the Editor of the *French Review,* Cornell University, Ithaca, N. Y.

All correspondence concerning advertising should be forwarded to Edward O. Perry, Business Manager of the *French Review,* George Washington High School, 192nd St., New York City.

Kindly notify the Business Manager of any change in address.

All books, texts, publications which may interest the teacher of French will receive mention in the bibliography or critical comment, if a copy is sent to a member of the editorial staff. Literary and scholarly works should be forwarded to A. G. H. Spiers, Columbia University, New York City, while texts and other publications should be sent to Dr. Hélène Harvitt, 1309 Carroll Street, Brooklyn, N. Y.

Exchange of the *French Review* with other journals may be arranged by addressing the Editor of the *French Review,* Ithaca, N. Y.

American Association of Teachers of French

THE FRENCH REVIEW

EDITORIAL BOARD

THE FRENCH REVIEW

VOL. I MARCH, 1928 No. 3

CERTAIN OF OUR PROBLEMS

By CHARLES C. CLARKE

"Why Teach French?" is the title of an article by Colman Dudley Frank, in the November number of the *French Review*. It seems to me that a sufficient answer would have been, "because of the great and ever increasing demand"; for that demand is increasing, despite the dissatisfaction expressed from time to time with the results obtained by those who have "taken" French or by those who have paid for their children's lessons in the language. This dissatisfaction I take to be a sign of healthy interest, and at the same time the outcome of misunderstanding.

Some years ago, in 1914, in one of his reports President Nicholas Murray Butler expressed himself as follows:

"Elaborate arguments are made by men of weight and authority to the effect that the ability to speak French and to speak German is much less important than the ability to read those languages, and the possession of some general knowledge of their literatures. This is a sadly perverted point of view. The man who is able to read a page of Taine or perhaps of Anatole France, and who finds himself in a French business house or a French drawing-room without the ability to express his wants or his thought in a single well formed and intelligible sentence, feels like a fool; and he deserves to feel like a fool. The man who cannot speak and write French and German does not know French and German, and it is sheer folly to suppose that this lack of ability to use a great educational instrument and a vitally important tool in business and social intercourse is compensated for by a more or less superficial knowledge of the classical literature of the French and German peoples..... Indeed it would be highly advantageous if all instruction in the French, German, Spanish, or Italian languages and literatures were conducted in those languages after the first year of college work in them."

This utterance was deemed in 1914 almost revolutionary, although it was meant to be helpful, and although its suggestion as to classroom use of French has become the rule in our better schools. It was then most astonishing that a man of President Butler's education and experience should seem to expect such a product from the processes used in American schools and colleges and under the conditions prevailing among us. The processes have been greatly changed, but still criticism of teachers comes from students and their parents. I do not speak of the careless parent who thinks that when tuition is paid his duty is done, nor of the too plentiful "student" whose resistance to teaching effort is proverbial. The fault finding of serious persons is deserving of serious reply. They devote time, money, and labor to the study of French and they often feel that they have got small return therefor.

How many of these critics know what it means to learn a foreign language, not to learn many interesting linguistic facts about it, not to commit to memory the rules of its syntax, not to be able to read it by substituting English words for the foreign words printed for the eye,—but to learn the language so that it can be understood by them aurally and can be made comprehensible to others, in fine, so that it becomes an almost natural second means of communication? Such a feat is rarely accomplished in a school by anyone after he has learned his mother tongue, and the teacher who aids in bringing about such a success has cause for self-congratulation. He should not be expected to repeat the success often. With differences of course, the acquisition of French, in the way one should wish to acquire it, is comparable in discriminating mental labor to the achievement of a science or a profession. But among all the students of chemistry or of history, many thousands of them yearly in our institutions of learning, how often can the best teacher turn out a real chemist or a real historian? Yet this is a feat about equivalent to what seems to be required of a teacher of French, with all pupils.

It is owing to a too general misunderstanding of the problem that its successful solution is demanded by the public. In the first place, French, even if a near relative of our own language, offers our learners many difficulties. It is hard for a person who has grown up, if only part way, in a language whose verb has almost nothing which can be called a conjugation, whose nouns have only natural gender and whose adjectives have none, whose adjectives and pronouns have fixed positions, as well as many other simplifications—it is hard indeed for such a person to acquire the comparative complication of French in these respects. And there is the pronunciation, a study in itself, and a most baffling one for a people whose vowel system has separated itself so widely from the general "continental" scheme, and whose consonants—well, pupils do not "get as far as that", and their teachers seldom try to drive them there.

With these and other stumbling blocks to overcome, it is wonderful that the school or college teacher occasionally produces something like a finished article, a fairly correct speaker and good general student of French; but he or she does this sometimes, just as the professor of chemistry or of history makes a chemist or an historian. What is really more indicative of our teachers' success is their effect upon the average pupil. To quote myself in a recent letter to the *New York Herald-Tribune,* "one has only to look at audiences at the lectures supplied by the Alliance Française to notice the understanding of French by larger and larger numbers of Americans; and in Europe I, at least, am impressed by the great increase in the ranks of American travelers who speak French, and often speak it pretty well.

However, it must be admitted that greater proficiency in speaking French might be acquired, if it were possible to obviate all or even some of the difficulties which now militate against success in thoroughly learning the language.

In the first place, the American learner has his expectations set too high. He supposes that the acquisition of a foreign tongue is largely a matter of vocabulary, a substitution of a foreign word for an English one. The truth is that French presents many difficulties which must be overcome one at a time, and the process cannot be hurried beyond a certain point. The brain cells of the learner must be drilled to act from a new stimulus, the new word as seen or heard.

As a rule, our schools and even our higher institutions of study either underestimate the time needed for learning a foreign language, or cannot give a large enough proportion of the school time to it. Three short hours, or, in rare cases, five, a week will not give to even a single student much fluency in French, let alone to a class of twenty or thirty, unless conditions are extremely favorable outside of the classroom. And in this country outside conditions are the reverse of favorable. In Europe, that is to say, on most of the Continent, French is of constant use socially and in all commercial relations. The majority of people "need it in their business". Or, if that is not the case, they hear it spoken by persons about them; and in travel they cannot fail to hear French and to read signs and notices in it, and to employ it as a sort of universal language. We may travel anywhere in all North America, except in a certain part of Canada, and not meet any one demanding a word of French, or proffering one."

The American is as a rule denied all contact with French except in classroom and through his instructor. And what is the nature of this contact and how long a time is it spread over? At the best, the relation is only that of master and pupil, and is shared by a number much larger than is tolerated in private classes or in schools exclusively devoted to languages.

Some of the hard things in French may not exist for those of us whose acquaintance with them began in early childhood; but the adult and the adolescent have lost the young child's imitative power, and it is just these grown up people that the average teacher is called upon to guide and stimulate. They are the ones who are so often disappointed after three or four *years* of the study of French. From the old grammar and translation way they would have gained nothing of practical, useful knowledge of the language; but how little they find they have acquired, in spite of their hopes, and the best semi-direct method, the method evidently desired by President Butler!

I have put *years* in Italics, for I must ask what kind of years is meant. Let us assume that most students of French have five classroom sessions a week, which is, in fact, an unusually large allowance. The classes are big, the *hours* not quite sixty minutes each, and the preparatory study is not likely to average more than two hours per classroom exercise. We may calculate fifteen hours a week given to French, and about forty working weeks in the school or college year, that is, six hundred hours given to French in 365 days, or about as much time as a person studying French in France, and living among the French exclusively, would devote to the language in the waking hours of forty days. This is supposing that an American student in France would be under the influence of the language fifteen hours a day. At that rate four years of American school or college French, *in time actually given to the language,* would be equivalent to 160 days in a French school and in purely French surroundings. If a student feels that three or four years of French in an American classroom, on leaving which daily he must at once resume the use of his native tongue, take up other studies requiring his attention, and probably try also to make a name for himself in extra-curriculum pursuits, ought to be enough to give him real control of French both written and spoken, that student is asking more than he would ask of 160 days in France. He would not expect a year in France, 365 days of 15 hours each, of contact with French, to produce the result which he blames some method or some teacher for not having produced. It is marvelous that once in a while success is attained, and a pupil of parts learns to read, write, and speak French acceptably, usually because he has supplemented the labors of his instructor by intelligent and hard study, and by extra-school contacts with French people, at plays, lectures, conversation clubs, and the like. The teacher can never do all that is needful; and it is time that we were realizing what Europeans have long known, that to get a firm mastery of a foreign language one must go and reside for some length of time in a country where that language is spoken by the population. The present procedure in teaching French in our better educational institutions can be depended upon to give the average student a considerable degree of fluency, and so render him fit for residence in France, with a foundation for further study and advancement. For others, who aim merely to travel, it provides a certain ability to "get along" and to enjoy many features of life in France to which they would otherwise be oblivious. And on all it confers the power of reading French, something which the old methods, in which reading was the chief expedient, did not really accomplish. Of course I am not speaking here of schools devoted to foreign languages, or of the wonderful systems advertised, by which, in a few short weeks and without effort,, "perfect" French is yours for a very modest cash payment. Such announcements would make us think of the Philosophers' Stone, if we were not reminded first of the trade in patent medicines. It is a pity that reputable newspapers sell them space.

But with our actual handicaps in time and in surroundings, if our teachers were better we might do more. As in the last twenty years there has been an immense improvement in the quality of American teachers of French, we may expect greater accomplishment in the near future. And French teachers of their native language are coming to us in appreciable numbers. These men and women are, or should be if they realize their proper rôles, of the greatest value in our instruction. Of various kinds, they can be a great inspiration to all but the most indifferent students, and an invaluable aid to our younger teachers. When educated in French universities they are likely to have a better general literary and historical background than our college graduates usually exhibit. Often their usefulness is hampered by their failure to allow for the careless mental habits of the American youth; and they are apt to assume too much knowedge of French on the part of their pupils. It is evident, however valuable they may be, that their numbers can never be sufficient to prevent the American teacher of French from being our main dependence.

With better teachers, even handicapped as we are by the shortness of the time devoted to the study, and by unfavorable surroundings, could not more be done for our students? There can be no question as to this.

As far as criticism of our teachers is sincere, it must be welcomed sincerely. It is true that many American-born teachers of French are not properly prepared for what they undertake. And this is largely due to the want of care exercised by school and college heads in employing instructors. Owing to the great demand, half prepared candidates are tempted to offer themselves, and are too easily accepted. If, as is now common, the would-be teacher can assert that he has had the advantage of a sojourn in France, this is apt to be taken in lieu of proof of fitness. The length, the place, and the character as regards study, of his stay abroad should be looked into, but they seldom are. Unhappily, the secondary school head is too ready to engage any one who can get the boys and girls past the college entrance examination. He looks no farther.

This contentment with imperfect work would quickly disappear from the secondary school man's mind if the College Entrance Examination Board could set a kind of test which would show whether first, second and third year French had been rationally taught. As long as so large a part of the college entrance paper is devoted to reading and composition, i. e., translation, and to syntax questions, with so great a proportion of the credits based upon that part, the present style of preparatory teaching will prevail, and the inadequate teacher with good drilling power will retain his job. If the pronunciation questions, now so unimportant a part of the examination, were reformed and reinforced by the use of the generally accepted phonetic alphabet, and oral and aural tests added, the candidate's practical control of French would invariably be known, and his teacher's deficiencies or strong points as well. The reaction upon the preparation of teachers themselves would be most favorable. In turn, the influence of a better teacher would be exerted to make better pupils, and a circle would thus be established which we could deem quite the reverse of *vicious*.

Another thing which is often damaging to good teaching of French is the effect upon promising teachers of the necessity of becoming Doctors of Philosophy. The praise-worthy desire of university and college trustees and presidents to uplift American scholarship, and to have only men and women of erudition in their faculties, makes the degree of Ph. D. indispensable to all ambitious college instructors, men or women, who hope for permanent positions. If the ability to do some "research", and to publish something which will advertise his or her institution, outside the realm of sport, is added, so much the better; but the degree is obligatory. Now an aspirant to professorial rank, who has specialized in French and intends to continue to do so in his teaching finds that most of his time and strength for several years must be given to the study of the other Romance languages plus German; and on top of these the labor of a year at least has to go to the production of a thesis which he may very probably not desire to write. During all this time what becomes of his French and his possible progress in it toward perfection, and his consequent ability to teach it in all its refinements? This situation is beyond the control of anyone, and our teachers must accept it. The best they can do is to take very slowly their studies in the related languages, while they attend strictly to their main interest, i. e., French in all its aspects. But the effect of the division of effort is undeniably harmful to the Doctor of Philosophy *viewed as a teacher of French,* and therefore entails a loss to his pupils.

By no means all of our problems have been stated in this article; the other thousand and one confront us after the bell has struck and the classroom door has been closed. Then comes the question of rousing interest and of adapting controverted teaching principles to the varied minds before us. If the dissatisfied could help us to obviate the difficulties which I have mentioned, the excellence in teaching which I maintain exists in our best institutions would soon spread to all of them.

Yale University.

ENSEIGNONS DES MOTS... ET DES IDÉES

Par Marcel Moraud

Certains estimeront sans doute que c'est une entreprise superflue, et même présomptueuse, que de vouloir apporter du nouveau sur un sujet qui pendant deux années a retenu l'attention d'une légion d'experts et de collègues remplis de zèle, sinon d'enthousiasme. La Commission d'Enquête de la Fondation Carnegie [1] a rassemblé tant de renseignements, et elle en a si heureusement tiré parti, qu'il semblerait que, pour le moment, il ne nous reste qu'à profiter des résultats acquis. A quoi bon soulever de nouveaux problèmes ? Pourquoi donc suggérer une besogne nouvelle, quand on vient à peine d'en compléter une, qui n'a pas du reste été tellement facile ? Notre situation n'est pas déjà si brillante.

L'enseignement des langues vivantes a de tout temps, nous le savons tous, été une tâche ingrate, en un sens du moins : "Languages are no career for a man of any ability", écrivait plus spirituellement que justement Galsworthy, il y a une quinzaine d'années. Aujourd'hui encore nous avons à lutter, même dans les Universités les plus modernes, contre une sorte de préjugé. Les scientifiques, du haut de leurs laboratoires dispendieux, et qui trop souvent absorbent le plus clair de la "substentifique moelle" de l'Université, nous regardent un peu comme des gens sans asile. Les mathématiciens laissent tomber sur nous des regards pleins de l'assurance et de la calme dignité que leur enseignement est sensé conférer. Les psychologues, les philosophes, en penseurs qu'ils se croient, font la moue devant les parleurs que nous sommes. Au fond, ils ne sont pas très sûrs que nous soyons indispensables. Ils lisent tous, tant bien que mal, les œuvres des savants étrangers, les com-

[1] The writer refers to the Modern Foreign Language Study which has been carried on under the auspices of the American Council of Education. The investigation was made possible by a very liberal grant from the Carnegie Corporation. *Ed.*

mentent, certains sans toujours les comprendre, j'entends les comprendre à fond, mais il leur semble qu'une "reading knowledge" des langues étrangères, celle qu'ils ont acquise eux-mêmes, à coup de dictionnaire et de grammaire, suffirait bien, après tout.

Entre cette "reading knowledge" de nos collègues philosophes ou scientifiques et cette "speaking knowledge" qui a tant préoccupé la Commission d'enquête, ne pourrait-on trouver un juste milieu ? Ne pouvons-nous prendre place dans la communauté universitaire et apporter, nous aussi, notre contribution à la formation intellectuelle des jeunes générations ? L'acquisition d'une langue étrangère est une chose très désirable et fort louable en elle-même, mais enfin devons-nous limiter là nos efforts, même dans les premières années où nous enseignons cette langue ?

Il ne s'agit nullement ici de suggérer que nos collègues de la Commission Carnegie n'ont pas achevé leur besogne. Ils ont, dans la limite de leurs moyens, fait ce qu'ils avaient entrepris. Mais devons-nous et pouvons-nous nous en tenir là ?

Nous venons de faire un grand progrès. Nous savons maintenant à peu près, comment déterminer les aptitudes de nos étudiants à apprendre telle ou telle langue étrangère. On nous donne de précieux renseignements sur la façon de développer ces aptitudes. Voilà qui est fort bien. On a essayé d'établir le minimum indispensable pour parler une langue étrangère. Voilà qui est encore mieux. On a enfin tenté de nous indiquer les mots dont l'usage est le plus courant dans cette langue. Là, évidemment, on a entrepris une tâche fort délicate. La fréquence de certains mots peut à la rigueur se déterminer chez tel ou tel écrivain, et en examinant avec soin un groupe d'écrivains, on arrivera sans doute à établir les mots le plus fréquemment employés par ces écrivains. Mais il n'est nullement certain que cette méthode de compilation suivie de statistiques ne donnerait pas des résultats tout différents, si on prenait un autre groupe d'écrivains.

Un collègue, fort spirituel, d'une grande université du Nord, m'assurait que les statistiques ont prouvé que le mot "casquette" s'emploie plus fréquemment en français que le mot "chapeau". C'est possible, après tout, et il est fort probable que "casquette" se rencontre plus souvent chez Zola que chez Anatole France. Mais puisque nos législateurs en linguistique ont sagement évité de nous dire quand on doit employer la casquette et quand au contraire il convient d'arborer l'autre couvre-chef, plus aristocratique, je ne m'insurge point, pas même contre les statistiques.

Il y a forcément dans ces statistiques quelque chose de mécanique; elles ont cela de décevant qu'elles ne vous montrent qu'un côté de la vérité et ne vous laissent pas soupçonner qu'il peut en exister un autre. Je me demande donc si des recherches conduites à coup de statistiques n'ont pas quelque chose d'un peu sec et de limité.

Dans toutes les enquêtes qu'on a menées ces dernières années, tant en Angleterre qu'aux Etats-Unis, je vois un effort très louable pour organiser, d'une façon moderne et scientifique, un enseignement qui avait jusqu'ici été laissé à la routine, à des méthodes surannées ou à des initiatives privées et des tentatives nullement contrôlées.

En ce sens, la tâche accomplie par nos collègues ne mérite que des éloges et surtout lorsqu'on se rend compte des difficultés qu'ils ont eu à surmonter. Partis de rien, sans outillage d'aucune sorte, sans contact avec les bonnes volontés qu'ils se proposaient d'utiliser, ils ont, je crois, fait le maximum. Leur but a été, me semble-t-il, de faciliter la tâche du maître qui, enseignant une langue étrangère et s'étant assuré que ses étudiants sont aptes à l'étude de cette langue, veut arriver à la leur faire connaître et parler aussi rapidement que possible, et cela, en évitant tout effort superflu.

C'est là l'ambition qu'ont eue en Europe tous ceux qui, depuis des années et des années, ont cherché un moyen pratique d'enseigner les langues vivantes. Leur unique but a été sans cesse de découvrir le minimum strictement nécessaire pour s'exprimer dans une langue étrangère, sur un nombre limité de sujets. L'art suprême du professeur d'école Berlitz, ou de toute autre institution de ce genre, est de donner à ses étudiants l'illusion qu'ils savent la langue qu'ils étudient et de leur permettre de voyager sans trop de difficultés.

Ce qu'on remarque dans toutes ces méthodes tant vantées, Berlitz qui est une des meilleures, Gouin ou toute autre, c'est qu'elles sont excellentes pendant les quinze ou vingt premières leçons.

L'élève fait des progrès étonnants. Le cercle dans lequel on le fait se mouvoir est si limité, qu'il s'y sent parfaitement à l'aise et en sécurité. Mais, passé ces vingt leçons, ces méthodes sont inutilisables. On a beau pousser et presser l'étudiant, il ne sort plus de son cercle enchanté. Ces méthodes ne se renouvellent pas. Leur valeur littéraire est inexistante, et elles ne reçoivent aucun secours de la littérature qu'elles ignorent totalement.

On le comprend du reste, ce sont des méthodes commerciales et on ne saurait reprocher à leurs auteurs de ne pas s'être souciés de la formation intellectuelle des touristes qu'ils préparaient. Autre danger, presque aussi grave que celui-là, surtout quand nous nous adressons à des étudiants qui ne sont pas stimulés par l'idée de visiter le pays dont ils apprennent la langue; ces méthodes, en dehors de la satisfaction et de l'illusion qu'elles donnent au début, n'offrent bientôt qu'un enseignement sans intérêt, car leurs auteurs semblent ignorer même le pays auquel elles sont destinées. Elles sont à peu près uniformes. Vous voulez aller à Londres ? Très bien, voilà une méthode anglaise. Vous vous dirigez vers Paris ? Parfait, voilà, presque dans les mêmes mots une méthode française. Vous voulez visiter Berlin, encore mieux, voilà une méthode allemande qui vous y conduira tout droit comme votre billet. Vous pourrez aller à l'hôtel, retenir une chambre, la faire aérer, commander votre repas au restaurant, faire quelques emplettes, prendre un billet, et même aller au théâtre, à condition toutefois que vous ne cherchiez pas à comprendre la pièce. Vous pourrez échanger quelques mots avec le gérant de l'hôtel, les garçons, la concierge, le tailleur, ou la modiste; mais n'allez pas vous aviser de glisser quelques remarques à votre voisine au parterre. Vous ne la comprendrez pas, si elle ne parle pas Berlitz ou Gouin, et si elle vous comprend, vous lui semblerez horriblement plat, sec, ennuyeux, une véritable mécanique s'exprimant pratiquement, correctement peut-être, mais sans vie et sans âme.

Bien plus, si vous ne voyagez pas, et si vous vous en tenez à votre méthode pratique vous ne saurez que des mots, vous ferez sur Paris les mêmes remarques que sur Berlin et sur Londres. Qu'il s'agisse de la rue, des magasins, des théâtres, du jour, de la nuit, des parcs, on vous en dit la même chose; et cependant l'aspect d'une rue de Londres n'est pas celui d'une rue de Berlin et encore moins d'un boulevard parisien. Quant aux parcs et jardins, ceux de Paris sont 'ouverts le jour" et "fermés la nuit" alors que ceux de Londres, du moins certains, sont fort hospitalièrement ouverts le jour et... la nuit, comme chacun le sait.

L'inconvénient des méthodes pratiques et simplifiées à l'extrême est, en général, qu'elles ne tiennent aucun compte de la vie et de la pensée du peuple dont elles enseignent la langue.

Je sais bien que nos enquêteurs ont procédé d'une autre façon et qu'ils se sont occupés de chaque langue séparément. Mais la difficulté n'en est pas moins là. Ces méthodes toutes tant qu'elles sont, étouffent la pensée. Je me demande comment avec un certain nombre de mots bien choisis et une connaissance suffisante des règles de la langue, on va initier un étudiant à la vie d'une nation étrangère, comment on va l'intéresser à la vie matérielle de son peuple, puis peu à peu à sa pensée et enfin à sa littérature et à son art.

Car c'est bien de cela qu'il s'agit, n'est-ce pas, dans l'enseignement d'une Université ? Le professeur d'école secondaire, et à plus forte raison, le professeur d'université n'est pas une gouvernante répétant à des enfants des mots et des phrases d'une langue étrangère et les leur faisant répéter. Il n'est pas non plus un professeur de conversation. Il ne peut en aucune façon être le Professeur d'Ecole Berlitz, qui en vingt leçons prépare ses étudiants à faire un tour d'Europe. J'en demande bien pardon à Berlitz, dont la méthode est excellente pour le but qu'elle se propose, mais ce but ne peut pas être le nôtre, car s'il l'est, alors! "Accourez philosophes, mathématiciens..." "Et tout ce que les universités ont fourni de savant". Accablez-nous de votre mépris trop justifié, je renonce à notre défense.

S'il s'agit au contraire d'une initiation intelligente et savamment graduée à d'autres façons de vivre, de penser et de s'exprimer, car on pense généralement avant de s'exprimer, alors nous reprenons notre place dans l'université, nous apportons justement cette facilité d'adaptation, cette largeur de vue, cette curiosité toujours en éveil, souple et tolérante qu'un enseignement scientifique ne donnera jamais.

La vie de chaque jour n'est pas la même dans les différents pays. L'aspect des villes, l'allure des habitants, les repas, les mets, les fêtes de famille ou nationales, la vie des écoles, les amusements privés ou publics, la vie des villes, celle des campagnes diffèrent sensiblement dans chaque pays. Quant aux rêves, aux joies, aux souffrances, ils ne s'expriment pas de la même manière. La nature elle-même ne parle pas de la même façon au cœur du poète allemand, qu'à celui du poète français ou anglais.

Et puis, il faut tenir compte des traditions, de l'éducation, de tout ce qui peu à peu vient meubler l'esprit et former la sensibilité d'un peuple; or on ne s'intéressera à ce peuple, on ne le comprendra, on n'appréciera son art et sa littérature que lorsqu'on sera entré en contact, non pas avec des mots, mais avec sa vie et sa pensée.

Peut-on espérer que l'enquête qui se termine ne sera qu'un premier pas et que celui-ci sera suivi d'un nouvel effort pour établir, à côté des mots et des constructions indispensables, le maximum de connaissances nécessaires pour s'initier à la vie d'un peuple et s'approcher peu à peu, intelligemment, de sa littérature ?

Que ce soit au moyen de petits poèmes, de descriptions, de récits, de courts passages, tirés de pièces de théâtre ou de romans, de revues, de journaux même, peu importe pourvu que les passages choisis soient représentatifs et qu'ils donnent une juste idée du peuple dont il s'agit. Il n'est pas nécessaire qu'ils soient ni longs, ni difficiles; ils devront en tout cas être judicieusement gradués. Il en faudra pour les différentes étapes de cette acquisition de la langue étrangère. Ils pourront différer, mais l'essentiel sera qu'ils attirent l'attention de l'étudiant sur les aspects caractéristiques de la vie et de la pensée du pays dont on s'occupera. Les livres contenant ces extraits, appelons-les des "readers" ou tout ce que vous voudrez, devront bient entendu être suivis de textes également choisis avec le même soin judicieux et dans le même esprit. Pour ces choix, il faudra faire, encore une fois, appel à de nombreuses bonnes volontés. Il nous faudra des collègues moins préoccupés de méthodes et de mots que d'idées. Des lectures abondantes, un goût très sûr, une connaissance remarquable de la littérature seront indispensables pour en tirer ce qui semblera le plus représentatif tout en restant le plus heureusement conçu et le plus artistement présenté. Il y a là me semble-t-il une tâche utile et urgente à remplir. Elle devra l'être en dehors de toutes les préoccupations personnelles et commerciales qui dictent certains des "readers" trop hâtivement composés que trop souvent nous rencontrons aujourd'hui.

Quand cette tâche sera accomplie et que nous en pourrons utiliser les résultats, conjointement avec ceux de l'enquête Carnegie qui se termine, l'enseignement de langues vivantes qui vient de faire un pas sérieux aux Etats-Unis, en aura fait un autre, encore plus grand.

The Rice Institute.

FOREIGN LITERATURE IN THE CLASS-ROOM[1]

By Albert D. Menut

This is an anniversary year in the history of modern language teaching in the United States. Exactly a half-century ago, in July, 1877, Dr. Lambert Sauveur established at Amherst College a summer course in foreign language methods. His was the first successful attempt to create a special pedagogy in this field. In the years that have followed this modest beginning much water has flowed under the bridge. Not only has the number of students and teachers multiplied in geometric proportion, but the methods themselves have increased, until today there are almost as many methods as text-books. The incidental literature dealing with language methods bids fair to overwhelm us; its volume alone is a certain assurance that interest in this subject has never been more alive than at the present time.

It was wholly logical that the attention of methodologists should have been directed at the outset to the fundamental matter of discovering the most effective means of imparting to the student the ability to read, write and understand a particular idiom. Indeed, so intense has been their concentration upon this central problem that a hasty scanning of the bibliography on the subject reveals little else than this. Fully ninety-five percent of the books and articles published in our field are concerned with language methods alone. This narrowing of our field of interest, more notable than ever since the War, must indicate that we have come to consider language as an end in itself, rather than as a means to an end. If the pioneers in the field could see no farther than this, the magnitude of their task sufficiently excuses them. It has been shown however, that the practical benefits derived by high-school students from the study of modern foreign languages are largely illusory. The time has come for us to look beyond the mechanism itself and to behold the significant creation of language through-

[1] Abstract of address before Central New York section, A. A. T. F.

out the centuries. Language is the key to literature and ought to be taught as such. This has been admitted long since in the teaching of English; several excellent studies stressing the literary aspect of that language have appeared since the War. If the total effect of this movement in English instruction has been negligeable thus far, at least a beginning has been made. Of such a movement the field of foreign language instruction has remained up until the present time virtually innocent.

It may be fairly claimed that the teaching of literature belongs in the college and not in the high-school; that time is lacking for more than the present burden of grammar, composition and translation; further, that eighty percent of the students will not go beyond high-school, and that attention must be centered upon this overwhelming majority. These are but a few of a multitude of objections that will occur to every one—objections that seem at first sight wholly insurmountable. Let us for a moment test their validity.

There is no possible doubt that the college is the proper place for literary studies of an intensive nature. No one would venture to suggest that a survey of French literature, for instance, should be imposed upon the high-schools. Nor is there any need to add courses of any kind to the already overcrowded curriculum. The problem is rather to take advantage of the remarkable opportunity afforded by the courses now being given. Today this opportunity is seldom used effectively, because it is rarely emphasized by methodologists and almost never receives the recognition it deserves from those real and final arbiters of the teaching standards in our secondary schools,—the makers of official examination papers. All that is needed to bring about the revision of values here suggested is the inclusion in the high-school reading list of foreign language texts of representative authors of different epochs and ample instruction of the student in translating with regard to the fundamental social and philosophical background that explains in large part the ideational content of a given text. This does not mean that the twenty-five minutes per day alloted to translation should be transformed into a lecture by the teacher on history, sociology or philosophy. It means simply that the literary aspect of the text should be fully discussed during the period of reading, in such a way that the author's ideas become clarified in the student's mind so that their relation to his own knowledge of life will be evident to him. In this way his meagre stock of mental associations will be set in motion with a view to comparing contemporary thought and custom with those of the period described in the text. It means also that the indefensible practise of carefully extracting the linguistic element from a text and leaving the literary element behind as a useless by-product would yield place to a recognition of both these elements on a basis of absolute equality.

Obviously, the first requisite for a revision in the sense here indicated would be the adoption of and adherence to a list of reading texts of unquestionable literary worth. It is too evident that at the present time the tendency in selecting texts for high-schools is in the contrary direction. To be sure, the sempiternal *Tulipe noire* is still a very popular favorite, along with *Colomba, Tartarin de Tarascon* and *Le Voyage de M. Perrichon.* But to the Frenchman, these are not the great masterpieces of his literature, nor are they indicative of the more serious aspects of French thought and life. It is not to be doubted that they are entertaining and have the right to a place somewhere early in the curriculum. The same may be said of the numerous collections of short stories, which since the War have found such favor with high-school teachers. To the casual observer, nothing is more striking than the rapidity with which the publishers have won the language teachers away from the old standard text-books to these *contes* and *nouvelles* of slight literary value and negligeable ideational content. It is a somewhat painful experience to find that students who have studied French three or even four years in high-school have never heard of Balzac, Hugo, Flaubert, Zola or Anatole France. By common consent, these are the great names of modern French letters; yet it is evident that their works are those least favored in the secondary schools. Experience has shown that less than two per cent of the high-school graduates having spent three and four years studying French are able to identify the name of Molière; he is commonly presumed to have lived in the early nineteenth century and to have written fairy stories. As for Hugo, his career is variously held to have fallen anywhere between the twelfth and the twentieth century. The omission of Molière from the high-school reading list would seem to indicate a strange incomprehension of values. Probably no other available texts in the French language offer such an adequate picture of a full century of civilization in so small a compass as *Les Précieuses ridicules* and *Le Bourgeois gentilhomme.*

There is no reason to suspect that conditions are measureably better among students of German or Spanish. The methods employed being practically identical, it is difficult to conceive of any notable difference in results obtained. Besides, it is only fair to inquire what must be the situation as regards that large majority of high-school students whose literary knowledge is never tested, in as much as they never enter any higher institution of learning. If we admit that the students who gain entrance to our colleges are the intellectual flower of our high-school student body, it becomes painful to surmise the status of that vast residue of tender plants that never bloom on any campus.

A recent questionnaire conducted by the Board of Regents of the State of New York revealed the fact that, in spite of their avowed preference for modern languages over every other subject, less than one half of third year students desired to continue the study of French, while 30% of fourth year students expressed a desire to discontinue the subject. In commenting upon this situation, Mr. Ben D. Wood, of Columbia University, asks this pertinent question: "Why do French teachers fail to impart a living interest in the French language and in the history, literature and culture of France, even after having students in their classes 2, 3, or 4 years?" Perhaps it is possible to answer Mr. Wood's question by transposing his word-order and slightly enlarging upon it: Because teachers fail to impart a knowledge of the history, literature and culture of France, even after having students in their classes 3 or 4 years which would tend to arouse in them a living interest in the French language as the most effective means for understanding French thought and culture.

The objection that time is lacking for this type of instruction seems to be based on the false assumption that the time allotted to translation is insufficient for anything more than a hasty reading of the text. But what benefit is derived from this reading if it is not associated with general ideas already familiar to students in the class? It would seem that if we fail to make absolutely clear the ideational significance of a text by adequate commentary and discussion—by a method less detailed, but at all events approximating the excellent method so long in use in French lycées, known as *explication de textes*—if we fail to do this with some degree of thoroughness, we have only ourselves to blame when the students lose interest and show an almost total absence of that most precious acquisition of civilized man,—namely, a sense of history. The time actually required for adequate discussion of these matters is infinitesimal as compared to the benefits to be derived thereby. Better fewer texts better understood than a larger number merely "skimmed over".

Every year sees the penetration of new texts into our curriculum, and every year we cater more to the vulgar taste in the act of choosing. More and more we seek to hold the student's attention by offering him "thrills and startles" rather than to take upon ourselves the trouble to train his tastes toward serious literature. So fearful are we lest we cause mental indigestion in our wards that we continue to feed them a diet of intellectual gruel long after they are man-grown. The result is that peculiarly American malady, which an eminent psychiatrist has aptly named "adult-infantilism". Of what use is it to complain of this malady on the one hand, while on the other we continue to purvey to the young student nothing more profound in the class-room?

This situation gives rise to a serious social problem which has not escaped the purview of several prominent educators. Each year many thousands of students leave the high-school never to pursue further the studies begun there. What have these future citizens benefited by their study of one or more foreign language which will remain with them as an enduring value either practically or culturally? These constitute the large majority of students upon whom it is stated that the public schools must center their attention. The recent report of Professor O'Shea on the extent to which those who have pursued modern foreign languages in high-school read these languages after graduation must cause consternation in the ranks of those who have proclaimed the practical as opposed to the cultural benefits derived from such study. With these negative results before them, is it strange that the maintenance of foreign languages in the secondary schools encounters increasingly the opprobrium of many thoughtful educators, the disdain of parents and the growing opposition of governing bodies? Basing their judgment on the supposedly practical results obtained, these individuals are threatening to divert the millions now expended on foreign language instruction into the teaching of commercial subjects, handicrafts and household arts. To make matters worse, of late the psychologists have bereft us of our traditional argument in favor of language study as a facultative discipline.

To such an impasse have we been led by following too closely and too long the narrow path of practicality. It is high time to overhaul the traditional methodology based too exclusively on the immediately practical and to inject into our methods something like a frank recognition of the cultural element inherent in language study. Many teachers have been doing exactly this thing for many years past; but their number is thus far too small and their influence too feeble to affect the general application of this criticism. There is, of course, no guarantee that the reform suggested here will prove wholly successful. Of this we cannot be assured until the experiment has been tested on a far wider scale than heretofore. It seems self-evident, however, that the study of modern foreign languages could be used effectively as a means to introduce our youth to the rich treasures of foreign literature. If we continue to disregard this opportunity, placed so conveniently within our hands, we may have reason to fear the onslaught of our critics; if, on the other hand, we set about improving our opportunity in this direction we can at least demand from them that they give us time to prove the worth or waste of the experiment.

In the history of foreign language teaching in our secondary schools nothing is more notable than the tenacity with which we have clung to the practical ideals of the pioneers. Greatly as they vary in detail, the pedagogical methods have scarcely deviated from the fundamental principles laid down by the methodologists of a half-century ago. Grammar methods, direct methods with realia, etc., have been widely tested for themselves and in selective combinations. Within the narrow range of their elemental purpose each of these methods has achieved notably successful results. The purpose of all is essentially the same, and it is with this purpose that we are here concerned. To question the worth of a long established and venerable ideal must appear to require considerable temerity, since it involves the use of seemingly destructive criticism. But the change of purpose suggested here is in no sense revolutionary, nor does it mean the discarding of present practices in language teaching. We shall always need all the intensive linguistic training that we now have, preferably more than less; but we need also to recognize that such training is an incidental means to an end, rather than an end in itself. We need to broaden the scope of our instruction by revision in two directions; first, by employing only those reading-texts that possess an indubitable educational value in a cultural as well as a mechanical sense; secondly, we need to inculcate an intelligent appreciation of the significant ideas in these texts, stressing always the relative application of these ideas to the life of the present generation of men.

Fifty years ago it was the colleges of this country, under the leadership of President Eliot of Harvard, which brought about the introduction of modern language courses in the high-schools. In the present circumstances it is only natural to look to the colleges to take the lead in an organized attempt to effect a qualitative improvement of foreign language instruction. A few questions on the various official and semi-official college entrance examinations would probably go a long way towards accomplishing the desired results.

Syracuse University.

FOREIGN STUDY FELLOWSHIP OPPORTUNITIES
FOR TEACHERS OF FRENCH

By Archie M. Palmer
Assistant Director
of the Institute of International Education

Some years ago at a meeting of international societies the late Andrew Carnegie remarked that in time there would be no place in the world for the peace societies which he had founded, but that there would always be need for organizations which would bring different countries together in points of intellectual contact.

Whether one is a foe or a friend of internationalism, whether one believes in a society of nations or thinks that the human race will prosper best when parcelled into small, assertive nationalities, one must admit that in the future, as in the past, nations will be stimulated by the contact of one civilization with another. The understanding and appreciation of one's neighbors can be best realized through a comprehension of their culture, of their social life, and of their psychology. In what more effective way can this end be attained than through the interchange of students and teachers, thereby effecting the interpretation through the observing eyes of critical youth?

Ever since the days when Benjamin Franklin and Thomas Jefferson were exerting themselves in the interest of an *entente cordiale* between France and the struggling young American Republic, there has been gradually evolving a strong intellectual sympathy between the two countries. The late World War has contributed to a greater extent than any other single event in arousing and bringing the American people to a full realization of the wealth of intellectual and inspirational opportunities available in France for Americans.

With this awakening has come a more adequate knowledge and appreciation by Americans of the contributions made by France in all fields of modern knowledge. During the Eighteenth and Nineteenth Centuries France produced many great masters in literature, in science and in art. These outstanding figures were usually skilful teachers as well as creators and they had many capable young disciples who spread abroad the ideas and visions of their masters, thereby prolonging and extending their influence by supplying the needed interpretations and elaborations. In many fields these young scholars set the pace of intellectual progress in Europe.

The tremendous increase in recent years of interest in the study of the Romance Languages, and particularly of French, has caused many an American student to cast a longing eye on the possibilities of study in France. With the traditional background provided by the significant achievements of French savants, it is not at all surprising that young American scholars should respond to the attractions of such foreign study.

Value of Foreign Study

Teachers of French can benefit greatly from a period of study in France where they can observe and learn at first hand the spirit and culture and the institutions of the country whose literature they interpret to their own students in the classroom and from the lecture platform. Not merely do the teachers themselves profit from this experience but they carry back to their own people an intelligent and sympathetic understanding and appreciation of their subject matter.

It is not always possible for the ambitious young teacher who is devoting himself to a life of service in the field of education to provide from his meagre earnings the necessary funds for a trip abroad, much as he may recognize and cherish its value to him personally and to the enhancement of his professional advancement. Opportunity for such deserving scholars to enjoy the advantages of foreign study is made possible through a number of fellowships and scholarships established by farsighted individuals, foundations, colleges and universities, and other institutions.

The fundamental idea behind practically all these foreign study opportunities is the desire to make it possible for America to broaden her horizon and to promote international goodwill through a better mutual understanding between the United States and foreign countries. That the furtherance of this ideal is being realized is clearly manifest in the activities of those who have returned after an enjoyment of these opportunities and the increasing breadth of vision and of interest in international affairs on the part of our people generally and of our youth particularly.

Liberal Opportunities Available

One of the most liberal opportunities that teachers of French find open to them for foreign study is that offered under the John Simon Guggenheim Memorial Foundation. The specific objects of this foundation, which was established in 1925, are "to add to the educational literary, artistic and scientific power of this country and also to provide for the cause of better international understanding." It aids scholars of exceptional aptitude and artists with creative ability of a high order, making no restrictions as to subject or place of study and offering equal opportunities to both sexes, married or single, of any race, color or creed. Every year some fifty fellowships, each carrying a stipend of $2,500 a year, are filled, many of them by teachers or professors on sabbatical leave.

Another interesting group of fellowships are those awarded under the Kahn Foundation for "the Foreign Travel of Teachers, founded on the conviction that the cause of civilization may be greatly encouraged and promoted by travel on the part of teachers, scholars and investigators." These fellowships are open to men only, preferably to professors in our colleges and universities, between twenty-five and thirty-five years of age, with records of success in their studies that prove their capacity for strenuous work, and not only capable of independent observation and constructive thought but also able to communicate to others the results of their observations.

The Kahn fellowships provide for a year of foreign travel and study, the incumbents being expected to visit the various countries of Europe and Egypt, India, China, Japan, Ceylon and Java. The yearly stipend for such travel is about $5,000 and it is expected that the fellowship will enable its holder "to issue from the world of books and their narrow sphere of habitual interests into the broader world of various civilizations and such human interests, struggles and endeavors as go to the making of general civilization."

It is in order to develop a more complete realization and consideration of the contributions made by the great minds of France to science and learning that an organization known as the American Field Service Fellowships for French universities was established shortly after the World War. It was also "in order to provide an enduring memorial to the one hundred twenty-seven Field Service men who gave their lives to the cause and to perpetuate among future generations the mutual understanding and fraternity of spirit which marked their relations during the war" that the organization has continued activities. Each year awards are made of a series of Fellowships for advanced study in France to qualified candidates selected from among the graduates of American colleges and universities and from the technical and industrial field, each carrying a stipend of $1,200.

These fellowships, which at present are open only to men, are offered for study in the universities and faculties and other institutions of higher learning in Paris and in the sixteen provincial universities. The candidate may designate his choice of the institution in which to pursue his work but the desirability of a period of residence in a provincial university is strongly recommended.

International Exchange Fellowships

In the realization of its aim, to develop international goodwill and understanding through educational agencies, the Institute of International Education has now for a number of years been making it possible for foreign students to come to the United States on international exchange fellowships and for American students to study in European universities on reciprocal fellowships. Prominent among the exchanges administered by the Institute is the Franco-American Exchange which provides for the bringing over of fine French scholars to the United States to study in American colleges and universities and the sending of a group of American students to France to study on scholarships offered at the French universities. These scholarships, offered to American students by the Ministry of Public Instruction and the universities of France, cover in most instances board, lodging and tuition, although some of them provide free tuition only. Under either arrangement the successful scholarship holders enjoy a number of excellent advantages at the French universities by virtue of their status as Franco-American scholars. These scholarships are open both to men and to women.

For the past few years the French Ministry of Public Instruction has offered to American men through the Institute of International Education a number of teaching positions in French lycées and écoles normales, known as "postes d'Assistant d'Anglais" if in the former, or as "postes de Répétiteur d'Anglais" if in the latter. The function of the assistant is to give lessons in conversational Engish to his French pupils two hours daily. There is no salary connected with these positions but the assistant receives room, board, light and heat free. He occupies an academic position which is just below that of the professors and chargés de cours. These posts offer exceptional opportunities for improvement in the language and for understanding the people, especially for those who contemplate the teaching of French. The assistant is given the privilege of attending courses at the institution where he is teaching or, if within commuting distance, at a university.

The American Association of University Women administers a number of foreign study fellowships for women graduates of our American colleges and universities. Their International Fellowship, which is open to all members of the associations and federations of university women forming branches of the international federation, carries a stipend of $1,200 and enables the winner to study in any approved university or institution in a country other than that in which the Fellow had received her previous education or habitually resides.

The Anna C. Brackett Memorial Fellowship, which is awarded every third year (the next award will be made this year) and which has a stipend of $1,000, is awarded through the Association to an American woman having a degree in art, science or literature who intends to make teaching her profession. In general, preference is given to applicants who have had successful experience in teaching and in addition have completed at least two years of graduate study. Similarly, the $1,000 Julia C. G. Pratt Memorial Fellowship is awarded every third year, the last award having been made in 1927.

The Association administers the Alice Freeman Parker Memorial Fellowship, which is open to women holding the degree of Ph. D. or D. Sc., who are able to present evidence of distinctive subsequent accomplishment in research. The Phi Mu Fellowship of $1,000, which is awarded to an American woman having a degree from a college or university in which Phi Mu has a chapter, is also offered under the aegis of the Association.

The Association's $1,200 European Fellowship is open to women having a degree in art, science or literature who have met all the requirements of the Ph. D. degree, with the possible exception of completion of the dissertation, and who show promise of distinction.

Information about Opportunities

A number of colleges and universities offer foreign study fellowship opportunities to their own graduates and in some instances consider applications from graduates of other colleges of recognized standing. Also, fellowships originally intended for graduate study at a particular American college or university may under certain circumstances be used for foreign study. As each of these opportunities entails a specific relationship to the institution in question, the teachers interested in them might well consult their alma maters or the particular colleges concerned.

In a bulletin on "Fellowships and Scholarships Open to American Students For Study In Foreign Countries", published by the Institute of International Education, detailed information about these various fellowships will be found. The Institute also publishes a number of bulletins of interest and value to teachers and students, such as the "Handbook for American Students in France" and treatises on the systems of higher education in other countries of Europe.

The fellowships cited above are all for graduate study abroad. In general, graduate students profit most from such foreign study opportunities. There are certain very obvious reasons for this. The organization of education in the European countries is very different from that in our own country. This makes it somewhat difficult for an undergraduate from the United States to fit in almost anywhere in any of their systems. The average undergraduate who goes to such a country as France or Germany for purposes of study usually wastes his time from the standpoint of systematic study, however much general culture he may get from his experience. He will not be accepted as a student at the university and he is a complete misfit at the secondary school such as the lycée or gymnasium.

Even the graduate student from the United States has considerable difficulty at first in making his orientation. The European university is a place of research in which the student is thrown almost wholly upon himself. There is very little of the cooperation or even guidance on the part of the professor which characterizes graduate study in the American university.

Naturally, the educational authorities in the European countries do not look with favor upon the advent of isolated undergraduate students. Since the War the Universities in most of the European countries have become overcrowded. They are glad to welcome foreign students but only such as are mature scholars who can carry on their own studies and research without supervision and guidance.

The "Junior Year Abroad"

Nevertheless the movement described by the term "Junior Year Abroad", when participated in by organized groups under well-defined supervision, has won the hearty approval of all the factors concerned in its operation, the French educational authorities, the American college faculties, and the students themselves. It has passed out of the experimental stage and has now apparently become a permanent factor in international education. The student participating in it becomes so steeped in the French culture and civilization as to become a unique product of American and French education.

Through the generosity of a group of interested persons, a number of scholarships are awarded by the Institute of International Education, through its Committee on Foreign Travel and Study, to American college students desiring spend the junior year abroad studying in a foreign university, not necessarily limited to study in France. These scholarships, which carry a stipend of $1,000 each, are open both to men and to women. A candidate for one of them must be not less than eighteen years of age, must have been in residence for at least two academic years in an American institution approved by the Institute and must intend to return to his American college to take his degree. He plans his course of study in France in such a way that he may be able to resume his college work regularly with his class when he returns to the United States.

In addition there have recently been turned over to the Institute for administration, some twenty or so competitive scholarships in the amount of $300 each. These scholarships, which are open both to men and to women, are for study in France only and they are intended to be used for the purpose of enhancing and spreading the "Junior Year Abroad" idea throughout the colleges of the country. These scholarships are intended to cover the cost of the ocean passage both ways and of a certain amount of travel in France, which are the principal items of expense incurred by a scholarship holder, beyond the usual cost of the year in college in this country.

The American student abroad, be he graduate or undergraduate, enjoys the opportunity to study a "civilization other than his own" in the making, and is enabled to interpret and compare his own nation and its institutions with another nation and its institutions. Rich opportunities in every field of study and research are afforded in the universities of France providing an invaluable supplement to our own educational resources. The graduate of an American college who desires to proceed to an advanced degree will find that a French university degree equivalent in standing to the Ph. D. of an American university of recognized standing and declared by the French university authorities to have the same scientific and academic value as the state doctorate (doctorat d'Etat) can now be obtained in all of the faculties of the University of Paris and at all of the other sixteen French universities, while opportunities for study in the specialized national and independent institutions are also available to him.

PRONUNCIATION ANALYSIS

By Florence M. Baker

When we are told that we have a good French accent the resultant sentiment is one of undivided pleasure. When we are told—less blatantly—that we have a poor French accent the reaction is one of depression varying in degree and in kind according to the temperament of the listener. The one regrets it, but with a feeling of hopelessness. "I always knew that," he will say, "I simply can't get the pronunciation. Languages always were very difficult for me", etc., etc. The other will mingle with his regret a certain feeling of resentment. "Yes," he says, "I suppose my pronunciation is poor, but I don't know what to do about it. Why does not the instructor tell me how to improve it? What is wrong with my accent anyway? I should like to have a better one but I don't know how to get it," etc., etc.

And the complaint is a very just one. No one, at least no teacher, should tell a student that his pronunciation is poor unless he is also ready to show him what is wrong with it. For evidently it is not all wrong or we couldn't have understood it at all. A bad French accent is simply a collection of mistakes repeated *ad infinitum.* But each mistake can be isolated, given the correct treatment and ultimately cured if the patient co-operates with courage and industry. To isolate these difficulties, however, needs special training on the part of the instructor and native teachers of French are no better equipped by nature in this respect than are Americans. They are able to remark mispronunciations more easily than can American teachers but, on the other hand, they are more inclined to accept mistakes as being the natural condition of a foreigner and to feel that not much can be done about it. American teachers who take lessons from French people will testify as to this fact. Their primary aim is to acquire a good accent and yet after a few lessons there arises a feeling of doubt, of wonder as to whether one is making any progress and the following conversation usually ensues:

"How is my pronunciation?"

"It is very good, yes, really, quite good."

"But I make mistakes, do I not?"

"Why yes, yes, a good many."

"Well, won't you tell me what these mistakes are so that I can correct them."

Here come gesticulations followed by protestations that the pronunciation is not at all bad. But in the end the pupil is no wiser than he was at the beginning, except in realizing that his faults are probably there to stay. This is not the fault of the French Instructor. He has not had the necessary training in practical phonetics to diagnose errors and to offer a remedy. In the face of a poor pronunciation he is as helpless as a layman in the presence of a case of appendicitis. Nor is this condition confined to one nationality. We do the very same thing to the foreigners within our gates. If after a residence of several years with us they speak English distinctly and agreeably it is due far more to their perseverance or their natural ability in adapting the organs of speech, than to any tangible help we have given them in pronunciation. The teachers of English for Foreigners in this country are generally as little trained in the sound production of their native tongue. It is only to be expected that the last study one would take up would be the phonetics of one's own language, for it is hard to understand how an activity which we acquired unconsciously can present so many difficulties for someone else.

These difficulties are of many varieties. They are not only difficulties of intonation, of word-grouping, of individual words in the sentence, but they come down very frequently to separate letters in the word itself. When a word is badly pronounced it means that one letter, or several letters or possibly all the letters in the world are wrongly produced. The only way to rectify this is to isolate the letter or letters and learn the pronunciation of each separately. Let us take, for instance, the rather simple word "poli". It seems easy enough but it is possible that many first year and even second year students would pronounce it so that they would be recognized at once as foreigners. Let us see what errors could arise in the pronunciation of such a word:

"p" may be too aspirate. It then becomes much harsher than in the accent of the French people.

"o" may be long instead of short.

"l" may be too palatal.

"i" is probably the most correct letter in the word. The only danger here is that the student accents the last syllable too much and thereby turns the vowel into a diphtong.

This word can be best learnt if the two syllables "po" and "li" are divided and practised separately.

Learning the pronunciation of words by individual vowels and consonants may seem a long and ardous business but it is really more efficient in the long run. The student who spends his time in studying the pronunciation of separate words has learned in the end only the total of those words, whereas the student who studies the individual letters or syllables has learned them for all possible combinations of these sounds.

The making of a Pronunciation Analysis even for a large class is not as formidable as it may seem at first glance. It must be borne in mind that a class will vary widely in the quality of its pronunciation from those who speak with a comprehensible and agreeable accent down to those who pronounce in the grand manner. But there are a certain number of mistakes which can be expected among American pupils and except in rare instances errors will fall into certain groups. These errors we shall classify under the titles of Phrase Errors and Unit Errors. It will be noticed that the individual word is not given much attention in this grouping. That is because, as we have tried to show earlier in this article, the individual word is rarely wrong entirely but is wrong either in its relation to other words in the sentence or is wrong in parts of its make-up.

I. Phrase errors—this includes all the mistakes that interfere with the easy flow of the sentence, or rather the phrase; such as:

a. Liaison, which may be neglected or overdone
b. Too heavy tonic accent

c. Neglect of the syllables which would be unaccented in similar English words.

II. Unit Errors—includes all faulty individual letters in the word. These are:

A. Vowels:

open "a", "u".

Closed "e" at the end of words (which may be written é, er, ez, et)

Substitution of a Diphthong for the pure vowel.

B. Consonants

"r" insufficiently trilled

"t, d, p, b, c(k) too aspirate

"l" too palatal.

It will be found that most of the errors of pronunciation will fall into these groups. The list given here was arrived at by several years of checking on the pronunciation of American pupils in French classes and by comparative studies made abroad of the respective pronunciation problems of different nationalities. The number may seem discouragingly large but it must be remembered that one student does not necessarily possess all the defects here listed and it must also be borne in mind that they can be corrected in due time. The writer has used with considerable success the following plan for analyzing pronunciation and keeping a record of the student's improvement. If the class is entering the second year of French a piece of very simple prose is selected which will include a wide variety of phonetic sounds. Each student reads it in turn while the rest of the class can be occupied with some other work. After the test is completed his attention is drawn to the outstanding defects of his pronunciation. He then constructs some form of chart similar to the one below which will enable him to study his progress in improving himself. He is given a list of words or phrases suited to his needs, which are to be used for practice, and at the end of a month he is given another test, not a general pronunciation test, however, but one designed to judge solely the items on which he has been working. He is given a mark for each item and notes it on his chart making curves in different colors for the different items. He is thus enabled to see how he stands and if he finds the curve descending he must plan to do some extra practising.

If the class is beginning French the first test is not made until the end of the second month, but in other respects it is carried out in the same way as the second year chart. From one month to another regular work is done in pronunciation and the student's attention called to his faults occasionally, but the regular test is not given more than every four weeks. The actual work thrown upon the teacher is slight. The students make and take care of their own charts and the time required for the monthly test need not take more than one period unless the class is very large.

The chart shown here is one made by a girl in the Second Year in High School and represents her pronunciation growth during her second year of French. It must not be concluded that the four curves depicted represent her only faults and that her accent is otherwise one hundred percent French. By no means. The chart simply shows her most marked defects of pronunciation, that is, those which contribute towards making her spoken French incomprehensible. She began work in September after a vacation of three months in which no French was spoken and as the previous year had been devoted largely to grammar it is not surprising that the curves began at so low a point.

The improvement shown by the vowel "u" is the most striking, but not at all unusual. For the "u" though entirely foreign to English-speaking people is easily gained and once acquired seems to remain intact. Its very foreignness is perhaps a protection as having no near equivalents in English it can remain unaffected by the native tongue. The curve illustrating Liaison takes its rather hesitant shape from the fact that the student after once realizing the importance of Liaison began to exaggerate its use until the next month's test showed her the error of her ways. The two other curves show a rather average improvement, due to faithful though not extensive drill.

This chart is only one of several methods of keeping individual records of pronunciation. Another very practical method for Unit Errors is to chart all the vowels and consonants in their correct phonetic classifications and then mark with a blue pencil each

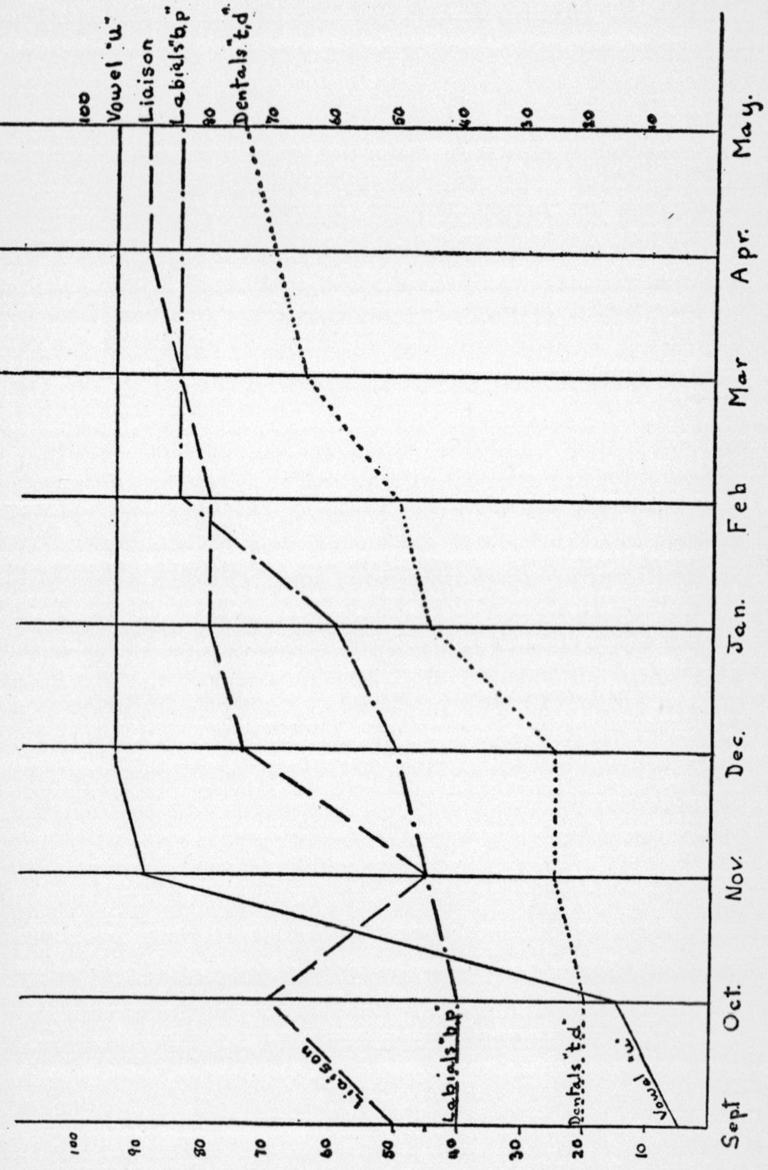

Chart showing improvement made during school year in four Pronunciation Units: 1. Liaison; 2. Labial Consonants *p* and *b*; 3. Dental Consonants *t* and *d*; 4. The Vowel *u*.

unit as soon as it is pronounced correctly. This has the drawback of not showing growth very clearly but, on the other hand, it is more desirable when there are a great many errors to tackle as a network of curves might excite feelings of despair rather than encouragement. Where a pupil is timid in the speaking of the language it is best to make the analysis gradually and not to draw attention to too many of his errors at once.

It is not the purpose of this article to treat of the exercises necessary for the correction of pronunciation errors. That forms in itself an extensive study. Pronunciation analysis is only one branch of the teaching of French pronunciation but it is a very important one for it starts the student on the right track and it lays the responsibility directly on the shoulders of the individual. The big majority of the French students in our schools have passed the age when their organs of speech are so adaptable that they can produce foreign sounds without effort. They are also past the age when they can learn by imitation. They must be told how to produce the sounds and their work must be checked frequently to see if they are producing them correctly. When they are shown what their particular weak points are, and not the weak points of the whole class, it is seldom indeed that a desire for improvement does not awaken. Most students are anxious to pronounce French nicely and they are doubly so when they see the possibilities of attaining their aim so closely within their reach and when they realize that their work is not all bad but has defects that can be remedied by help from their instructors and by industry on their own part.

New York City.

MA VISITE A ANDREW D. WHITE

Par FERNAND BALDENSPERGER

L'hiver s'attardait à fond sur Ithaca et ses environs, lorsqu'en mars 1914, au retour de l'Ouest, je fus invité à m'arrêter à Cornell University en venant de Buffalo et de Cleveland. Toute la contrée était, comme certains dessins persans, un damier noir et blanc irrégulier: les sombres lignes de sapins, sur les pentes, se débarrassaient à peine de la neige qui avait chargé leurs branches. Aussi ai-je gardé surtout, de l'octogénaire vigoureux qui voulut bien m'accueillir au passage, le souvenir d'un courtois vieillard en pelisse et bonnet fourré qui, ancien ambassadeur à Pétersbourg, retrouvait aisément des habitudes et un costume d'hivernage.

J'avais visité le 5 mars, comme il convient, l'Ecole ménagère et l'Institut agronomique, admiré à la Bibliothèque les richesses des collections italiennes et islandaises, et fait sous les auspices de mon collègue Comfort une conférence dont je me rappelle le sujet : *Chateaubriand et son voyage aux Etats-Unis*. Episode assez controversé à cette époque, et qu'il n'était pas sans intérêt de mettre au point, pour tenir une balance équitable entre les allégations d'un voyageur trop gourmand et les dénégations d'une critique soupçonneuse : double attrait pour un conférencier qui arrivait du Niagara!

Présenté par un de mes collègues, à l'issue de cette conférence à laquelle il avait bien voulu assister, je fus prié par M. White de lui donner quelques instants le lendemain matin, avant de retourner à New-York. Ce fut donc assez tôt dans la matinée que mon aimable hôte M. James F. Mason m'accompagna jusqu'à la maison de l'ancien Président: et j'admirai la belle santé d'un homme qui se trouvait prêt d'aussi bonne heure à faire les honneurs de ses livres et de ses riches souvenirs à un voyageur de passage.

La causerie alla bon train. Telles des anecdotes dont je me souviens se trouvent, plus ou moins identiques, dans cette *Autobiogra-*

phy of A. D. White dont les deux volumes sont, encore aujourd'hui, fort curieux à consulter; encore était-il possible de trouver, dans la tournure qu'elles prenaient sur ces lèvres souriantes, un léger changement d'interprétation, peut-être inconscient de la part du narrateur lui-même. Et je dirais aussi que le choix qu'il faisait, dans une longue vie si remplie, de tel souvenir plutôt que de tel autre, avait au moins une valeur de symptôme.

Etudiant d'histoire, A. D. White, on le sait, avait fait à Paris et Berlin, en 1853 et 1854, des études et des recherches. La faible organisation de l'enseignement supérieur français à cette époque ne l'avait pas empêché de suivre, à la Sorbonne et au Collège de France, les cours publics qui constituaient alors une grande partie de la vie intellectuelle permise au pays. Il avait été très frappé, me disait-il, de la rapidité avec laquelle toutes les allusions possibles d'un orateur universitaire étaient saisies par l'auditoire bigarré assis au pied de la chaire. Il se rappelait en particulier un cours où Saint-Marc Girardin ayant fait allusion aux vertus d'honneur et d'héroïsme illustrées par les légendes épiques du moyen âge, des applaudissements avaient aussitôt éclaté dans la salle, à peine réprimées par le conférencier protestant avec mollesse: "Mais, Messieurs! Mais, Messieurs!..."

De la France du Second Empire, les souvenirs passaient aisément à la Prusse bismarckienne. On sait que le premier Président de Cornell University avait été une première fois ministre à Berlin de 1879 à 1881, pour y retourner de 1897 à 1902. De ce second séjour, je n'ai pas le souvenir que mon hôte ait fait particulièrement mention; l'autre lui avait laissé au contraire dans la mémoire deux anecdotes bien caractéristiques.

Un jour, le Chancelier de fer, grippé, rencontre le diplomate américain, avec lequel il avait pris l'habitude de prendre un ton mi-cordial, mi-railleur, auquel A. D. White répondait par un tranquille humour. Ce jour-là, il conseilla à son interlocuteur de se remonter en buvant quelques verres de Saint-Emilion. Bismarck ne regimbe pas à l'ordonnance, et s'informe seulement des heures où il semble qu'elle doive faire le meilleur effet.

A quelques jours de là, nouvelle rencontre: le colosse semble pâle et défait. Le bordeaux n'opérerait-il pas sur le chancelier de l'Empire d'Allemagne ? Le diplomate s'informe avec sollicitude, et reçoit cette réponse: "Je ne sais pas si les bouteilles étaient éventées, mais il y a trois jours que j'absorbe tous les matins, à jeun, toute une bouteille de Saint-Emilion, et c'est le contraire d'un réconfort que j'en ai éprouvé jusqu'ici!"

Autre anecdote qui n'avait rien d'inédit sans doute, mais qu'il était plaisant d'entendre conter à un témoin—faut-il dire à une victime ? Le ministre des Etats-Unis, en visite chez le Chancelier, demande à celui-ci comment il peut bien faire pour empêcher les fâcheux de s'éterniser dans son cabinet. Oh! c'est bien simple, répond Bismarck. Ma femme, dans la pièce voisine, sait à quel moment l'indiscrétion commence, et elle y met fin en me rappelant que c'est soi-disant pour moi le moment de prendre médecine." Il n'avait pas fini de parler que la porte s'entrebaillait et que la princesse de Bismarck, d'une voix de léger reproche, disait à son mari :

"Otto, n'oublies-tu pas que c'est l'heure d'absorber ton médicament?"

Deux diplomates français qu'A. D. White avait connus à Berlin, Noailles et Saint-Vallier, lui avaient laissé les meilleurs souvenirs. En revanche, il ne semblait pas enchanté de ses relations avec le lecteur français de l'impératrice, l'ami de Gambetta, M. Gérard, que pour mon compte j'avais trouvé à Tokyo en 1912, et sur lequel il partageait peut-être certaines préventions régnant à Berlin; ou si quelques affectations qu'on a reprochées à un homme entré par hasard dans la diplomatie répugnaient à la simplicité du ministre des Etats-Unis.

La Russie permettait dès cette heure-là, à M. White qui la connaissait bien, d'exercer une perspicacité que j'ai admirée depuis. Car ses jugements sur le comte Witte, et sur le rôle peu loyal qu'il jouait auprès du souverain, me sont souvent revenus à l'esprit...

Université de Paris.

VARIA

By J. F. MASON

It is unfortunate that in American schools and colleges the spirit of rivalry and competition counts for so much in athletics and non-scholastic activities and for so little in the class-room. The establishment of prizes, in spite of many obvious difficulties in supervision and control, offers a legitimate means of stimulating interest among high school pupils and college students.

The newspaper *La Prensa* of New York City has for the fourth year in succession announced a prize competition of 203 prizes amounting to $3,500.00. There is an elaborate scheme of distribution in the control of a group of well-known Spanish scholars. Thanks to the generosity of *La Prensa* the study of Spanish is bound to be stimulated.

The Briand Speech Competition was conducted last spring with much success and aroused a great deal of interest among students of French. The committee in charge now announces the publication of a booklet containing the names of all the college and high-school students who received honors, in addition to the French text of M. Briand's speech, and a composite translation of the same which embodies the happiest phrases from all the papers that received prizes and honorable mention, together with a history of the contest.

Let us hope that a large number of generous prizes for excellence in the study of French may be established to encourage and reward our better students. Human nature being what it is, both in and out of academic circles, competitions will always serve a definite purpose.

* * *

In the *Educational Review* for January 1928, James B. Taylor discusses the question of objectives in modern foreign language study in an article entitled "Why study a foreign language?" "The practical educational truth is that one comes more under the influence of the characteristics of other nations by travelling to the heart of their language than by travelling to the heart of their country. The practical aspect of the study of modern foreign languages is to be found in the opportunity which they offer us to lay "side by side with our experiences other experiences which touch us and will be profitable for us to know." Instruction in the modern foreign languages is defective in America because the pupil is not taught to "make the foreign language a part of himself, he is taught about the language as extraneous matter." We are behind European countries in making the knowledge of a foreign anguage a liquid asset. The author finds in the direct method, which is only in the experimental stage in America, a solution of our difficulties, and advocates the use of the gramophone.

* * *

The increasing interest in objective tests has led the University of the State of New York to publish in its Bulletin of Feb. 1, 1928 (Bulletin No. 893) a manual on the local construction and uses of objective tests by J. S. Orleans. This manual is a conscious effort to encourage and assist teachers to construct objective tests and to use the results profitably. Suggestions are given as to the form and arrangement of such tests with instructions for giving and scoring the same. The statistical treatment of the test results receives careful explanation. There is a full description of the various types of objective questions, such as the 'multiple choice-single response', 'multiple choice-plural response', 'true-false', 'completion', 'matching', 'short answer,' etc. The formula for computing the median of a distribution of scores is fully explained.

While the examples of tests are in such subjects as reading, geography, arithmetic, etc., the teacher of French can easily use this manual to construct similar tests in French. The Bulletin is supplied by the New York State Department of Education, Albany, New York, for ten cents.

* * *

At the annual meeting of the New York State Modern Language Association held in Syracuse last October, it was unanimously voted to change the name of the organization to the New

York State Federation of Modern Language Associations. The latter title seems more appropriate and exact, now that the American Association of Teachers of French and the American Association of Teachers of German have come into existence to take their place beside the American Association of Teachers of Spanish and the American Association of Teachers of Italian. The change of name does not imply any radical change in policy or organization. The annual and sectional meetings for teachers of modern foreign languages will be held as usual and, as in the past, some time will be devoted to papers and discussions of interest to all teachers of modern foreign languages, but particular attention will be paid to a division of the meeting into groups for the various languages. In the past the attempt to have programs of general interest has not met with much success. The officers of the N. Y. S. Federation of Modern Language Associations, who were elected for a triannual period, are as follows: J. F. Mason, president; Evie M. Grimes, First Vice-President; F. A. Casassa, Second Vice-President; F. F. Di Bartolo, Secretary and Treasurer, with the Board of Directors, which is composed of the Chairman and officers of each section and Genevieve Brooks, A. G. Host, F. C. Barnes, C. Holzwarth.

* * *

On December 10, 1927, a group of persons interested in the Junior Year Abroad Plan, as initiated and developed by the University of Delaware and Smith College, met in New York City at the invitation of Dr. Stephen P. Duggan, Director of the Institute of International Education, for the purpose of considering ways and means of fostering and developing the wider extension of the Junior Year Abroad idea and of administering certain scholarships for undergraduate foreign study. As a result of this meeting the Committee on the Junior Year Abroad of the Institute of International Education was created with the following membership: Dr. S. P. Duggan, Director of the Institute of International Education, *Chairman;* A. M. Palmer, Assistant Director of the Institute of International Education, *Secretary;* President W. Hullihen, of the University of Deaware, President W. A. Neilson of Smith College, Dorothy W. Dennis of Wellesley

College, C. A. Downer of the College of the City of New York, Margaret E. N. Fraser of Randolph Macon Woman's College, J. F. Mason of Cornell University, H. E. Smith of Brown University, Mary L. Waite of the Institute of International Education, Raymond Weeks of Columbia University, Florence D. White of Vassar College, B. E. Young of Indiana University, Mary V. Young of Mount Holyoke College.

This Committee has recently sent to a large number of college officials and teachers of French an open letter of the Junior Year in France. In this pamphlet are presented the arguments in favor of the plan, a brief outline of the program of work available in French, and the announcement of the establishment of a number of scholarships of $300.00 each. Copies of this pamphlet and further information may be secured from the Secretary of the Committee of Undergraduate Study in France, Institute of International Education, 2 West 45th Street, New York City, or from any member of the above-mentioned committee.

Cornell University.

* * *

In the *School Review* for November, 1927, the article, entitled *The Use of prognostic Tests in Modern Languages* throws some light on the selective function of modern high school instruction. After a description of experiments with the Wilkins Prognostic Test in Modern Languages at the Okmulzee (Oklahama) high School, the results of the investigation are summed up as follows: "While some of the percentages are fairly low, it is believed that the correlations are high enough to justify the use of prognostic tests. Although pupils who have scored below 300 on the Wilkins tests, or even 240, have not actually been refused admission to modern language courses, such pupils have been urged to take a different type of subject unless a language is required for admission to the college they expect to attend. The Freshman have been advised to postpone the modern language requirement until the last part of their high school work. It has been explained to them that, according to the Wilkins test, their chances of failure are 3 out of 4 and that, according to the Terman test in modern language, they have been made to realize that a great amount of effort is necessary.

If prognostic or mental-ability tests are used, many pupils will be saved from a year of failure and discouragement in a modern language, and the efforts of the teachers will be spared for the more capable pupils".

In the same number of *School Review* Louis H. Limper writes on *The Effect of having Studied a Foreign Language in High School on the Ability of College Freshmen to use English Correctly,* which continues the controversy of transfer values. The results of certain tests given the entering class at the Kansas State Agricultural College are not conclusive. "Although the difference in scores in the English test between the students who had not studied any foreign language and those who had studied a foreign language two or more years is sufficient to have statistical value, this difference is not sufficiently great to be of any real consequence." Further tests indicate that "the superiority of those who had studied a foreign language two or more years over those who had not studied any foreign language was greater in most cases than the improvement made during a year of college rhetoric."

While neither of these articles bring very definite results, they show the tendency of modern language teachers to carry on experiments in order to arrive at an objective truth. Professor Fife of the Modern Foreign Language Study, writing in the *Educational Review* for October, 1927 emphacises this point: "An active body of modern language teachers can no longer listen with patience to a program which consists of the iteration of individual opinion regarding methods or organization or the setting forth of results unless success has been measured by reliable tools, such as standarized tests. It is now recognized that the only way to break up the indescribably boring characted of teachers' conferences on methods is to demand that every exponent allow his wares to be tested." "Opinion subjectively formed is valueless unless supported by finding from tests."

A. Gazool.

BOOK REVIEWS

MARJORIE LOUISE HENRY

La Contribution d'un Américain au symbolisme français Stuart Merrill (1)

La vie de Stuart Merrill, qui, né à Hampstead, L. I., fut élevé en France, revint dans son pays natal à plusieurs reprises, puis se décida à vivre et à écrire en France, a été excellemment étudiée par Miss Marjorie Louise Henry.

Peut-être faudrait-il lui reprocher de n'avoir pas rendu assez vivante cette personnalité si sympathique. Miss Henry s'est procuré un nombre considérable d'inédits, et il semble bien qu'elle ait épuisé les documents nécessaires à son travail. Elle a accumulé faits et détails et je doute qu'on puisse trouver dans son livre d'importantes omissions. Cependant, par un excès de réserve, elle a passé sous silence quelques évènements de la vie sentimentale du poète qui eurent sur son œuvre une influence certaine. Au lieu de nous dire: "Le lycée n'étant guère à plus de vingt minutes de l'avenue d'Eylau, l'écolier pouvait deux fois par jour faire le trajet à pied", elle aurait dû nous parler plus franchement de "la mauvaise reine qui inspira *Les Fastes*", et surtout d'une autre "qui depuis bien des années l'accompagnait dans l'existence", et qui inspira *Les Quatre Saisons*. Il semble que Miss Henry ait mal choisi ses détails, ils ne sont que rarement pittoresques.

Mais c'est là un défaut presque inhérent aux travaux universitaires; et il faut louer dans cette thèse la précision dans l'analyse de l'œuvre, l'étude excellente de la technique, et de l'effort de Merrill pour adapter au français la prosodie de l'anglais. Dans *Les Quatre Saisons,* il chercha à transplanter le vers employé par Coleridge dans *Christobel.*

Un des problèmes que posait l'étude de Stuart Merrill, c'était justement celle des origines étrangères du symbolisme. On a re-

(1) Paris, H. Champion, 1927.

proché aux symbolistes d'agir contre la tradition française, de créer une technique qui n'était pas faite pour la langue. Mais la contribution de l'Américain Stuart Merrill, malgré les efforts de Miss Henry pour prouver le contraire, se borne à peu; quelques poèmes en vers blancs, quelques légendes empruntées à Tennyson et à Swinburne, quelques souvenirs de Whitman. Si d'autre part on considère ce qu'il doit à la France, aucun doute ne reste: Merrill a suivi les maîtres symbolistes de très près et il s'inspire de Verlaine et de Mallarmé beaucoup plus que de ces Anglais.

Quand Miss Henry explique ses tendances idèalistes ou même socialistes par ses origines américaines, on peut lui répondre que toute cette génération se donna à l'idéalisme et aux aspirations libérales. Je me représente mal, pour ma part, un Américain-type mené au poste "pour avoir manifesté trop ouvertement sa sympathie pour les anarchistes", et je me le représente encore moins comme un violent dreyfusard.

Stuart Merrill, qui écrivait aussi parfaitement l'anglais que le français, qui avait des amis parmi les poètes d'Amérique et ceux d'Europe, devait se sentir plus de sympathie pour ceux de France, qui, à cette époque, déployaient une vigueur et une originalité magnifiques. Ce que Miss Henry ne veut pas dire, c'est que Stuart Merrill appartient à la longue liste des artistes américains notoires qui s'expatrièrent pour trouver une terre artistique. Il rejoint ainsi Henry James, Sargent, Vielé Griffin, dans le passé; T. S. Eliot, Ezra Pound et bien d'autres aujourd'hui.

RENE TAUPIN.

BOOK REVIEW IN EDUCATION

"The Classroom Teacher"

We are glad to call the attention of Junior High School Teachers to a recent publication in the field of Education, conceived according to an entirely new plan. The Teachers who did not have an opportunity to study modern and progressive methods of teaching with the leading educators of the country will find in this work the best professional advice and guidance.

The chapters on the teaching of Modern Languages will be found in volume 12. Each volume can be bought separately.

The Classroom Teacher, edited by Milo B. Hillegas, William C. Bagley, and Thomas H. Briggs, Chicago, The Classroom Teacher, Inc., 1927, in 12 volumes, over 7,000 pages, illustrated with color plates. "What the American classroom teacher needs is a complete exposition of the American school, its management, its life, its curriculum, and the best that we know of how to teach it. We need a balanced treatment, scientifically accurate and in good taste. This is the function of "The Classroom Teacher. Here we find a collection of books dealing with the elementary school and the Junior High School. The editors are the outstanding leaders of the profession, and the various sections are written by those best qualified to speak. No one school of thought is emphasized. No individual hobby is stressed. The leading teacher-training institutions are represented. The teacher who uses these books may rest assured that the statements are authoritative in the light of the best theory and practice to date." (Dean William F. Russell, Teachers College, Columbia University.)

* * *

"Whatever training a teacher may have had, there is need for the stimulus of new ideas that professional growth may result. Every teacher tends to settle down to routines of instruction. However good these at any time may be, they become increasingly less effective. Every one needs new points of view, new suggestions, some of which will of course be rejected, others accepted fully, and still others modified so as to contribute to the specific tasks that are to be accomplished." (Thomas H. Briggs).

RECENT TEXTS

LABICHE ET MARTIN. *Le Voyage de Monsieur Perrichon.* Edited with Notes, Exercises, and Vocabulary by Ralph W. Haller. New York, Globe Book Co., (1927), v + 188 pp.

Another avatar of the immortal Perrichon, conceived "in the hope that the features of the appended exercises will be an added attraction to an already popular text." The attraction would have been more pronounced had these exercises been benefited by greater editorial care and competence. This is evinced by the fact that, whereas the text proper is comparatively free from errors, the "exercises" teem with mistakes, typographical (?) and otherwise, which average to two per page. To list them all would be supererogatory. Suffice it to class most of them, albeit somewhat arbitrarily, as follows:

(1) Faulty or unidiomatic French: *se conférant avec* (101); *Qu'est-ce que Daniel a-t-il préparé* (139); *plutôt* (for *plus tôt,* 122); *si non* (144); *à la point nommé* (135). Let us hope that *que mon éducation fût terminé* (137), *toute à l'heure* (106 and 102), *tu sais tous* (123), *se faire fort le* (135), are misprints. The editor should have avoided directions worded like the following: "Des verbes ci-dessous indiqués écrivez à toutes personnes les temps suivants" (89), and remembered the function of *en* in writing directions of this kind: "(a) Apprenez la signification de chaque locution; (b) Employez chacune dans une courte phrase française" (92). A more idiomatic headline than "Notre citoyen revient" could reasonably be expected of a French home-town paper, and mooted construction as "Qu'est-ce qu'*il* arrive lorsqu'on" etc. (100) easily avoided.

(2) Anglicized spelling: Throughout these exercises *Mme* and *Mlle* are written with a period, *commandant* is capitalized, while *adresser* and *exemple* have a hybrid double *d* and an *a* respectively. Similary, we find *approacher* (97); *mechanique* (103); *exercise* (108); *échaper* (115); *désire* (noun, 117); *advantageuse* (118).

Further, wrong divisions: *cour-age* (122); *conven-able* (132); *ex-ample* (sic, 132). One may include here *Vous dire "adieu"* (95) with un-French quotation marks, such abbreviations as *5ième* (on one line), etc.

(3) Various misprints: The most numerous involve the omission of accents: *parentheses* (90); *suggerées* (91); *proteger* (99); *eloigner* (102); *etend* (104); *lievre* (105); *seriuex* (sic, 105); *ecrit* (111); *inquieter* (112); *regulier* (127); *decouverte* and *etre charge de* (134); *a l'instant fixe* (135). The spellings *diner* (124), *bruler* (129), *connaitre* (138), and *dites le lui* (143) are not intentional. Other instances of wrong accentuation are *extrème* (118, and in the vocabulary, 168); *où* for *ou* (124); *rélatifs* (twice, 103). Obvious misprints are *hommés* (98); *á* for *à* (120); *umprunter* (88); *phrase savec* (87); *boaucoup* (90; *fair* (94); *Que'st-ce* (100); *unrhume* (109); *douteaux* (123); *nourir* (106); *servánt* (112); *due* (for *du,* 113); *exqliquez* (127); *expermiees* (133); *était-it, veut-it* (95, 100); *ca* for *ça* (102); further, *cantonnade* (109); *chifres,* (90), etc.

(4) Miscellaneous imperfections: "Nous lisons ce livre depuis (il y a) un quart d'heure" (114) is misleading to the student. It is likewise misleading to infer from "ça me fait du bien (act. II, sc. III) that "se faire du bien = se sentir mieux" (107).—"Henriette" is given with mute *h* in the Vocabulary, as is normally the case, yet the student will be puzzled to read "de Henriette" (141).—To ask a student, "Quelle idée Madame Perrichon avait-elle de la rencontre?" (*i. e.,* Perrichon's duel, 105) is, I fear me, to condemn him in advance to silence: the question is too generally worded.—*Dévergondage* (*grammatical*) (118) is too loosely glossed as as "erreur extrème" (sic), perhaps through the editor's misgiving that the pupils' morals might be endangered by a more accurate explanation. (The Vocabulary renders *dévergondage* as "impertinence".)—The distinction between *approcher de* and *s'approcher de* (109) is but partially correct.—"So" in "so he said" is not *puis* (122).—The first and third rules governing conditional phrases are mechanical and inaccurate (131).

The "Notes" which follow the "Exercises" are very scanty; so scanty, in fact, that the well-known allusions to the *récit de Théramène* and to Napoleon's speech before the Pyramids are not explained (unless we are to regard as explanation the bald statement, in the Vocabulary, that Théramène is a character in Racine's Phèdre). The same neglect is suffered by such words and expressions as *notaire, attrape!"* (how delighted the students would be to be told that it means "stung!"), *zouave* (explained in the Vocabulary merely as "a class of French soldiers"), *musée de Versailles* (to state, simply, that Versailles is a city near Paris is insufficient), etc. It does not appear that the editor is aware of the difference between *ça and çà* (148, 149). Both in the text and notes he has seemingly attempted to correct "Il est plus vrai que nature" to "*la* nature".

Follow a few additional remarks concerning the Vocabulary on which more care has been bestowed than on the exercises. Misprints: *Ah ça! aie!, paris* (*s. v.* Beauce), *a* for *la* (*s. v.* calotte),, *extrème, frêre, héroique, portfeuille, Phedre* (*s. v.* Théramène), *verité.*—It is hardly advisable in an elementary school text to enter *pleurs* under the rare singular *"pleur."*—The months are given with the article prefixed.—Neither under *coeur* nor under *gens* is mention made of the locution *gens de coeur,* explained (129) inaccurately (for its context) as "courageux, braves."—*Gradé* might better be explained as "non-com" than as "having the rank of an officer," whereby the point is missed—*avoir de l'ordre,* glossed as "to be orderly", is rather "to be a good manager" (177). —And, finally, there is no reason for giving *estomac* a second meaning of "body" just because Madame Perrichon uses the word in a picturesque expression.

FELIX VEXLER.

James Madison High School.

BAZIN, René. *Madame Corentine.* With Introduction, Notes and Vocabulary by Edwin B. Place, Ph. D. Alfred A. Knopf, 1928.

The problem of choosing modern texts to edit for classroom use is a rather delicate one. We seem to be putting a sort of stamp of official approval on any book thus edited so that it comes to the student with the authority of a classic. Yet we need to teach modern books. The student should be given some idea of the good contemporary writers and the teacher needs to depart from the old standbys in order to put new life in his teaching. The need however should not keep us from realizing the responsibility which our authority gives us to set a very high standard of literary excellence for our choice. *Madame Corentine* does not perhaps meet quite such a standard as one would hope to see set up. Even the editor does not claim that it is a neglected masterpiece. But it is a human story well told. It has a picturesque setting in Brittany, that most interesting of French provinces. The plot is not too obvious, the people live and move naturally. For this and many other literary reasons, *Madame Corentine* is worth the agonizing effort which is sometimes necessary for the poor student who, with an imperfect knowledge of the language tries to appreciate its literature. But why does the editor spoil it all with the unfortunate disclosure in his introduction to the effect that he has selected the book for a moral value, that he considers it a "wholesome work to place in the hands of young students"? Possibly it is a good motive, but it is one to be silent about. What young student wants to be told about the wholesome influences to which he is being subjected?

Madame Corentine is a study of a family problem, and one which is familiar in literature; a young wife and a managing mother-in-law are at the foundation of the inevitable domestic tragedy. This particular young wife was a country belle who married a rich townsman, and this particular mother-in-law had complete charge of her son's personal and business affairs since her husband's premature death. The country belle, though she loves her husband, has not married to settle down and seeks a wider field for a career of harmless enough pleasure in the added wealth and social position she has acquired. The mother, who is the type of woman traditionally associated with New England villages, is personally jealous, suspicious of the love of pleasure, and irritated at her son's inattention to business, and finally succeeds in tormenting her daughter-in-law beyond endurance. The terms of the separation give to the young wife the custody of a baby daughter, and the supposedly frivolous girl goes to Jersey where she makes a small fortune with a souvenir shop. The final reconciliation which we have been expecting all along is effected by the almost grown up daughter, and the happy ending is just saved from too much banality by the departure of grand mother who cannot forgive, and who will finish her life in bitter solitude. Certainly a story morally above reproach, but not so commonplace as the bare plot would seem to show. Bazin has charm and so have his characters. The local color is delightful and serves as a good companion piece to *Pêcheur d'Islande* which leaves us with the impression that all Brittany is one remote fishing village. The sea is ever present in *Madame Corentine* but it is not everything.

The presentation for classroom use is for the most part good. Those of us who expect our students to do all their written work in French cannot but regret that the introduction is in English. The language of the explanatory notes is a matter of indifference. The purpose being to explain a French phrase the means is unimportant. But if the student is questioned in French in a critical discussion of his author, it is difficult for him to answer well if his chief source of information has been in English. One thing that most teachers will be grateful for is the absence of "suggestions to teachers." If the teacher is one who needs such aids he does not like to have the student let into the secret, so he dares not use them in any case.

The question of the location of the notes is a real problem to an editor. He does not wish to spoil a fair page of the story by tiresome-looking footnotes, nor numbered references, and yet I often wonder if the notes which lie between the text and the vocabulary are not safely interred beyond disturbance. Curiosity after all does not lead us very far. As I read the story I had a vague impulse to look up some nautical terms which were unfamiliar to me, but it would have taken the fear of a very exacting teacher to make me really seek far for those words which I may never see again. If they had been at the bottom of the page I should have been glad of the information.

Every teacher will be glad for the questions which suggest conversation, although they are not all models of French style. "Qu'est-ce que Marie Anne a en apprenant que le projet est accepté?" is awkward to say the least and sins with a dreadful hiatus. But faults are always to be found by those who are on the scent of them and should not be exaggerated. We are glad to welcome to the bibliography of classroom texts a good story, well, but not over-edited.

EDITH PHILIPS.

Goucher College.

Moritz **LÉVI.** *Reading, Writing and Speaking French.* Henry Holt and Co, New York, 1927.

There is nothing new about Prof. Levi's new book but the title. Messrs. Bierman and Frank did the same thing in 1921 in their Conversational French Reader (Allyn and Bacon, New York, 1921). However, Prof. Levi's book, identical with the earlier work in method, is fuller in treatment and intended for more advanced pupils.

The book is a collection of short stories, a few excerpts from plays, fairy tales, letters, and some longer short stories. The stories are illuminated by copious notes, by questionnaires, by drill on verbs, on word families, on synonyms, antonyms, homonyms, by *thèmes, révisions, dictées,* and a myriad multitude of other devices for drilling and revamping the text.

All the old familiar favorites are here,—the peasant who wants glasses that will teach him to read, the little girl who is seven at home and only five when traveling, the Englishman who is not sure whether he has a wife or is merely hungry, the traveler who wants to see "Complet", the postman who is advised by his doctor to walk more, the two boys who dispute over the found nut, La Fontaine's poisoned apple, Red Riding Hood, Cinderella. M. Perrichon, Sganarelle, and the two roasted chickens in the Calabrian hut, all pass in review like Joe Miller's jokes on the vaudeville stage.

There is one element of novelty about this book. It departs from its prototypes, both preceding and contemporary, in that the author and the publishers have been brave enough to omit the usual photographs of the Place de la Concorde, the Place de l'Opéra, the Amiens Cathedral and Victor Hugo. The professor of French in the Podonk high school (who is really a teacher of physics, but having had a year of French in college, is taking the French classes, too) will hardly recognize this as a French book without the customary familiar pictures.

While the book lacks photographs, it does not fail to give a picture of France. You meet Frenchmen in restaurants, in church, on the street; you sense the play of their ready wit; you are introduced to Louis XIV, Napoléon, the Empress Eugénie, Mme de Sévigné, the Dumas père et fils, Pascal, Diderot, to mention only a few of the historical characters that figure in its pages.

There is much that is excellent in this book; it is a meaty and delectable volume. No work from the pen of so competent and experienced a teacher as Prof. Levi could fail to be worthwhile. Yet, just because Prof. Levi has long been one of the most capable, appreciated and revered of the teachers of French in this country, we are disappointed in not finding his work richer in aids for the teacher as well as for the learner.

Prof. Levi uses his Preface for a historical review of methods of teaching modern languages (most of which he finds faulty), rather than to give a hint of the best method of using this book and for whom it is intended.

Prof. Levi decries the old-fashioned method of answering ready-made questions on the text, yet thruout his book each story is followed by a questionnaire for the pupils to answer. In theory he favors a method of encouraging pupils to frame their own questions, but in practice he never suggests such an exercise. In connection with this constructive impulse, i. e., showing the pupil how the thing is done and leaving the rest to his own efforts, he quotes from Bertrand Russell's *Education and Life,* "the prospect of doing something venturesome with one's knowledge ought to be held before all the able young men and women". One can not resist the temptation to add "and before gifted teachers who write books".

Prof. Levi in his Preface emphasizes the value of conversation in the classroom and says "it is advisable to have pupils talk at times among themselves under the supervision of the teacher about the things of immediate interest to them". Is it not surprising, then, to find no suggestion in the book for dramatizing the stories or for dialoguing them?

Prof. Levi modestly absolves his readers from any thought of getting ideas out of his book. In his Preface he says (p. viii), "During the first two years the chief object should be the acquisition of the language—not the study of ideas", and on p. xiv, "the present book is intended to be read and studied carefully, intensively, not extensively—not for the ideas contained therein, but for the purpose of laying a sound foundation for future work."

The greatest fault one can find with this book is its lack of gradation. On page 12 there is a fairly long, not easy story "Un Malheur Complet". On page 22, a week or two later, the pupil meets the far simpler "Quel est votre âge?". And several weeks later, when he is supposed to have gained in vocabulary and in grammatical proficiency, he is given the still simpler five-line anecdote "A la Campagne", of which the easy vocabulary, the brevity, the use of the present tense, all argue for an earlier position in the collection. It is the same with the exercises. On p. 10, [7], almost at the beginning of the work, the pupil is asked to answer the question "Que feriez-vous si vous aviez affaire à un pauvre diable hors d'état de vous payer?", quite a long, complicated, idiomatic sentence; and twenty or twenty-five lessons later, (p. 55) the pupil is drilled on the present and future of "avoir", and even later (p. 68), he gets the simple present of *être, penser,* and *porter.*

In the Notes, there is the same lack of grading or failure to give thotful attention to it. For example, early in the book (p. 17), a note on the past participle feminine plural, reads "Expliquez l'accord (agreement) du participe passé." Much later, after the pupil has advanced in knowledge, a similar note (p. 55) and again (p. 68) is accompanied by the English translation, "Expliquez l'accord du participe passé. Explain the agreement of the past participle." Still later (p. 144), only the English is given. Surely if the English is needed at all, it is in the earlier not the later cases.

It is difficult to understand the theory on which the notes were built. For example (p. 129, n. 7), on the Subjunctive, asks the question, and asks it in French "Pourquoi le subjonctif!". In later cases, instead of putting it up to the pupil to explain the use of the subjunctive, the rule is told him and is told him in English (p. 169, 20; p. 170, 6; p. 259, 6).

Other examples might be mentioned of this carelessness or lack of method in framing the notes: p. 169, n. 10, reads in English "Translate literally" and (p. 169, n. 14), again in English, "Give the literal translation", but earlier than these cases (p. 163, n. 32), reads in French "Quelle est la traduction littérale?" If the pupil understood the French on p. 163, it is hard to see the reason for reverting to English on p. 169.

On p. 15, n. 10, we find "Donnez plusieurs sens de ce mot" all in French without English help. When the pupil gets on to p. 28, n. 6, he again reads "Donnez deux sens de ce verbe" again all in French. On p. 59, n. 1, there is a concession made to his acquirement of French, for the meaning of the word *sens* is given in English, "Donnez plusieurs sens (meanings) de cet adverbe". But when he reaches the later lessons (p. 72, n. 2) he finds the note all in English "Give several meanings of this verb" and (p. 72, n. 5) "Give several meanings of this adjective". In other words, the theory seems to be that if French is used in the rules in the earlier stages of learning the American pupil will be able to understand the rules if given in English in the later stages.

On pp. 110-111, there are two full pages of notes, sixty of them, all in English, all save one, No. 4, which for some inexplicable reason is put in French, "En France les femmes emploient assez souvent *mon* ou *cher ami* en parlant à leur mari". Where is the ryme or reason in this sort of thing? And is there any pedagogic principle or value served in inserting the single French word "ici" in an English note? (p. 17, n. 3) "faire. Ici; to cook or prepare food."

Repetition is so frequent in this book as to be almost a vice. Prof. Levi says in his Preface (p. xiii) "all teachers who have looked into the matter know that the average student remembers but little today of what he has learned only yesterday". Of course Prof. Levi doesn't believe that; neither does any teacher who has stuck to his job more than a year, for certainly that statement deals sure death to all hope of success in ever teaching anything. Yet this idea is probably Prof. Levi's justification for his constant repetitions. He seems to have certain fetiches, grammatical points that he, no doubt, has had difficulty thru the years in getting into the minds of his students. Open the pages at random to any body of notes and you will find one on the following points; —*brave,* its meaning before and after its noun, pp. 59, 158, 163, 271, 285; *venir de* infinitive, pp. 52, 158, 226, 283, 11; *faire* infinitive, pp. 64, 237, 251; *blesser* vs. *bénir,* pp. 259, 268; subjunctives, pp. 8, 50, 99, 110, 129, 144, 163, 169, 170, 252, 259, 264, 262, 301; *pleurer* vs. *crier,* pp. 250, 251, 262, 268, 271, 291; *assister* vs. *assister à,* pp. 150, 257, 262; the definite article with parts of the body, pp. 8, 17, 92, 111, 150, 251, 226, 239, 203; *marcher,* to walk; *milit.* to march, pp. 11, 239; agreement of the past participle, pp. 15, 17, 50, 55, 68, 77, 78, 144, 190.

Prof. Levi's faith in his pupils' ability to learn and to retain is lamentably weak and not very flattering to the pupil. Otherwise, why would he find it necessary to repeat incessantly the English meaning in the note (p. 41, p. 77) "Employez un temps quelconque (use any suitable tense)", and even on page 137 and again on page 143? Surely there must be some time when even the thickest numskull can be expected to grasp the sense of a French sentence repeated incessantly, without the necessity of giving him the English translation. It is not good pedagogy. It makes for laziness and slovenly thinking.

Prof. Levi is not always felicitous in his definitions; as, for example, when he calls a *commissionnaire,* "an errand porter" (p. 15, n. 4), an expression that has probably never been heard from Maine to California. And instead of explaining (p. 144, n. 3) that the *lycée* is "an establishment of secondary education under the direction of the State" (the same statement occurs in French p. 153, n. 13, and sounds as tho it were taken out of a dictionary) would it not have been more informing to have stated that the *lycée* is the nearest thing in France to the High School in the United States?

Typographically, the pages are very attractive, the choice of type varied and explicative. For convenience of reference, it would have been wise to have numbered the stories. The story "Excuse Malheureuse" (p. 44) might better have been omitted. It is neither elevated in style nor in moral tone; neither does it contribute a valuable vocabulary. It falls far below the level of the majority of the stories. Compare it with the "Une Paire de Bas de Soie" (p. 57) and you realize what a little tale can offer in high ethics, in universal appeal, in wealth of vocabulary.

Prof. Levi, who is such a provocative, inspiring, informing class-room teacher, let an opportunity slip by in his notes on historical personages in not giving enough information. Diderot, Renard, Courier, are all alike set down as "écrivain français". Occasionally certain personages receive fuller treatment—Glück, Madame de Sévigné, Buffon, but the learned professor here missed his chance to kindle and interest in French literature and history.

Colman D. Frank.

De Witt Clinton High School, New York.

Charles HOLZWARTH and William R. PRICE. D. C. Heath & Co., *Intermediate French.*

This book, designed for use in the second and third years, is an entirely satisfactory complement to the authors' much praised Beginners' French. Each lesson divided, as in the elementary book into two convenient parts, presentation (Premier Jour) and exercise (Second Jour) deals clearly with a single point in grammar, developed inductively in the text, then presented simply in explanation with examples; followed (Second Jour) with sufficient exercises in French and English to clinch the point with very little extra explanation or additional exercise demanded of the teacher. More or less logically every sixth lesson or so a review lesson contains questions and exercises demanding a summing up and reemphasis of material just covered. All of this is neatly topped off by an unusually clean-cut grammatical appendix which not only contains the usual verb paradigms (preceded incidentally, by a very useful explanation of use and formation of tenses), but also a complete and easily accessible restatement of all grammatical material presented in the book. This is very useful for general review. This book may be used without accompanying texts. Part I of the book (Lessons 1-18) consists of constructed texts giving with reasonably large vocabulary and moderation of idiom the general experiences of a high school boy. Part II is based on Laurie's *Mémoires d'un Collégien,* with the text sometimes too contorted in order to present grammatical material inductively. This contortion is pardonable only in that it makes it possible for the authors to do two things at once: (1) present their material inductively; (2) keep the interest of the students by use of a connected text. The job of adaptation is done fairly well. The forcing into it of grammatical examples would probably go unnoticed by the student. Accompanying texts however, may be used if the teacher so desires.

The chief value of the Intermediate French is that it is easy to work with. The authors, while offering every opportunity for general use of French in class, have wisely recognized the limitations, particularly for absorbing vocabulary and idiom, of the normal student. I would not say that vocabulary and idiom are sparse in this book. I would say rather that they are sufficient to be assimilated in the second and third years of French. The book is a decided and pleasant contrast to those frantic, laborious, and formless volumes which attempt to give the student knowledge of vocabulary and idioms out of proportion to his capacity or to the extremely limited time which he has at his disposal to "learn" a foreign language. A working knowledge of the language is offered here, the "high spots" of grammar pertinently and clearly presented, the exercises short and definite, sufficient opportunity for oral work, the whole compact, clear, easy to handle.

EDWIN J. MORGAN.

Thomas Jefferson High School,
Brooklyn, New York.

FRENCH GRAMMAR, by A. Béziat, W. M. Dey, Editor and Collaborator in Part. Published by Lafayette Series, 1927.

Qu'est-on en droit d'exiger d'une grammaire? D'abord, être un objet d'intérêt et non d'ennui pour l'élève. Peut-on demander à celui-ci de trouver un plaisir quelconque à apprendre par cœur une suite de règles insuffisamment éclaircies par de rares exemples, puis à traduire un exercice, la chance jouant un plus grand rôle que la connaissance, sur des règles mi-comprises?

De plus une grammaire, au lieu d'être un corps inanimé, doit parler à l'élève et à ses facultés, être vivante en un mot.

Enfin une grammaire doit enseigner le français, et par là j'entends une langue parlée; car, un élève, après deux ou trois ans d'étude, doit être à même de prononcer, lire, écrire la langue apprise, s'exprimer et converser.

Notre nouvelle grammaire répond à toutes les qualifications cidessus énumérées. Le livre contient trente chapitres, divisés chacun en trois ou quatre leçons, constituant chacune une unité. L'auteur donne au commencement un chapitre d'introduction sur une science discutée qui prend à l'époque actuelle une valeur de plus en plus scientifique, grâce à des expériences multiples : la phonétique. Les exercices correspondants sont bien choisis, basés sur les difficultés avec lesquelles les élèves anglo-saxons sont aux prises dans la prononciation du français. Chaque chapitre de la grammaire proprement dite traite un sujet entier en lui-même. Il commence par un vocabulaire usuel, dont l'élève aura besoin dans la vie courante; puis, prennent place, des règles claires, simples, bien énoncées et *en français,* complétées par des exemples judicieusement choisis. Une page de lecture, non une de ces anecdotes banales et démodées, mais un morceau intéressant puis, soit chez les classiques, soit au dix-huitième siècle et mis à la portée des élèves vient renforcer les règles énoncées. La leçon se continue par des questions assez serrées sur la lecture, suivies par un ou deux exercices en français, le deuxième se rapportant à une des leçons précédentes, et complétée par un exercice de traduction d'anglais en français.

Quelques critiques me paraissent cependant nécessaires : Par exemple, le livre réunit en un seul chapitre (chapitre 11) tous les pronoms personnels, conjonctifs et disjonctifs. Comment un élève moyen arrivera-t-il à comprendre, classifier et retenir tous ces pronoms ainsi appris?

D'autre part le chapitre 17, réunissant les pronoms possessifs et démonstratifs, est d'une étude ardue.

De même, les pronoms relatifs et interrogatifs me paraissent trop difficiles pour être traités aussi rapidement.

Un des modes d'emploi de l'imparfait paraît confus ainsi exprimé : L'imparfait indique *la durée* d'une action passée. Le mot "durée", cher aux élèves par rapport à l'imparfait, semble une source féconde d'erreurs pour la majorité des étudiants.

Par contre les auteurs donnent du conditionnel un des modes d'emploi trouvé dans des grammaires dont on se sert en France, mais rarement encore mentionné dans des manuels à l'usage de nos étudiants: "Le conditionnel exprime souvent une idée de futur dans le passé." Exemple: Il dit qu'il viendra; il a dit qu'il viendrait. Le livre est rendu encore plus attrayant par un certain nombre d'images représentant diverses parties connues de la France, telles que le petit Trianon, la Cathédrale de Chartres, etc., qui donnent lieu, au gré du professeur, à des conférences historiques.

Le vocabulaire donne non seulement la traduction et la prononciation en lettres phonétiques, mais en plus une véritable définition en français de chaque mot.

Enfin la grammaire est complétée par un petit album, "Laboratory Manuel". Ce petit livre est composé de soixante larges pages, correspondant aux trente chapitres de la grammaire.

De nombreux exercices oraux contribuent en grande partie à rendre notre grammaire absolument vivante; ce n'est plus seulement un ensemble de règles et d'exercices, mais une sorte d'encyclopédie de la langue française.—Combien de personnes, après plusieurs années d'études d'une langue étrangère se plaignent de savoir la grammaire et de s'en tenir là; combien d'élèves à l'heure actuelle ne voient dans la grammaire qu'une succession de règles ennuyeuses à retenir dans l'unique but de ne pas échouer à leur examen.

Messieurs Béziat et Dey auront contribué au changement radical de l'étude et de l'enseignement du français.

Un élève intelligent peut se servir seul de ce livre et en tirer le plus grand profit. Un professeur inexpérimenté n'aura qu'à suivre leçon par leçon une méthode toute tracée. Quant au bon professeur quelle source d'intérêts pour ses élèves et pour lui-même ne trouvera-t-il pas dans cet excellent volume, que, dès qu'ils le connaîtront, les professeurs remercieront l'auteur de leur avoir donné.

EDWARD S. DE CHAMPLON.

De Witt Clinton High School.

Pierre LOTI. — *Pêcheur d'Islande.* — Adapted for the use of schools with Introduction, Notes and Glossary by J. Senior, Oxford University Press, American Branch, New York, 1927. 198 pages (152 of text), 70 cents.

The readers first comment on learning of this latest edition of Loti's most famous work is likely to be, "what is its justification", since we have already had several satisfactory American editions. After examining Mr. Senior's work, the reviewer finds some difficulty in answering this very pertinent question. The appearance of the book, printed in France, is to be sure rather attractive and suggestive of the library rather than of the class room. It contains furthermore an attractive frontispiece representing Loti in naval uniform, and also as end pieces excellent maps of Brittany and French Indo-China, where much of the scene of this story is laid. It can hardly be said, however, that there are any other features of this text which mark an advance on earlier editions. No attempt has even been made to appeal to the apparent demand of recent modern language pedagogy for the inclusion of elaborate composition and conversational exercises, tho this reviewer, for one, is far from reproaching the editor with the omission!

In his short but well written introduction the editor has succeeded in giving the student an idea of the peculiar genius of Pierre Loti, of his temperament and style of writing. We might wish however for a little more biographical material than his opening paragraph contains, as well as for some slight treatment of Loti's other notable works, such for instance as *Ramuntcho* and *Matelot*. I am not sure whether it is good pedagogy to devote most of the space given to *Pêcheur d'Islande* to a résumé of the story. Unless one is cynical enough to feel that our students never look at introductions anyway, one wonders whether this résumé will not dampen the interest of the reader. Finally, it is perhaps difficult to agree with Mr. Senior that the chief reason for the popularity of *Pêcheur d'Islande* is its absence of an intimately personal note. This argument would scarcely explain why critics almost unanimously rank the *Pêcheur* above an equally impersonal work such as *Ramuntcho.*

On the whole, the editor has performed his task of preparing vocabulary and notes with considerable care. Since most words similar in appearance and meaning in both languages have been omitted, such as *tendresse* (p. 12, line 24) and *gigantesques* (p. 17, line 11), as well as many common words, it might have been well to have stated this fact above the vocabulary. There are, however, a few serious omissions such as *troubles* (adj.) p. 14, line 26, and *goudronnée,* p. 10, line 28. Mr. Senior has had the original idea of giving us two separate sets of notes, the first referring to geographical, literary and historical allusions, and the second set, separated from them by vocabulary, to "Phrases and idioms." This method has the advantage of bringing into the open, where they can be hunted down by the diligent student, those most elusive things known as French idioms, but it may be questioned whether many of our students will be able to use this parallel set of notes without confusion. Mr. Senior himself seems at times to be a little unsteady in his separation of the sheep from the goats, for he gives us in the notes such expressions as *venait de s'écrier, plein leur poitrine, d'en avoir le cœur net,* etc., which we might rather have expected in "Phrases and Idioms". Mr. Senior's notes are in general informative, scholarly and interesting. In "Phrases and Idioms" there are, however, several omissions, such as *tant que vous êtes* (p. 16, line 7), *elle avait eu beau faire* (p. 68 line 3), *elle n'en pouvait plus* (p. 68 line 18) and *s'était mise à tomber* (p. 76 line 26). *Faire le tour de* which is explained for page 20, line 9, is an expression which is first met on page 17, line 6. It is however practically impossible to prevent such minor errors in the first edition, and no one who has ever edited a text can afford to judge harshly. The proof reading seems to have been done with remarkable care.

Maxwell A. Shith.

University of Chattanooga.

BIBLIOGRAPHY

SCHOOL TEXTS

BAZIN, René. *Les Oberlé.* Edited with Introduction, Direct-Method Exercises and Vocabulary by I. H. B. Spiers and Mary C. Burchinal. D. C. Heath and Co., 1927, x-235 pp. Price, 88 cents.

FRANCE, Anatole. *Abeille et autres Contes.* With Notes, Direct-Method Exercises and Vocabulary. By George Neely Henning. D. C. Heath and Co., 1927, vi-260 pp. Price, $1.08.

GAUTHIER, Théophile. *Selections from Théophile Gauthier.* Edited with Introduction, Notes and Vocabulary by Aaron Schaffer and S. A. Rhodes. The Century Company, 1928, xix-185 pp. Price, $1.10.

MARCHAND, E. *La Famille Dupont.* Oxford University Press, 1927. Price, $1.00.

MERCIER, L. *Junior French.* Silver, Burdett and Co., 1927, xxvii-376 pp. Price, $1.78.

MICHAUD, R. and MARINONI, A. *France.* Macmillan, 1927. Price, $1.20.

ROGERS, W. G. *Fluent French for Beginners.* Sanborn, 1927, 191 pp. Price, $1.12.

THEURIET, André. *Mon Oncle Flo.* With Notes, Direct-Method Exercises and Vocabulary by E. A. Méras and L. R. Méras. D. C. Heath and Co., Contemporary French Texts, 1927, xiv-303 pp. Price, $1.16.

GENERAL

DILLINGHAM, Louise Bulkley. *The Creative Imagination of Théophile Gauthier.* A study in Literary Psychology. Psychological Monograps, Vol. VIII, No. 1 (whole No. 170), 1927.

MALET, A. *Histoire de France.* Doubleday, Doran and Co., 1927, pp. ix-489.

PALMER, J. L. *Studies in the Contemporary Theatre.* Little, New York, vii-189 pp. Price, $2.75.

PLATTARD, J. *Anthologie du XVIe siècle français.* Nelson, New York, 1927, 256 pp.

RITCHIE, R. L. G. *A First French book of Poetry.* Nelson, New York, 1927, 199 pp.

STEWART, D. L. *Anatole France the Parisian.* Dodd Mead and Co., 1927, xiv-394 pp.

PERIODICALS

GAY, Lucy M. *Reflections on the Henmon Word Book.* Mod. Lang. Journal, Vol. XII, No. 5, Feb., pp. 365-369.

RICE, George A. *An Evaluation of the Factors which Condition Success in the Study of a Second Foreign Language.* California Quarterly of Secondary Education, Jan. 1928, pp. 155-159.

YOUNG, C. E., and LAUS, J. M. *An Experiment in First Year French.* Mod. Lang. Journal, Vol. XII, No. 5, Feb. 1928, pp. 356-364.

WARSHAW, J. *Literature versus Language in the College.* Mod. Lang. Journal, Vo. XII, No. 4, Jan. 1928, pp. 281-291.

WERNER, Oscar H. *Influence of the Study of Modern Foreign Languages on the Development of Abilities in English.* Mod. Lang. Journal, Vol. XII, No. 4, Jan. 1926, pp. 241-260.

FOREIGN PUBLICATIONS

JALOUX, E. *De Pascal à Barrès.* Plon, 1927, 264 pp.

LOANNIDÈS. *La Comédie française* (1926). Plon, 1927, 40 pp.

MORNET, D. *Histoire de la littérature et de la pensée françaises contemporaines.* Larousse, 1927, 261 pp.

VILLARD, Louis. *Le Théâtre contemporain en Amérique.* Revue des Cours et Conférences, 15 déc., 1927, pp. 60 et seq. 5 (1).

THE LIBRARIAN'S CORNER

Dear Sir,

I should like to know which sets of photographs of the mouth in the various positions for French vowels you consider the best, where they may be obtained, and what the cost is. They are to be used in teaching elementary French in the High School.

F. W. Brooklyn, N.Y.

Answer: The best charts showing mouth positions for French vowels are those by D. Jones & F. Raush. Besides the fact that these charts treat each vowel from several angles (full view, profile, position of lips and tongue, angle of jaws), they have the advantage of being neatly and clearly printed, so that they can be seen easily from every point of the class-room.

These charts are obtainable from E. P. Dutton & Co., or from G. E. Stechert & Co., Price, $6.00 for the set of nine charts.

I am undertaking to teach French to a child of nine who is in the fourth grade in school. None of the beginner's texts that I know would be simple enough. Could you suggest any?

E. C. K. Cobleskill, N. Y.

Answer: There should be no formal study of grammar, of course. In this grade, pupils are best trained in hearing and speaking the languages (for which they are very alert), by means of games, songs pictures and charts. Correct pronunciation must be required, and care should be taken that the child is not acquiring bad language habits. When the child is familiar with the fundamental sounds of French, the following texts may be used:

Chapuzet & Daniel: Mes premiers pas en Français.

Soltoft-Ballard: Children's French. World Book Co.

THE LIBRARY

The following books have been received by the Librarian for the Library of the A. A. T. F. In the name of the Association, I have sent our very cordial thanks to the publishers whose names appear below, who have so generously responded to my call for reference books for teachers of French. Most of these books are valuable to the teacher who is looking for suggestions and inspiration.

I. LIBRAIRIE HATIER, 8, Rue d'Assas, Paris

Ch. M. Des Granges: Pages de Littérature, 1800-1820. Ed. luxe; 1040 p., illustré.

Histoire illustrée de la Littérature française, 975 p.

An Illustrated History of French Literature, 956 p., translated from the French by Louise M. Still.

Histoire de la Littérature française, in-12, 1041 p.

Précis de la Littérature française, in-16, 414 p.

La Littérature expliquée, (modèles de lecture expliquée) xxxv-508 p.

Le même ouvrage, livre du maître, 1019 p.

Les Grand Ecrivains Français des origines à nos jours, histoire littéraire et textes, 920 p.

Morceaux choisis des Auteurs Français, classes de lettres, xii-1410 p.

Morceaux choisis des Auteurs Français, classes de grammaire.

Collection d'Auteurs Français, publiée sous la direction de Ch. M. Des Granges.

Œuvres choisies, 14 volumes, reliés toile souple. Introduction, bibliographie notes, grammaire, lexique et illustrations documentaires:

Montaigne; chefs-d'œuvres poétiques du XVIe siècle; Corneille; Racine; Molière; Boileau; La Fontaine; Bossuet; Fénelon; La Bruyère; Mme de Sévigné; Voltaire; Chateaubriand; Lamartine.

Guibillon: La littérature anglaise par les textes, 622 p.

Georgin: Histoire illustrée de la littérature latine, 498 p.

Les Latins: Morceaux choisis, 1200 p.

Grammaire latine élémentaire, 448 p.

Homère illustré, 446 p.

Delaruelle: Tite-Live, œuvres choisies.

Ponchont: César, œuvres choisies, éditions illustrées.

Dictionnaires (Collection portefeuille): français; français-espagnol; latin-français; anglais-espagnol.

II. LIBRAIRIE LAROUSSE, 13, Rue Montparnasse, Paris

Nouveau Petit Larousse Illustré.

E. Breuil: Leçons illustrées de Français, du Cours préparatoire au Cours supérieur, 5 volumes in-16.

Pinloche: Vocabulaire par l'image.
Martinon: Comment on parle en français, 600 p.
Comment on prononce le français, 414 p.
Daniel Mornet: Histoire de la Littérature et de la Pensée françaises contemporaines, 1870-1925.
A. Weil: Choix de poésies du XIVe siècle.
Weil & Chénin: Contes et récits du XIXe siècle.
H. Bornecque: Les chefs-d'œuvres de la langue française. Prose.
Les chefs-d'œuvres de la langue française. Poésie.
M. Morel: La Fontaine: Fables illustrées. 2 volumes.
P. Mérimée: Colomba, Mateo Falcone, Vision de Charles XI, La Vénus d'Ille.
Emile Saillens: Toute la France: sa terre, son peuple, ses travaux, les œuvres de son génie, in-16, 447 p.
Contes et romans pour tous: Alexandre Dumas, La Colombe, H. Bernay, Le Scolopendre.

III. LIBRAIRIE HACHETTE, 79, Boulevard St.-Germain, Paris

Clédat: Dictionnaire étymologique de la langue française.
Radouant: Grammaire Française.
Exercices sur la grammaire française.
Régnier: Théâtre Classique.
Chevaillier & Audiat: Les Textes français, 16e, 17e, 18e siècles. 3 vol.
C. Jullian: Extraits des historiens français du XIXe siècle.
A. de Vigny: Poésies complètes et Servitude et Grandeur Militaires. 1 vol.
Seguin: Jeannot et Jeannette. Livre de lecture, Cours élémentaire.
Gabet & Gillard: Vocabulaire et méthode d'orthographe; Cours moyen.
Fontenille et Roy: Cent Récits; Livre de lecture, Cours moyen.
V. Bouillot: Le Français par les Textes; lecture expliquée; Cours moyen.
Maquet, Flot & Roy: Cours de Langue française, Cours moyen.
De Plinval: Résumé Aide-Mémoire. Histoire de la Littérature française.
Encyclopédie par l'image: Le Romantisme.

IV. LIBRAIRIE DELAGRAVE, 15, Rue Soufflot, Paris

Petit Larive & Fleury: Dictionnaire encyclopédique illustré.
V. Fleury: Anthologie Générale de Littérature étrangère.
E. Maynial: Précis de Littérature française moderne (1815-1925).
Collection Estève: Les Auteurs français du programme. 2 volumes: Tome I, Moyen Age, XVIe et XVIIe siècles. Tome II, XVIIIe et XIXe siècles.
L. Sudre: Grammaire française; Cours moyen.
Grammaire française; Cours supérieur.
F. Chadeyras: Belles lectures françaises: Cours préparatoire, Cours élémentaire et Cours moyen. 3 volumes illustrés.

Boitel & Coquet: Le français par la lecture: Cours élémentaire, moyen, supérieur et complémentaire. 4 volumes illustrés.
Galandy & Balaignac: Vocabulaire analogique. Sections enfantines, cours élémentaires, cours moyen et supérieur, cours complémentaire. 4 vol. illustrés.

V. LIBRAIRIE ARMAND COLIN, 103, Blvrd. St.-Michel, Paris

M. Braunschvig: Notre Littérature étudiée dans les textes.
I. Des origines à la fin du XVIIe siècle; II. Le XVIIIe et le XIXe siècle; III. La Littérature française contemporaine, 1850-1925.
Jean Giraud: L'Ecole Romantique française.

The Librarian has also received the following books from Miss Amelia Waller, Fort Lee High School, N. J.:

L'abbé Rousselot et Laclotte: Précis de prononciation française.
Otto Bond: The Sounds of French.
Vietor & Ripman: Elements of Phonetics.
Nitze & E. Wikins: A handbook of French Phonetics.
Numville: Elements of French Pronunciation and Diction.
Martin: Essentials of French Pronunciation.
J. Matzke: A. Primer of French Pronunciation.
Cousins & Ward: Student's Handbook of French Pronunciation.
Martinon: Comment on prononce le français.
Grammont: Traité pratique de prononciation française.

ALBERT L. CRU.

The above volumes are placed at the disposal of all the members of the A. A. T. F. A nominal charge to cover the expense of postage will be made.

THE FRENCH TEACHER'S FORUM

Too much clerical work for teachers

True to our policy of offering to teachers an opportunity to discuss any subject of vital interest to their profession, we quote the following alarming statement made by a teacher in one of the public high schools:

One of the greatest obstacles to efficient teaching is "paper work"; in our school, half of a teacher's time is devoted to clerical work.

The Forum will be glad to receive and to publish further information upon this important matter. It will print comments not exceeding 250 *words in length.*

The Forum Resolution, November 1927.

Resolved that students in our High Schools are not sufficiently advanced to read with profit the French classics of the seventeenth century such as Corneille, Racine and Molière.

Teachers are Builders. Our materials differ from those of other Builders, but still we are Builders. And while we are often inclined to place ourselves on a higher level than carpenters, still we could with profit follow some of their methods.

When a carpenter builds a house he works according to a very well defined plan. It is on paper and he knows just what he is doing. He knows that he must first excavate, then erect a firm foundation, and then add the different stories in a logical sequence, the second after the first, the third after the second. Nor does he attempt to put on the roof until he has something to which he can attach it.

Our courses of study for French should follow just as systematic a plan. In a high school offering four years of French have we had an opportunity to excavate for our foundation, build our foundation, add nough floors to still be able to attach the roof represented in the classics of the Seventeenth Century? Scarcely! And where less than four years of the language are offered it is still more impossible to offer the classics with any profit to the students or with any satisfaction to the instructor.

Olives Reeves Foster,
Whatcom High School,
Bellingham, Washington.

Je suis entièrement en faveur de la résolution proposée dans le premier numéro de la "French Review", concernant la lecture des grands classiques français du dix-septième siècle dans les High Schools.

L'enseignement du français dans ces écoles devrait, à mon avis, être limité à la langue moderne. Le champ me paraît déjà assez vaste.

Un très petit nombre d'élèves, parmi les centaines qui entrent au Collège de la Ville de New-York où j'enseigne, sont en état, au sortir des High Schools, d'écrire une phrase correcte en français. Pourquoi leur mettre entre les mains des œuvres dont le vocabulaire n'est plus toujours celui d'aujourd'hui, dont quelques formes grammaticales ne sont plus admises et dont la syntaxe diffère à bien des égards des règles qu'on leur demande d'observer?

Qu'on leur dise en fin d'études quelques mots des grands classiques, je n'y vois aucun inconvénient; tout au contraire, car il est bon de leur inspirer le désir de lire les chefs d'œuvre de Corneille, Racine et Molière, quand leur préparation antérieure leur permettra de profiter de l'enseignement donné au collège, et qu'ils posséderont une connaissance sûre de la langue moderne.

Felix Weill,
Secrétaire Général, Alliance Française.

The Classics in High School

The angle from which I must approach this question is fixed by my experience, which has been with College Freshmen. They are ready, but only just ready, to read the classics. A certain number have read some plays, oftenest le Cid, in high school, and almost without exception they have not appreciated such literature, frequently the plays have been, at least for the time, spoiled for them. They testify: "I used to hate the Cid, but now I love it." There are three reasons for this lack of appreciation at the high school age: 1) the text was too difficult, all the student's powers were taken up with the words, with the syntax; 2) the students were not mature enough-even a year is a large fraction of the intellectual life of a person of 18; 3) the literary background for the plays was lacking, as few preparatory schools can give any history of literature.

I regret seeing the cream taken off classics in the earlier years of their study of French.

Mary Vance Young.

Mount Holyoke College

A. A. T. F. NEWS

On Jan. 29 the members of the Executive Council dined at the Hotel Brevoort as the guests of President Charles A. Downer. At the conclusion of the dinner the Council met for discussion and the reading of reports by the President, the Secretary, and the Treasurer of the Association and the Editor-in-Chief, the Business Manager, and the Librarian of *The French Review*. These reports all pointed to a very remarkable progress and development of the A. A. T. F.

The membership passed the limit of 1,000 some time ago and now is well on the way to 2,000 with a geographical distribution extending over 32 states in the Union and one foreign country. The members of the Council have been most gratified at the encouragement received from all quarters and especially from the aid and assistance rendered by teachers and educators thruout the country. The very successful efforts of Dr. William R. Price of the Department of Education of the State of New York in furthering the organization of the nine chapters of the Association in the State of New York outside of the metropolitan district were recognized by a vote of thanks and special mention was made of Professor James Geddes of Boston University, Dr. E. B. de Sauzé, Director of Modern Languages of the Board of Education of Cleveland, Professor Hugh A. Smith of the University of Wisconsin, and M. Samson of Washington, D. C., all of whom have rendered very valuable assistance to the officers of the Association.

Plans were formulated for an active campaign to increase the membership and enlarge the scope of the work of the Association. Tentative arrangements have been made to render service to the teachers of French along a number of lines which will demonstrate beyond the question of a doubt the urgent necessity that has existed for bringing into existence an association which would serve in every respect the best interests of teachers of French.

The first Annual Meeting of the A. A. T. F. held at Hunter College, New York City on Saturday, March 10 was probably the most successful of all the meetings of the Association. It was opened by a word of greeting by Professor Downer to all those present, especially representatives of chapters other than the Metropolitan. The President then continued his address by explaining his ideal of the teacher. He concluded his address with an introduction of Mr. Mongendre, Consul General of France who spoke briefly of the delicate mission intrusted to teachers of French as the interpreters of the clearest and most logical language of the contemporary world, "the language of peace". His address was followed by the report of the secretary who announced the latest official membership of the Assoliation as 1270, with eleven chapters, the latest having been formed by Dr. James Geddes in Boston. He also announced the projected formation of three new chapters in Ohio by Professor de Sauzé. He reported that at the present, the Association has members in all but ten States in the Union and two members in France. The Treasurer reported a good surplus in the treasury but also expressed his willingness to receive more funds. These reports concluded, Professor Downer introduced President Glenn Kelly of the Westchester Chapter who read a very instructive paper, the result of some ten years' research, on "French, a Language of Precision." The very exact and in some cases almost mathematical conclusions were offered with delightful touches of humor that broke the serious tenor of the meeting. Mr. Kelly's address was followed by a very practical discussion of methods of teaching composition, by Professor Félix Weill of the College of the City of New York. In brief, he explained that he had adapted the well-tried method of Professor Lanson of the Ecole Normale to the needs of American students and had found the results excellent. The last address of the morning was given by Professor Feuillerat of the University of Rennes and at present visiting professor at Columbia.

M. Feuillerat gave a brief account of the economic situation in France, explaining how and why the financial problem was so acute in spite of the miraculous changes wrought by the present government. He concluded his address by saying that despite the very pessimistic outlook, he felt that France would solve her problem in some way just as she had so often done before.

After the meeting a luncheon was held at Hunter college for the guests of the day. The organization of the meeting and luncheon was under the direction of Professor Claudine Gray of Hunter College.

THE AMERICAN ASSOCIATION

OF

TEACHERS OF FRENCH

Last spring nine Chapters of the A. A. T. F. were organized outside of the Metropolitan District in the State of New York. During the past autumn large and enthusiastic meetings were held by all of these Chapters and the officers of each Chapter are as follows:

Westchester Chapter

President: Glen M. Kelly, White Plains High Schoo.l
Vice-President: Miss Caroline Burgevin, Portchester.
Secretary: Miss Edna Palmer, Mount Vernon High School.
Treasurer: Miss Anita Piatti, White Plains High School.

Hudson Valley Chapter

President: Miss Charlotte Loeb, State College, Albany, N. Y.
First Vice-President: Arthur de Pierpont, R. P. I., Troy, N. Y.
Second Vice-President: Genevieve Brook, High School, Schenectady, N. Y.
Third Vice-President: Louise Stocker, Arlington High School, Poughkeepsie, N. Y.
Secretary: Glenn M. Davis, High School, Albany, N. Y.
Treasurer: Emily M. Cavanaugh, High School, Troy, N. Y.
Directors:
Florence White, Vassar College, Poughkeepsie, N. Y.
Florence B. Hayes, Russell Sage College, Troy, N. Y.
Charlotte Loeb, State College, Albany, N. Y.

Western New York Chapter

President: Miss Alice M. Finn, Niagara Falls High School.
First Vice-President: Mr. Felix Casassa, Hutchinson High School, Buffalo. Buffalo.
Second Vice-President: Miss Lucretia Terry, Bennet High School, Buffalo.
Third Vice-President: Mr. George Schneider, Technical High School, Buffalo.
Treasurer: Mr. Francis Sweet, South Park High School, Buffalo.
Director: Professor J. P. Rice, University of Buffalo.

Utica Chapter

President : Miss Zoe Ward, Utica Free Academy.
First Vice-President: Mrs. M. C. Parkhurst, Peterboro High School.

Second Vice-President: Frances Dossert, Oneida High School.
Third Vice-President: Frances Wright, Munnsville High School.
Secretary: Mary Sullivan, Ilion High School.
Treasurer: Mr. Ralph Johnson, Oriskany Falls High School.
Director: Professor F. M. Jones, Colgate University.

St. Lawrence Chapter

President: Mrs. Beatrice Wheater, Chateauguay High School.
First Vice-President: Miss Anna Sparks, Old Forge High School.
Second Vice-President: Miss Ethel Hogan, Watertown High School.
Third Vice-President: Sister St. Ives de Blois, Tupper Lake.
Secretary: Miss Teresa Owens, Malone High School.
Treasurer: Mr. Harold P. Hayden, Antwerp High School.
Director: Professor S. Plaisance, St. Lawrence University.

Fingerlake Chapter

President: Harriet Kellogg, 1417 W. Water St., Elmira, N. Y.
First Vice-President: Marie I. Henderson, Hartwick Seminary, New York.
Second Vice-President: Nellie B. Rogers, 59 Oak St., Binghamton, New York.
Third Vice-President: Marie Landon, 124 Main St., Penn Yan, New York.
Director: E. Margaret Grimes, Elmira College, Elmira, N. Y.
Secretary: M. Louise Henderson, 18 Ferguson Av., Port Jervis, New York.
Treasurer: Ruth L. Miller, 218 University Av., Ithaca N. Y.

Long Island Chapter

President: Ada C. Smith, Huntington, New York.
Director: Mary Louise Smith, Freeport, New York.
Secretary: Doris Benson, Lawrence, New York.
Treasurer: Julie Franchi, Bay Shore, New York.
Vice-Presidents:
E. Lillian Ranquist, Freeport, New York.
Alice E Koch, Smithtown Branch, New York.
Helen E. Corkey, Amityville, New York.

Rochester Chapter

President: Mrs. Jane D. Dunham, East High School, Rochester.
Director: Dr. C. H. Holzwarth, Monroe High School, Rochester.
Secretary: Miss Florence Broxholm, Washington Junior High School, Rochester.
Treasurer: Louis Meinhardt West High School, Rochester.

Vice-Presidents:
Miss Elfrieda Hill, University of Rochester.
Verne Edegcumbe, West High School, Rochester.
Miss Madeline Marshall, Spencerport High School, Spencerport, N. Y.

Central New York Chapter

President: William Schaffrath, Central High School, Syracuse, New York.
Secreteary: Mrs. G. H. Daniels, North High School, Syracuse, New York.
Treasurer: Mr. David M. Dougherty, The Manlius School, Manlius, New York.
Directors:
Professor L. W. Crawford, Syracuse University, Syracuse, New York.
Professor A. D. Menut, Syracuse University, Syracuse N. Y.
First Vice-President: Professor Jean Gerard, Syracuse University, Syracuse, N. Y.
Second Vice-President: Miss Isabella M. Lanigan, Central High School, Syracuse, N. Y.
Third Vice-President: Miss Margaret Le Roy, Oswego High School, Oswego, N. Y.

The New S. S. Ile de France

PRINTED IN U. S. A.
FRENCH PRINTING & PUBLISHING CO., 149 W. 24TH STREET, N. Y. C.

Vol. I MAY, 1928 No. 4

THE FRENCH REVIEW

Devoted to the Interests of Teachers of French

Published by the
American Association of Teachers of French

Vol. I MAI, 1928 No. 4

CONTENTS

THE LIBRARIAN'S CORNER 2
THE FRENCH REVIEW, *J. F. Mason* 7
THE CLEVELAND EXPERIMENT IN THE TEACHING OF FRENCH, *E. B. de Sauzé* 13
THE TEACHING OF FRENCH GRAMMAR AND THE TEACHING OF THE FRENCH LANGUAGE, *Osmond T. Robert* 27
WHAT IS INTERESTING TO MY CLASSES IN FRENCH, *Leah A. Huckans* 38
DISCOURS DE M. MONGENDRE 48
L'ÉTAT ACTUEL DE LA FRANCE, *Albert Feuillerat* 53
QUELQUES RÉSULTATS OBTENUS DANS UN COURS DE COMPOSITION AVANCÉE, *Félix Weill* 60
LE CENTENAIRE DE JULES VERNE, *Robert Fouré* 68
ITEMS FROM FRANCE, *Harry Kurz* 72
VARIA 74
RECENT TEXTS 78
BIBLIOGRAPHY 81
FRENCH TEACHER'S FORUM 82
A. A. T. F. NEWS 84
THE AMERICAN ASSOCIATION OF TEACHERS OF FRENCH 86

The *French Review* is the official journal of the American Association of Teachers of French and is published four times during the year, November, January, March, May.

Office of Publication, George Washington High School, Audubon Avenue and 192nd Street, New York City.

Entered at the Post Office, New York, N. Y., as second class matter.

The annual dues of the American Association of Teachers of French, including subscription to the *French Review*, are $2.50. Single copies. $.50 Applications for membership should be addressed to E. A. Méras, the Secretary of the Association, Adelphi College, Brooklyn, New York.

Communications to the editors, manuscripts, etc., should be addressed to the Editor of the *French Review*, Cornell University, Ithaca, N. Y.

All correspondence concerning advertising should be forwarded to Edward O. Perry, Business Manager of the *French Review*, George Washington High School, 192nd St., New York City.

Kindly notify the Business Manager of any change in address.

All books, texts, publications which may interest the teacher of French will receive mention in the bibliography or critical comment, if a copy is sent to a member of the editorial staff. Literary and scholarly works should be forwarded to A. G. H. Spiers, Columbia University, New York City, while texts and other publications should be sent to Dr. Hélène Harvitt, 1309 Carroll Street, Brooklyn, N. Y.

Exchange of the *French Review* with other journals may be arranged by addressing the Editor of the *French Review*, Ithaca, N. Y.

THE LIBRARIAN'S CORNER

THE LIBRARY

The following books have been received by the Librarian.

In the name of the A. A. T. F., I have sent our very cordial thanks to the Librairie Henri Didier who have so generously responded to my call for reference books.

Librairie Henri Didier, 4 et 6 Rue de la Sorbonne, Paris

La Littérature Française illustrée: Collection moderne de classiques, avec illustrations documentaires.
Corneille: Le Cid, Horace, Cinna, Polyeucte.
Racine: Andromaque, Britannicus, Mithridate, Esther, Les Plaideurs.
Molière: Le Misanthrope, Les Femmes Savantes, Les Precieuses Ridicules.
Fénelon: Choix de Fables et de Dialogues.
Histoire Illustrée de la Littérature Française, par Abry Audic et Crouzet, nouvelle édition, 746 pages.
Corneille: Théâtre choisi, 876 pages, avec commentaires et illustrations.
Molière: Scènes choisies, 404 pages.
La Bruyère: Les Caractères, 684 pages.
Boileau: Poésie et Prose, 608 pages.
G. Cayrou: Le Français classique; lexique de la langue du XVIIe siècle.
Montesquieu: Morceaux choisis, 380 pages.
J. J. Rousseau: Morceaux choisis, 375 pages.
Chateaubriand: Morceaux choisis, 549 pages.
H. de Balzac: Morceaux choisis, 509 pages.
Lamartine: Morceaux choisis, 1080 pages.
Musset: Morceaux choisis, 532 pages.
Vigny: Morceaux choisis, 592 pages.
Méthode française et exercices illustrés, par Crouzet, Berthet et Galliot, 1er volume et 2e volume.
Crouzet et Rouaix: Grammaire préparatoire; Théorie et exercices.
Grammaire élémentaire.
Grammaire française, simple et complète.
Camerlynck: France, première année de français.
France, deuxième année de français.
Au pays de France, troisième année de français.
Pour les petits, année préparatoire.
Parlons Français, the essentials of French conversation.

Ces cinq derniers ouvrages forment une série de Méthode directe de français, avec notation phonétique.

A. L. C.

The French Review

Vol. I — MAY, 1928 — No. 4

THE FRENCH REVIEW

By J. F. Mason

With the present issue, *The French Review* completes its first volume of four numbers and it might, therefore, be opportune to make a definite statement regarding its purpose and editorial policy. *The French Review* was founded to serve as the official organ of the American Association of Teachers of French and to furnish members of that organization with information regarding its activities. Furthermore, *The French Review* aims to present to teachers of French articles on the teaching of French in both high schools and colleges, articles of general interest regarding France and French literature, critical reviews of French texts, and a bibliography of our special field. It also offers in the French Teacher's Forum an opportunity for the discussion of any subject connected with the teaching of French and in the Librarian's Corner attempts to answer any question which a teacher of French may care to ask. The Editorial Board hopes to bring *The French Review* to the point where it will be indispensable to any progressive teacher of French who wishes to be well informed on the latest developments in his or her subject.

The French Review will always welcome any contribution of a serious nature but will endeavor to remain outside of any discussion. Subjects of such controversial nature as the 'natural method', the Dalton Plan as applied to modern foreign languages, phonetic transcription, immediate and ultimate objectives, the 'new-type' tests, may be discussed in *The French Review* by both supporters and opponents. Critical reviews of texts will be as unbiased as possible and, whenever so desired, the pages of *The French Review* will always be open to a reasonable reply on the part of an editor or author who disagrees with the reviewer.

On one subject, however, *The French Review* holds very definite views, namely, the importance of French in the curriculum of both high schools and colleges in America. We find the best expression of our position in the words of that friend of France, Professor Frederico de Onis, Professor of Spanish, at Columbia University, who says: "If one should try to determine which of the modern languages is of the greatest educational importance for the American student, I should unhesitatingly select French for reasons that are obvious to many, and over which I shall not linger." There still remain many who do not agree with Professor de Onis in regard to the importance of the study of French. In many cases inspectors of modern foreign languages, superintendents of schools, and other officials are called upon to make a decision as to the relative importance of several modern languages, and not infrequently they have arrived at decisions which appear to be based rather upon chance than logic. One can easily understand why local conditions give more importance to the study of Spanish than to French in California and Texas, and why there were in the spring term of 1927 almost as many pupils studying German in the high schools of Milwaukee as both French and Spanish combined, but it seems more difficult to determine why at the same time there were in Jersey City 2,110 pupils in French and 1,784 in Spanish, whereas in Newark there were 1,391 in French and 1,783 in Spanish. Chicago, altho closer geographically to French or German centers, nevertheless reports for the spring term of 1927 8,658 pupils in French and 11,510 in Spanish, while Cincinnati reports for the same period 1,347 in French and 1,800 in Spanish.

Tho naturally partial to French, *The French Review,* nevertheless, fully recognizes the danger which threatens us if we disagree among ourselves, and the ease with which an attack upon one modern foreign language may be transferred to another .Many educators group the modern foreign languages together and tolerate or exclude them *en masse* and not as individual languages. Consequently, one of the objects we shall strive for is harmony and co-operation among all teachers of modern foreign languages and *The French Review* will always be ready to lend assistance to any of the various federations of modern language associations now in existence.

Since the welfare of our own particular subject is closely dependent upon that of all the other allied subjects, *The French Review* considers it a duty to comment favorably or adversely not only upon the methods used by partisans of French, but also upon those used by partisans of the other modern foreign languages. For example, we must always deplore the activities of those teachers of Spanish who over-emphasize the importance of a knowledge of Spanish as a commercial asset and tend to 'confine the study of Spanish to a narrow utilitarianism.' If the public becomes accustomed to such arguments in favor of Spanish, we shall soon hear French defended on similar grounds. The only valid reason which we can advance for the study of Spanish in American schools and colleges is that it is the language of a great and noble race which has played a most important role in the history of the occidental world and still continues to do so. Commercial relations between Spanish-speaking countries and ourselves fluctuate, but our debt to Spanish culture remains the same. Many Spanish teachers have themselves seen the danger of some of the propaganda of their too zealous brothers, but they have not been able to stop it, and now, for other languages as well as Spanish, the public tends to forget the broader aspect of the study of a modern foreign language. 'To commercialize' the study of Spanish is to belittle all linguistic effort.

In a similar manner the teachers of German have, in their desire to increase the number of pupils in German, resorted to arguments as dangerous. German teachers are largely responsible for the view that modern foreign languages are not an end in themselves but merely tools necessary to the advanced students in other subjects, and to scientists in general. The German teachers have sold their birth-right for a mess of potage. That the language of Goethe and Schiller does not exist primarily for chemists and physicists is a fact that our German colleagues have not sufficiently impressed upon the public.

As for our own sins, we must confess some which may have had an unfavorable influence upon the other languages. The view which considers the acquaintance with a modern foreign language as an accomplishment rather than a necessity may probably be traced to teachers of French. Modern foreign languages have always seemed more appropriate to the distaff branch of the family, the girls studying French together with music and painting, while the boys did Greek and Latin and the sciences. French teachers have allowed their pupils to think of France in terms of *couturiers, restaurants, et vaudeville* and tried to teach them enough French 'to get along in Paris.' One can easily verify this by a chance examination of French introductory grammars and composition books. We spend too much time pointing out the picturesque villages and quaint costumes of a race which has produced scientists of the calibre of Fabre and Pasteur. French teachers are failing in their duties if they do not succeed in convincing their pupils that they study French because it is the language of a great race occupying an important position in the modern world.

Consequently the teachers of modern foreign languages must stand together not only against those from the outside who wish to belittle us but also against those from within who attempt to use methods and arguments which are bound in the end to do us harm. Good wine needs no brush and German, Italian, Spanish, and French have a right to a place in the curriculum for no other reason than that these four languages are the finest expression of four races, each in its own way playing an important role in the world of to-day.

Another unfortunate circumstance in modern foreign language work has to do with the present relations existing between the high school and the college teacher. The latter tends to retire to some academic ivory tower and view somewhat unsympathetically the efforts of the high school teacher. A better understanding between schools and colleges is absolutely necessary, if we are to make any progress along certain lines. If the college teachers would, for example, insist upon the futility of one or two years of a foreign language and demand a minimum of three years of any language to be counted as college entrance credit, high school teachers would be very grateful. *The French Review* hopes to suggest many ways by which the two groups of teachers of French, the college men and the school men, may lend one another assistance.

In regard to the character of *The French Review* in general and the nature of the articles which should be published in it, there is, of course, a certain diversity of opinion. The first volume has been to a certain extent tentative and the Editorial Board is only too anxious to receive suggestions from the members of the American Association of Teachers of French for changes and ameliorations. It will be difficult to maintain a balance between pedagogical and cultural articles which will satisfy every one. European reviews of the same type tend to devote more space to articles of a general nature than to special problems of teaching, while here in America there would seem to be a demand for discussion of practical aspects of teaching. We hope that teachers will send in such contributions but we recognize how few teachers have either the time or the funds necessary to carry on investigations to the point where they could produce results of sufficient validity to be of use to teachers of French in general. As Professor R. H. Fife, of the Modern Foreign Language Study, has said, "opinion subjectively formed is valueless unless supported by findings from tests."

The success of both *Hispania* and *Italica* has given us many suggestions and the recently founded *German Quarterly* in its first two numbers has set a very high standard of excellence, while the *Modern Language Journal* has served in a most efficient manner the purpose for which it was created. *The French Review* considers none of these contemporaries as rivals whose aims would be entagonistic to its own, but rather as friendly workers striving each in *its* own way to support the cause of the teaching of modern foreign languages in the schools and colleges of America. We sincerely hope that the Jeremiahs who 'viewed with alarm' the formation of the separate language associations may soon be willing to allow themselves to be converted gracefully to the point of view of those most interested in The American Association of Teachers of French and *The French Review,* i. e., that the separate language associations, each with its own publication, best solve the problem of the teachers of modern foreign languages in general and also of the teachers of each of the modern foreign languages now generally taught in American high schools and colleges.

THE CLEVELAND EXPERIMENT

IN THE

TEACHING OF FRENCH

By E. B. DE SAUZÉ
Director of Foreign Languages
Cleveland Board of Education

In 1916 the writer of this article was present at a meeting of romance language teachers. During the course of the discussion one of the college professors present was complaining of the insufficient preparation in French of the high school graduates entering the Freshman class of this particular college. Even when those students had pursued the study of that language for four years, they were woefully lacking in accuracy when writing, in real understanding when reading; few of them had ever used enough French orally in the class room to feel at ease in a class conducted in that language. Suddenly out of the large audience mainly composed of high school teachers, a voice was heard to say: "But professor, those students that are so poorly prepared were taught by graduates of your institution or some other college!" Indeed we seemed to be caught in a vicious circle, poor teaching or rather wrong methods in high schools were often but the logical consequence of the inadequate preparation, both in content and special technique, received by college graduates, who begin their task of teaching without a reasonable mastery of the subject to be taught and a grasp of the problems involved in its presentation to children of junior or senior high school age.

This incident started the writer in a study of the problem of methodology in the teaching of foreign languages. Even from a cursory view of the situation it was evident that we had no science of teaching Foreign Languages. We had proceeded empirically; Prophets had come, announcing to the modern language teacher that they had found at last the *great* method, the method that was to solve all his vexing problems, only to be followed by another prophet advocating another method usually the opposite of the previous one. The very variety of methods used in the foreign language class rooms all over the world is the most convincing proof that we have not yet evolved out of the chaos of conflicting theories a science of language teaching, a science based upon an exhaustive study of processes involved in learning a language, a study of the psychological mechanism which is put to work when an individual is applying himself to the learning, theoretical and practical, of a new tongue.

In 1918 the writer accepted an invitation to Cleveland to direct the teaching of foreign languages in the public schools. Cleveland offered an unusual opportunity to conduct, even on a modest scale, a study of at least some of the problems involved in the teaching of a foreign language. That school system, through an efficient centralized organization, could be transformed into a laboratory large enough to give validity to results and at the same time compact enough, responsive enough to supervision to assure control of the experiments. Because of lack of money, of time, and especially of measuring tests which could not very well be prepared in advance of the course of study, the results secured in those experiments are not available in terms of statistical percentages ; we had to content ourselves in many instances with the evidence when accepted as conclusive by the unanimous judgment of all teachers engaged in the experiment, this evidence based mainly upon comparison of present results with those of previous years. Our principal measuring tool was, and, still is, common sense, a tool now in disuse, even in disrepute in the wave of pseudo-scientific methods which is sweeping over some of our pedagogical institutions.

In no case were experiments conducted purely for the "sport" of the thing. We never lost sight of the fact that the children in the schools constitute raw material quite unlike wood or steel, that those children have only one chance for an education and that to subject them to an obviously wrong pedagogical practice just to demonstrate statistically the advantage of the opposite technique was most unfair to our trust and a betrayal of the confidence of parents.

Right at the start we felt the need of an agreement on a philosophy of education, of a common understanding of the aims to be achieved, of the contributions to be made to the education of the students through and by the study of foreign languages.

Since we were engaged in an educational enterprise, it seemed logical to start with an acceptable definition of education, in the name and for the sake of which we were conducting this experiment.

Education—e-ducere—educes or draws forth faculties.

Culture improves, refines and enlarges them after they have been brought out; "culture," somebody has said "is self-effectuation; it is not a natural gift, it implies tillage of the soil, artificial improvement."

Our teaching of foreign languages therefore should be so organized that it draws out certain faculties of the mind, instills certain mental habits, while endowing the student with certain fundamental skills which in due time will enable him to read, write, speak and understand the foreign language. Whenever he is in possession of those skills, he will "cultivate" his mind further through the varied contacts that his acquired knowledge makes possible in the field of literature, travel and interchange of ideas through oral or written language.

This conception of the function of the foreign language in the curriculum was the beacon light that illuminated our path when in search of fundamental principles and adequate technique.

This philosophy eliminated from consideration the teaching of a language purely through memorizations and habituation. It is true that a child has learned his mother tongue solely through that natural process, but it is impossible for schools to create the same intensity of contacts enjoyed by the child while learning his tongue, or by the adult when living in a foreign land. Furthermore, an intelligent adult is rarely successful in mastering a foreign language without learning in a functional way certain fundamental principles that govern the structure of that language and that enable him to generalize, to multiply his experience a thousand times. To know by memory even an ample stock of ready-made sentences in a language is not the same as to know that language. But even if that scheme of learning a language through habituation alone were possible, it would have little educational value in "drawing forth" faculties, specifically in developing the language sense.

It is obviously impossible in the length of this article to explain or even enumerate all the fundamental principles that our experiments have demonstrated to our satisfaction to constitute a safe and sound basis to a modern language pedagogy. It will suffice to present the most important ones, those that mainly control our present practice in Cleveland.

The most vital problem in any class room is how to stimulate and retain the interest of the pupils. Interest, attention, concentration, learning, cannot be separated and teaching or learning is indeed a dreary, almost an impossible task without them. Forcible feeding, mental as well as physical, is a nasty operation and is seldom successful. "The art of teaching," says A. France, "is only the art of interesting, of arousing curiosity, and curiosity is active only in happy minds." Interest is the oil of the machinery of education ; without it the wheels may go around, but there is friction, heat and prompt stopping. The doctrine of interest does not mean the emasculation of the subject by removing all difficulties ; the little girl who once told her teacher : "Now what are you going to amuse us with to-day," was perfectly conscious and pointedly critical of that type of teaching supposedly interesting. Students respect a teacher who makes them apply themselves and they enjoy a subject that has enough substance to challenge their efforts.

Interest is maintained when the material to be taught is carefully organized along sound laws of learning, when the students find in the subject a constant challenge to solve carefully graded difficulties, and when the technique of introducing the new elements follows correct psychological and pedagogical practice.

Let us examine the practical application of this doctrine of interest in the field of a foreign language. First of all how does it affect the selection of the material to be taught? It is an accepted principle that we deal well only with things that are within our range of experience. When a student learns a new language, he really is transferring his acquired experience from his mother tongue to the new language. He is learning a second mode of expressing this same experience. This transfer will be all the more easily and successfully effected if the elements are introduced along the same fundamental sequence and relation that prevailed when he learned his mother tongue. The topics introduced for reading or speaking must be a close counterpart of his experience ; they should at first center around his daily activities, home, school, sports, restaurants, amusements, etc.; later, when he already has mastered this expression of his elemental interests, his curiosity may be aroused into reading and speaking about the foreign nation. A safe and sane criterion to follow in establishing a vocabulary for a first year course of study, would be to group carefully the most elemental activities of a student of a given age, and to determine the vocabulary essential to the "living" again of each activity in the new language. Common sense here would save the tragic mistake of establishing a vocabulary for first year, not on that previous experience of the student, but on a word count of books to be read in advanced classes. This word count, scientific as it may seem at first glance, satisfactory as it may be to the educational expert who speculates at his desk, far from a close contact with the twelve to fourteen year old pupils, is after all a most unsatisfactory, unscientific approach to the problem. Every language is learned by a certain sequence which progresses upward not downward. To quote here Prof. Louis Marchand: "every Englishman learns "red" before "crimson," "end" before "extremity," "always" and the verb 'to last" before 'eternal," "to see" before "visible" and "vision." Furthermore, concrete expressions are not only learned first but are more easily explained and retained. It seems very poor pedagogy therefore to leave the important matter of the right vocabulary to be introduced first to the hazard of a word count based on probable "classics" to be read.

This fundamental vocabulary should be introduced not as detached words, but as a connected story. The unit in a language is the sentence. To require of a class to memorize a list of detached words is about as thrilling and as successful as learning a list of telephone numbers. Association is the fundamental law of memory. Since our aim is also to train the student to read, we must introduce him very early to a text that expresses thought and not to a haphazard collection of sentences that jump from the cow to the moon and create in the mind of the student the distinct impression that the new language is not capable of conveying thought, but only serves to illustrate grammatical relationship.

Let us see now how that carefully organized material may be introduced to the class in a manner that will again arouse and sustain the interest. We found some definite principles of pedagogy and psychology that apply closely to the learning of linguistic elements.

Every experiment conducted to determine the amount of grammatical material to introduce at one time demonstrated conclusively that considerable confusion was avoided and time ultimately was saved when we presented those elements one at a time, when we split them into small units, and when we even separated the exceptions from the rule. This practice which we labelled "single emphasis" focused the mind of the student on one difficulty instead of exposing it to several, causing thereby a blurring of the picture. In French, for example, it was found more efficient not to combine in one lesson even related elements like the contractions of the definite articles, the partitives, the exceptions to the rule of the partitives. In German only one gender is introduced at first and of course only in the nominative case. In Latin one declension and one case of that declension constitute a unit of presentation.

Not only should those elements be introduced one at a time, split to the smallest possible unit (and the younger the student, the smaller the unit), but we should linger long enough on that element to give the student time for assimilating, for mastering that element. We find another fundamental principle operating here, that of "incubation." A student should have not only an understanding of a rule, but he should have "assimilated" it through a sufficient series of drills, through repeated use until he has acquired a ready command of that rule. Difficulties still unconquered should not meet new difficulties on the way. To borrow an example from the field of physiology, we should not present the student with another meal merely because he has finished eating. Ample time should be allowed for digestion. As a rule the courses of study in languages have been unduly rich. We have conducted a mad "steeple-chase" through the text books, creating thereby an almost hopeless confusion of facts and impressions. In our experiments we calculated that it takes approximately five recitations in the Senior High School and seven to eight in the Junior High School before one unit of grammar skillfully woven into a connected text containing 30 new words may be said to be reasonably well mastered to the point where it is safe to proceed to the next unit.

One may object here that this careful procedure runs contrary to a tendency that has been noted in many schools and colleges and that emphasizes quantity rather than quality in the assignment and recitations of classes studying foreign languages. There are some who believe that extensive reading is more productive of results than the intensive process which is here advocated. It all depends upon the conception that one has of a "reading knowledge." Here as in all problems it may help to start with a definition. Reading from the standpoint of the reader is an instantaneous flashing of the meaning of the sentence read without the intermediary of the mother tongue. Any reading that is interrupted too often for looking up unknown elements or that is slowed up by being sensed first through English prevents the student from appreciating shades of meaning, beauty of form, esthetic value of the text read. In the early stages of instruction we are concerned primarily with the acquisition of "skills"; the reading "skill" in the sense of the above definition is best secured through careful study of limited material. The writer after examining many Freshmen entering French classes in several universities came to formulate the following proposition : the knowledge of a foreign language is in inverse ratio to the number of books read in a given time. It may be added that the perusing of countless pages just to discover the approximate meaning of those pages is not only grossly inefficient as a means of acquiring a real reading power, but it also leads the student into habits of carelessness, slovenliness, and into an unscientific attitude toward the whole problem of language study which he assumes to be one of purely habituation resulting from a series of unsystematic contacts. The writer is fearful for the future of American scholarship if such rapid reading should again be introduced into our halls of learning.

We noticed early in our experiment that learning by rote in

the conventional way elements of grammar such as conjugations, was causing wrong habituation through associations that inhibited spontaneous use of the particular person of the verb needed. Who has not observed the pathetic demeanor of the student who in order to find the French for "we go" has to start with the 1st, 2nd and 3rd singular before coming to the form wanted?

In attempting to find the most efficient, the most impressive way of introducing new elements of language, of crossing the bridge from the known to the unknown, we discovered the tremendous value of the principle of "challenge." All teachers who have been robbed of valuable time by students wasting a great deal of it solving puzzles or cross-words are painfully aware of the great fascination that such amusements hold for young and old. The psychological explanation for such a stubborn endeavor to find the answer to puzzles is very evidently to be found in the automatic, instinctive reaction of any one to a challenge. Our first movement is to take it up. This psychological reaction explains the superiority of the inductive process as a teaching device. Instead of presenting the student with a rule on a platter, we set up a few carefully chosen illustrations of that rule and we lead him to discover through skillful guidance the relationship of the new element to others previously mastered and to formulate his observations into a law governing those cases. The inductive process has the following advantages : it causes concentration, it sustains interest, it gives to the neurones the stimulation that comes from the satisfaction of having accomplished by one's own efforts a worthwhile and difficult task, it assists the memory which retains more easily and more permanently any element that has been carefully observed and stayed with. Another and an exceedingly valuable by-product resulting from the use of the "challenge" device is the training that the student receives in the most important tool of research: the inductive method. The writer has an unshakable belief that such mental habits are transferable not only to the related field of language, but to any situation requiring systematic observation, and careful generalization.

The same technique of challenge is used successfully in the teaching of new vocabulary elements incidental to reading. There are three ways of dealing with the genesis of unknown words : they may either be translated into the mother tongue, or be pointed to, or explained by paraphrasing. The first method alas! is the easiest and therefore still in general use in spite of the fact that it is most inefficient. Translation causes no challenge, it gives the fact too freely, and creates but a fleeting impression on the brain cells. The second method is better as it brings in visualization. The third one which consists in explaining new words with the help of elements previously taught is far superior to all others, as it is based on challenge and uses the inductive process. It has the added advantage of creating associations by linking the new word with others related to it and of framing it into the relationship of cause to effect or succession in time."

The "paraphrase" device solves also the most puzzling problem of language learning, repetition, by compelling almost automatically every teacher to review previously taught material. It prevents the creation of separate, uncommunicating compartments called lessons, each in turn seen, then left behind like stations along the railroad track. Repetition is necessary to produce habituation, that stage of spontaneous recognition or use of the language so essential if students are ever to read or speak fluently.

Spontaneity comes from repetition. We recognize two stages of knowledge of a language : the "conscious" one, during which we use the language slowly, applying rules of grammar, reasoning various relationships as we proceed. The second one, which I shall call the "automatic" stage, when we speak, read, write the language substantially like our mother tongue. It is very evident that students must reach that automatic stage if they are ever to read inelligently or speak or write with reasonable ease. In our experiments we found that an interval of eight weeks usually intervened between the introduction of a new form and a new vocabulary, and the "automatic" use of that form and vocabulary, provided, of course, those elements after being stayed with for five recitations had been repeated at least three times a week for the following seven weeks. The only satisfactory method of repetition that we succeeded in working out was the scheme of "paraphrase." As an illustration—suppose that I wish to explain the word "glace." Instead of saying: "Glace means ice," or pointing to a piece of ice in a picture, I may paraphrase it in the following manner, selecting, of course, only those words and forms previously taught: "En été l'eau du lac est liquide ; en hiver l'eau du lac n'est pas liquide, elle est solide ; l'eau solide est de la glace". This simple explanation contains all the challenge of a cross word puzzle or a conundrum, and it never fails to command attention and cause concentration. After repeating this description of the word "glace" two or three times, I notice through a gleam in the eyes of many students that the word has been understood. In order to check on this understanding, and for the purpose of imprinting "glace" in a deeper groove on the memory cells, the word is introduced further in a series of sentences such as: En quelle saison y a-t-il de la glace ? Y a-t-il de la glace au printemps ? en été ? en hiver ? Y a-t-il de la glace maintenant ? Fait-il chaud, quand il y a de la glace sur le lac? etc...

Of all the various devices of technique that we use in our teaching, the most efficient, the most stimulating, indeed the most essential to success is the oral and aural use of the language. Interest is maintained always as its highest pitch through speaking. It is without question the most natural way of satisfying the innate desire of the student of a language to use that language; with younger students it caters to their "love of doing," their desire to manipulate and put to use every material, every new acquisition. Every human being is endowed with the inherited ability to learn language by ear; because countless generations have dealt with language in terms of sounds and only comparatively recently has language become a matter of letters, all of us have an atavistic aptitude for receiving linguistic facts more vividly, more satisfyingly through the ear; the eye constitutes merely an auxiliary organ, one that should be used only as a second and never as a first organ of reception. One of our experiments showed that it takes an average child with his auditory and visual senses equally developed one hundred "seeings" of an abstract word before he has an automatic recognition of its written form, while twenty "hearings" plus five "seeings" are sufficient to imprint the same word in a deep groove upon the memory cells, and to make it available for purposes both of reading and conversing.

The form of oral practice we use is not a hit-or-miss series of questions without an object except possibly the increase of a stock of ready-made sentences. It is a "purposeful" exercise aiming at the mastery through oral use of fundamental principles of grammar and a connected topic. It may take the form not only of questions but also of dramatization, by taking advantage of the dramatic instinct which is so strong in the junior and even in the senior high school student.

While linguistic elements are received by the brain with greater vividness when they are presented through the ear, it is quite evident, however, that with students of high school age there is little automatic transfer from the sound to the written form, and that we must train the student to reason sounds in terms of letters through sufficient drill in reading and writing. The sequence that we found most efficient was the following: The ear receives a sound, the brain reasons that sound in terms of letters, the hand writes the word, the word is read aloud.

For educational reasons we are anxious to induce in the student habits of precision, accuracy, careful analysis and a scientific attitude toward language. We feel, therefore, that it is a dangerous practice to assign a so-called "classic," i. e., a book written by a Frenchman for Frenchmen, before the student has a sufficient knowledge of the fundamentals of the French language to enable him to account for the forms found and before he has mastered a sufficiently large vocabulary to read with some ease instead of painfully deciphering each word. To introduce such a reading text in the first year, even the apparently simple Contes de Fées, at a stage when it is obviously impossible for the student to reason out intelligently grammatical constructions met in the text, leads the student to habits of slovenliness and encourages him to adopt the comfortable practice of "ducking" under difficulties rather than of confronting them. We value so much this scientific attitude of our students toward the language that in our course of study we postpone all reading of such "classics" until the second year. During the first year reading is limited to a "prepared" text containing many pages of "lectures" each one carefully written around a topic and one major fundamental of grammar.

Very early in our experiment we found that classes in which

the foreign language was used exclusively as a medium of instruction were securing appreciably better results than others in which English was used part of the time. Students, particularly those in the junior high school, are very sensitive to this imponderable called the "class atmosphere." They take special pride in the fact that no English is allowed and in some instances they voluntarily impose a fine for any unnecessary English word. The only English permitted is the word or sentence introduced in the foreign language for the express purpose of clarifying a point of grammar or an idiomatic expression. Even rules of grammar may be dealt with in the foreign language, provided the teacher uses ingenuity and limits himself to simple expressions. We grant, of course, that the whole course of study must be organized with that technique in view. Some may object that we complicate the problem by introducing in French a number of useless words belonging to grammatical terminology. By actual count, however, we found only three or four expressions that might be said to belong exclusively to grammar; all others either were exactly like English in sound and spelling or belonged to a useful general vocabulary. We are convinced after eight years of experimentation (1) that it is possible to eliminate English entirely as a medium of instruction from the foreign language class-room; (2) that it saves considerable time to use the foreign language exclusively; (3) that it creates a wholesome atmosphere in the class-room; (4) that it stimulates both teacher and students to make the necessary efforts to express themselves in the foreign language; (5) that experience has shown that it is exceedingly difficult, not to say impossible, to limit oneself to a minimum of English; all administrators agree that the almost irresistible tendency is to increase the amount, five minutes today, ten tomorrow, ending with only ten minutes of the foreign language in a comparatively short time.

What about translation? While a limited amount of English into the foreign language has some value as a means of insuring more precision in the use of grammatical rules, translation into English is a hopelessly dull process that we can well afford to abandon. No one will deny the educational, the cultural value of rendering a page of French, for instance, into elegant English, with all the shadings of thought and beauty of form of the French; but such an exercise is exceedingly difficult and cannot be carried on successfully except in the solitude of one's room. Few people achieve success in this type of translation, which should be tried out only occasionally. The translation usually practiced in the foreign language class-room is a perfunctory rendering into very indifferent, if not wrong English, purely as a convenient device for reciting an assignment in reading. A skillful teacher, anxious to save valuable time and to excite the interest of the class in the work, will find judicious questioning in the foreign language, résumés, and dramatizations, a far more efficient, far less wasteful device. The constant practice in translation creates an inhibition to spontaneous reading by accustoming the reader to the use of the intermediary of English in a process that should proceed directly from the printed page to understanding. All our data show that the shortest road even to a mere reading knowledge of a foreign language is through a proper use of the oral approach.

There still remains much to be said about various points of technique, material and organization, but the writer has already exceeded the limit of space so wisely allotted to him. Those, however, are in the main the important fundamental principles that experimentation demonstrated to us as sound in the teaching of foreign languages. Those various principles grouped into an homogeneous scheme of teaching, into a body of technique came to be known among specialists as the Cleveland Plan for lack of a better label. We are all aware that this plan needs further improvement through continued research, but such as it is it has proved far more result-producing than any other scheme previously tried. It is satisfactory to our students who through its application acquire a practical command of the language which they treasure as an accomplishment of no mean value; it pleases also the parents who in Cleveland as well as elsewhere are demanding *practical* achievements of modern language teachers; it satisfies administrators who have seen problems of failures considerably lessened, articulations between schools and colleges greatly improved and the fear of the College Entrance Board examinations practically conquered. Most portentous result of all, it satisfies our teachers who have regained faith in the possibilities of their work and are laboring with renewed enthusiasm. They glean their reward and find new inspiration in the bubbling joy easily read on the faces of youths opening their eyes wide on the marvels of that new word: the new language.

THE TEACHING OF FRENCH GRAMMAR

AND THE

TEACHING OF THE FRENCH LANGUAGE [1]

By Osmond T. Robert

Much time, in French classes, is given to the teaching of grammar. The pupils memorize paradigms, rules, and exceptions. Their attention is constantly called to forms given them with the scantiest information about their meanings. When they come to apply the information thus obtained, it frequently happens that they forget some all important proviso, and therefore write nonsense or strained constructions upon which the teacher is obliged to spend much time in often futile correcting. It seems then that the only thing to do is to increase grammatical instruction; a separate subject is made of it; an increasing number of hours are devoted to it; and the results are often disappointing. The students fail to apply, when the time comes, the knowledge which they seemed to possess. Grammar has been presented to them as a science, but writing and speaking are arts, and the theoretical instruction which they have received proves to be difficult of practical application. What is more, the pupils work, during the hours of grammatical instruction, on a very limited and semantically "lean" vocabulary, and as soon as they begin to attempt to express their own thoughts or those suggested to them in texts set for translation, they need a vocabulary much wider and richer. That vocabulary they draw from their reading or from their dictionaries, and it is hardly be wondered at that they should so often apparently

[1] The following article is based on a paper read at a conference on French held by the Experiment Examination Board, at the Baldwin School, Bryn Mawr, Jan. 27, 1928.

forget[1] all about grammatical matters in using material which has for them no evident connection with the sources of their grammatical information.

We cannot here go into the study of the unfortunately very prevalent practice of separating the study of vocabulary from that of grammar, nor explain why, so often, the teaching of French grammar has ousted the teaching of the French language in French classes. We can only point out some of the weaknesses of formal grammar, as a means to language teaching, and suggest a presentation of grammar which shall tend to bridge the gap existing between it and language.

Formal grammar is deductive in method. It starts from definitions, gives rules, is general and abstract, and all that necessarily entails the use of a large highly technical vocabulary the meaning of which is not grasped until the matters to which it applies have come to have a real existence for the student, that is, until its usefulness as a means to teaching has largely ceased to be. Moreover grammatical terminology is sometimes positively misleading. Some of the matters to which it applies have so changed since its adoption that one is sometimes obliged to resort to ingenious

[1] When we say that they *forget,* we speak somewhat like the angler who says that he has *lost* a three pound trout which, in realty, he never securely hooked. *Remembering* is a matter of association. There can therefore be no *forgetting* where no association has been formed. In reading and translating, associations are formed between French forms and corresponding English ones through common meanings, but no association is necessarily formed between meanings expressed in English and French grammatical processes, — unless indeed the pupil has been trained or is helped by the teacher, to look out for such processes, and to link them up with meanings. When, therefore, the student applies English grammatical processes to French forms which he has learned to regard as mere allomorphs of English words, he has *forgotten* nothing; he has, on the contrary, made use of the associations which circumstances and weak pedagogy have formed in his mind. When the vocabulary is culled from texts, an observant student may be able to recall the grammatical processes which contributed to its meaning, but when it is culled from vocabularies or dictionaries, there is no reason why even the intelligent pupil should apply to it any other grammatical processes than those which he associates with the English forms expressing the meaning he must render. He is not conscious, *and there is no reason why he should be conscious,* that a new grammatical situation has arisen. And that is what is often referred to as "forgetting to apply knowledge".

explanations the main purpose of which seems to be to explain why the terms do not mean what it would be natural to suppose they do. This is surely a waste of the precious time which ought to be given to teaching French. As an example of this one might quote the terms "passé défini" and "passé indéfini" which really meant something when they were adopted because they corresponded to the usage of the day, a usage which in some respects is today the exact opposite of what it used to be. We say: "Louis XIV fit de Boileau son historiographe" and "Hier matin, à cinq heures cinq, je me suis réveillé", where in spite of the very definite time given it would be distinctly provincial to say "je me levai". The classifications of formal grammar were made partly according to function, partly according to form. Having decided that such a form as *viendrait* is conditional, and having defined the conditional as the mood of unreal consequence of an unreal supposition, the grammarian is hard put to account for the conditional in such a sentence as "Il m'a dit qu'il viendrait me voir". Most of our grammars merely point out that the "conditional" is used for the future in reported speech, and trust to the lack of interest or of intelligence in the pupils to get by with a rule of that kind. But one has heard of ingenious teachers who managed to justify that "conditional" by explaining that the accomplishment of the act was uncertain, or that there was a suppositive clause "s'il le pouvait" understood. That is, of course, very clever and saves the 'conditionality' of *viendrait,* but unfortunately it is contrary to the thought of the speaker who had no misgivings about the future, and never dreamt of making his promise conditional upon anything. What many grammarians have not understood is that we have here a tense of the indicative bearing the same relation to the past 'a dit' as the future tense (which the speaker used) bore to the present at the moment when he spoke. *Viendrait* is therefore not a conditional, but just a future-in-the-past indicative as will clarly be seen if one transposes the sentence into the present: "Il dit qu'il *viendra* me voir".

Formal grammar is necessarily abstract. It attempts to deal with linguistic material as mathematics deals with symbols and relations. But mathematical formulae have always the same connotation; a circle, whatever its size or position, is always πR^2, whereas the meanings of linguistic units are always changing and may acquire quite unexpected values when used,—albeit in perfectly correct grammatical relation,—with different units. It is always possible, if R be known, to determine the size of the circle, its circumference, the surface of an inscribed equilateral triangle, etc., and if R remain unknown the circle will nevertheless retain all the properties of a circle. On the other hand, it is quite impossible to deduce from the formula or rule of the derivation of adverbs what the meaning of *bonnement,* for instance,is likely to be, though we form it quite correctly and regularly from the adjective *bon* and know the meaning of *bon;* nor can we, from the rules governing the position of adjectives, foresee that *pauvre* will have very different meanings in the two expressions "un pauvre homme" and "un homme pauvre". When, as often happens, the language bursts the bonds of grammatical precepts, we have what grammarians have been pleased to call "exceptions." Those exceptions are, for the most part, perfectly regular and perfectly logical phenomena which have had the misfortune of not fitting into the grammarians' conception of what is "regular."

Enough has been said, I believe, to show why formal grammar can have but a very relative usefulness as a means of *teaching* a foreign language. One may add however that a further and not less grave defect, deriving from its method, is that it is not sufficiently interested in the meanings of the linguistic units it deals with. Its classifications were made for the benefit of those who already used the language. While it is certain that our knowledge of the mother tongue cannot be scientific until we have studied the grammar of it (for the study of grammar systematizes our knowledge), it is equally certain that it was not through a study of formal grammar that we acquired the power to speak, nor is it by that method that we increase our powers of speech. It seems highly probable that the Greeks spoke correctly long before Aristotle, and it is certain that French children speak French more correctly without any knowledge of formal grammar, than American students do though they know Fraser and Squair from cover to cover. This does not mean that the Greeks did not, nor that the French children do not, know grammar. To speak or write correctly is to speak or write grammatically. Many know grammar practically who lack the vocabulary or special training necessary to talk about it, just as some men play an excellent game of billiards who might be filled with amazement in hearing what even a poor player could tell them of the use they make in their clever play of momentum, friction, and angles of incidence.

Realizing the limitations of formal grammar as a means to the teaching of foreign languages, the proponents of the Direct Method went so far as to wish to do away with it altogether. They depended upon imitation—the method of nature *qui n'en peut mais* —to impart at least a speaking knowledge of the language. But there are limits to what can be done by mere imitation in the very short time at our disposal, and, what is more, when they begin their French studies in the High or in the Preparatory Schools, the pupils are of an age which rebels against mere imitation. They feel the need of grouping phenomena so as to learn faster; they want to use their intelligence as well as their memory. Are we therefore to give them instruction in the old type of formal grammar? De Saussure, Bally and a number of other grammarians in France, Switzerland and Germany, have attempted classifications of linguistic phenomena according to ideas, emotions, etc. They have studied the various processes wherby commands are given, assertions made, doubt expressed. They have based their classification on meanings, and grouped around those meanings the forms and processes which express them. They have therefore effected a *rapprochement* between meanings and forms and processes. Is such a treatment of grammar possible with our pupils? Only with the most advanced, I fear, for it also presupposes a vast practical knowledge of the language, and we cannot reproduce those conditions in the class room since the pupils are there not to systematize and perfect their knowledge of French, but to acquire the elements of the language. Brunot's conception of grammar is, however, illuminating. He describes it as that whereby we are able to understand everything and to express everything, and if we set about out grammatical teaching with the idea of making meanings clear and of giving to our pupils the means of clearly and correctly expressing meanings, we shall certainly do much to make our grammar teaching useful, and at the same time interesting and stimulating; but we shall find that it brings radical changes in our grammatical method. We cannot, in our classes, base much of our grammatical teaching on previously acquired knowledge (except in reviewing what has already been learned), neither can we successfully teach grammar *before* teaching the language, since this necessarily makes our teaching abstract and leads us back to definitions, rules and all the drawbacks of formal grammar; what we have to do is to teach grammar together with vocabulary, with a view to forming in the pupils very close associations between ideas, images, emotions, and the forms and processes which express them, so that when similar ideas, images, etc., arise in the minds of the pupils or are suggested to them, they shall recall the language, (vocabulary and processes) by which they are expressed.

As words, idiomatic expressions, verb forms, etc., have rich and definite meanings only in contexts, it is obviously only in texts which have been thoroughly studied and understood that we can hope to find intelligible grammatical material. Much grammar can indeed be practically acquired by observational exercises and by imitating the processes by which meanings are expressed, without resorting to abstract statements of what is being done. Little can be accomplished, on the other hand, by substituting to observation and imitation, abstract statements of what should be done. It is much more useful to show pupils how to use pronouns in imitation of the manner of the author under study, than to make them learn all the usual wonderful things about disjunctives and conjunctives which they certainly do not understand, and which they cannot understand until they are so familiar with pronominal construction that they can dispense with the rules. So also, any attempt to explain the why and wherefore of the use of prepositions, is necessarily beyond the powers of comprehension of the pupils—a knowledge of Old French being necessary even to reason about such things,—but they can and must, from the outset, learn to use the prepositions correctly nevertheless by associating word-groups with certain definite meanings.[1]

[1] Neither will it do to attribute definite meanings to the various French prepositions for they are translatable by almost any English preposition or by none at all. It is owing to the ficticious values attached to those dead words that pupils write "je pense de vous" for "à vous" or "j'ai emprunté ce crayon de mon frère" for "à mon frère".

The teaching of grammar should therefore consist first of all in pointing out the means used by an author to express his thought and not in saying such inane and aimless things as: "that *moi* is a disjunctive" or "that verb ending in *-ait* is in the imperfect," for that is surely doing grammar for grammar's sake. What *is* interesting, and what will throw light on the passage read and give the pupils a sense of the correct use of the tenses, is to point out that in using the imperfect the author has assigned a certain time to the act or state designated by the verb: has indicated its temporal relation to some other act. Then, when the pupil wishes to express a similar temporal relation between two acts, he will very probably turn to the imperfect, and for once use it correctly and intelligently.

Neither will it be sufficient to point out such relations once and let the matter rest. It will be necessary to give the pupils practice in analysing the thought and intention of the author, and in stating what the time relations are, for it is in the attempt to state, explain and justify by *reference to meanings,* that the thought gains clearness.

Let us suppose that the text under study has yielded such examples as the following:

Il m'a dit { qu'il était malade
qu'il n'avait que cinq sous
qu'il faisait beau quand il est parti.

Get the pupils to answer correctly questions such as the following:

"A quel moment était-il malade ? — "Au moment même où il me l'a dit".

"A quel moment n'avait-il que cinq sous ?"—"Au moment où il me l'a dit."

"Quand faisait-il beau?" — "Quand il est parti", and they will soon sense what grammarians have too often neglected to emphasize: that the imperfect is a tense the function of which is to indicate that an act is present with regard to some past. It matters little what name one gives it: present-in-the-past, imperfect, tense No. 2, the tense denoting habit in the past, or description in the past, past circumstances, etc., so long as the name given is not misleading. [1]

[1] The name "past continuous" however, which has come to be used of late

Work similar to the above should then be done with the pluperfect (the past-in-the-past), and with what we have already discussed: the future-in-the-past indicative. Likewise, the difference in *meaning* (not merely in use with or without *dès que, quand, aussitôt que,* etc.) of the two past-in-the-past tenses (the pluperfect and past anterior) should be pointed out and worked at as the text furnishes opportunity. Too much trust has generally been placed in paradigms and their translations into English. Indeed most of the stubborn mistakes committed by our students owe their origin and persistence to the use of the orthodox grammar book with its paradigms and English texts as media for teaching composition. The reasons for that are evident to anyone who gives a little thought to the matter. First, the functions of the English tenses do not correspond to the French. The perfect, for instance, is used in English to denote an act completed in a recent past, whereas the use of the French passé indéfini (which corresponds most closely in form to the English perfect), is governed by considerations of style (conversational, epistolary, etc.) and not by considerations of time alone. It is as common for a person of French origin and training to misuse the English perfect and imperfect as it is for our students to confuse those tenses in French: We have all heard French people say: "Yesterday I *have seen* your father" for "I saw" or "Every time I *was looking* at you I *was thinking of* what you had told me" for "Whenever I looked at you I thought . . . ". The lack of correspondence between the use of the tenses in English and in French, makes it necessary, in the translation of forms, the exact meaning of which is not made clear by a context, to offer a wide variety of possible renderings. The imperfect *je me levais,* for instance, may be rendered: I used to rise, I rose, I was rising, I would rise; while the English *he rose,* may be rendered into French by: il se levait, il se leva, il se fut levé, il se levât, se soit levé, etc., to say nothing of the participal renderings which might be cited. It is not to be wondered that students are puzzled when

---

is rather unfortunate in view of the fact that pupils are wont to interpret it as meaning that any extended and uninterrupted act in the past is to be rendered by the imperfect, e. g. "Les Romains *régnaient* (instead of *régnèrent*) sur le monde sans interruption pendant trois cents ans."

called upon to render sentences such as the following: "In those days, I would rise at five to go for a walk; he said he would rise at five; each day I rose at five; day after day I rose at five; I always rose at five; I didn't think that he rose at five; in spite of his cold he would rise at five; I said it so that he would rise at five."

In the paradigms one often finds English subjunctive forms given as the equivalents of French subjunctives although there is little in common between the two. English indicative forms must often be rendered into French by subjunctives, and some English subjunctives are rendered by indicavites in French. Translations of that kind are therefore misleading. One finds also renderings such as: "he will have risen" or " we shall have departed" which are more or less meaningless to Anglo-Saxon students who avoid the use of the past-in-the-future by using two simple futures joined by some adverbial expression such as *and* then. Realizing the predicament of learners, and the insufficiency of the information which grammars can afford them, the authors of composition books sometimes use forms such as "was rising" to hint that an imperfect is called for, or "has risen" to suggest the passé indéfini, or "shall have risen" to hint at the future anterior, and thereby often do violence to the English language. This constitutes a kind of prompting which in no way guarantees that mistakes will not be made when the student finds himself in presence of a text which has not been specially "doctored" for translation. Indeed, it is the surest way of leading the student into error; it debilitates his intellect by offering it a crutch instead of developing its strength by exercise. [1]

The *rapprochement* of meanings and of the forms and processes which express them, need not be confined to the study of syntax. The ways of negativing, for instance, in all degrees of strength should be pointed out, studied and practised as the texts under

[1] We must use, of course, every legitimate means which a lively imagination can suggest to attain our objective. The correct use of French by our pupils. The trick referred to above is, however, to be ruled out as illegitimate, for apart from the pedagogical unsoundness of it, it lends the sanction of print to strained English constructions, and the weakening of our pupils' precarious hold upon correct English is too heavy a price to pay even for progress in French.

study give one opportunity, and when a sufficient number of cases have been studied, and only then, a classification can be made which will greatly help the student to remember. One would avoid thus such common mistakes as the use of *seulement* for *ne que* in sentences such as: "J'ai *seulement* cinq sous dans ma bourse."

The same thing is true of certain matters which belong partly to vocabulary and partly to grammar: I mean idiomatic expressions and their use. If instead of saying, in the manner of the idiom list, that "avoir beau" means "to be in vain", one called attention, during the study of a text, to the mechanism of the full expression which, in French, conveys the idea that something happens (or does not happen) in spite of efforts to the contrary, one would avoid the occurrence of such translations as: "Je l'ai supplié de venir mais j'ai eu beau", with which all French teachers whose pupils consult lists of idiomatic expressions are only too familiar. Neither will it be sufficient to point out such matters. Observation will have to be followed by practice and a certain amount of manipulation. If the student has learned to say correctly: "J'ai eu beau le supplier de venir, il a refusé", he should be told to express that fact as if the action were taking place in the present: "J'ai beau le supplier . . . ", then as an habitual thing in the past: "J'avais beau le supplier . . . ", then in the future: "J'aurai beau le supplier . . .", then as a supposition: "J'aurais beau le supplier de venir, il refuserait". The same *cadre* should then be used to express other ideas: that, for instance, of the vanity of working since failure at the examinations is, was, or will be a foregone conclusion; or the idea that Father refuses, has always refused, usually has refused, or will refuse, to furnish funds though his daughter weep ever so pathetically. In that way, the student will discover that grammar is that which helps one to express real thoughts in French: thoughts which are not merely transcriptions of English thoughts which the wilfulness of French grammarians requires one to express in disobedience to all Anglo-Saxon (and therefore reasonable) habits of expression. They will come to see in fact that the French language exists for the purpose of expressing thoughts and not merely to consecrate the sacredness of apparently arbitrary and very unreasonables rules.

Grammar teaching of this observational and semantic type would give our pupils a firmer hold upon the language they are studying. It would, incidentally, develop their intelligence of the mother tongue, and their memories would not be burdened with a multitude of sterile facts having no clear connection with the foreign language they are attempting to understand and to master. The study of grammar would also gain in interest as all studies do which, through the exercise of the intelligence, lead to the accomplishment of good work.

WHAT IS INTERESTING TO MY CLASSES IN FRENCH

By LEAH A. HUCKANS

It is always with considerable misgiving that a teacher endeavors to analyze for herself or for others the methods that she uses in the classroom. Her little home-made devices then seem to her so petty and foolish as she jots them down, and yet each one is intricately woven into the fabric of her teaching. Certainly it is not theory that I endeavor to expound, but actual experiments that I have tried and found fairly successful. These methods may not always be in harmony with some accepted principles of pedagogy, but after all have they not a right to be called pedagogical if they are successful?

Each teacher must of course be a law unto herself when it comes to choosing the methods she can best use to make her pupils comprehend what she is so eager to have them learn. So, by telling you briefly of some of the simple things that I do, the mistakes I make, the success that I sometimes have, I may be able to convince you that your methods are not so bad after all. That would be surely accomplishing something worth while, for we all become discouraged often and thoroughly.

As I thought over what would be worthy of mention in such an article as this, I found it rather difficult to draw the line distinctly between what was actually interesting to my classes and what was interesting to me. I have often prepared assignments with infinite care and pains only to find that some expedient, thought up in a moment of necessity, is far more popular (and I must admit sometimes more worth while, if only because its popularity arouses interest.) Of one thing I am quite sure, that my mind must have the agility of a monkey, the patience of the Sphinx, the breadth and depth of the sea, and the humor of the ages to cope with all the demands put upon it.

In my youthful days, I believed if I told a class, "this is one of the most difficult things to learn in French," that they would of course buckle right down to it and endeavor to master it. But experience has taught me that that course is often poor psychology. The almost inevitable reaction is discouragement from the start, except in the case of the very bright who like to be told that they are really doing something difficult. With the wisdom of experience, I try to disguise as cleverly as possible that there is anything difficult in what I am explaining. Many times a subject can be approached casually, as an illustration of it occurs in a reading lesson, for example, and with just a short explanation and a few illustrations, behold a difficult point has been cleared up without any fuss at all. Drill is absolutely essential at times and the pupils actually enjoy it if the teacher can put some life into it. It is a reward in itself to see in the pupils the joy of accomplishment that manifests itself when once a subject is thoroughly understood. It is fine to feed the pupils a bit at a time on some occasions, but on the other hand there is the danger of giving it in such small installments that it has no effect.

Perhaps I may say that the keynote of my teaching is variety. I am not naturally an ingenious person. My sluggish nature would permit me to to the same thing in the same old way, if there were not somewhere within, an inner voice that bids me find a way out of the deadly monotony. The same ways, the same books, the same illustrations would be so much easier but I myself cannot stand monotony. I have heard pupils say of a teacher that she always told the same story in the same place and I am sure that I do not want to be like that. I prefer to have the pupils enjoy my "humor" as something they do not expect. I do not like to read the same books two terms in succession, not only for my own sake but because the pupils derive more benefit from new material that they have not heard their friends and relatives discuss. Naturally, this means more work for me, yet the preparation of new material is equipping me for what I want to do and be. The more I read, the greater is my vocabulary, the more illustrations do I have at my command, so that I may draw from them without pause. When I have several classes of the same grade, I like to and in fact find it imperative in order to preserve my own sanity, to keep such classes doing practically the same work. But I have to try out different methods in each class. Recently in teaching about personal pronoun objects, I tried a different method in each of three classes. To one I gave only French illustrations from which they worked out the rules ; to the second I gave the rules and then had the pupils translate from English to French sentences in which they made an attempt to apply these rules ; in the third I used both methods and found after two days that the boys and girls of that class had mastered the subject far more rapidly than the others. It was necessary to follow the same tactics with the first two classes before the horizon cleared. The final test was somewhat of a contest; the chagrin at failure, the rejoicing at success, the general enthousiasm and satisfaction — all this was my reward.

Beginning classes are my Waterloo, although I thoroughly enjoy them. There are always so many things I want to teach them that I almost stumble over myself to give new work and find that I am sacrificing accuracy on their part to amount of material. Then sometimes I slow down so that I am behind schedule. The beginners love conversation, love to hear me speak French to them. They get the thrill that comes once in a life time if I can give them directions in French and they are able to do what I tell them. I have formed the habit of teaching these beginners little snatches of conversation, or sometimes a bit of a poem. They enjoy talking with each other especially when they know that they are really saying the things the French say. To be able to say something in French and to say it correctly is marvelous. One of the first that I taught my class this term was the "formula" for a social introduction. As we were practicing the forms the first thing I knew, they were shaking hands and bowing to each other in real ernest. I do not always use the same conversations in each term. Usually some incident in class offers suggestion for some conversational form. Some pupil is always asking, "How do you say...... in French?" Often I will turn to the class and ask: "Would you like to learn to say that?" The response is always immediate and fervent and I find as much enjoyment in it as they. I chanced upon the introduction early this term in this way; I was asking different members of the class, "Qui est derrière vous ?" — "Qui est devant vous ?" — and I found to my surprise that they did not know each others names, which of course proved embarassing. So much to the amusement of the class I proceeded to introduce them to each other. From that I taught them what to say in reply and allowed them to introduce each other. Then I amused myself by pretending that the principal, the superintendent and even Dr. Price came to visit us and I presented the class to him. Various members of the class would enact the role of these people, and also of the teacher while the class would put on its best manners and intone in chorus "Nous sommes enchantés, Monsieur, de faire votre connaissance".

When I teach them to tell time, I have a Baby Ben alarm clock that I find more effective than a watch or the clock on the wall. I can turn the hands at will and the class can see readily. I often hold the clock so that the class can see the hands and ask them to tell me the time. Then I tell them in French where the hands should be at that time. I have to think quickly in order to make no mistake. A pleasant diversion is created by having one of the pupils take my place and the members of the class are on the alert to see that he makes no error. They like to have me ask them to figure out the time if I tell them the position of the hands.

To help fix numerals in mind, I spend some time in teaching addition, multiplication, and subtraction. The smaller numbers we do in our heads, there is always keen rivalry in figuring out the answer and expressing it in French. Again, I myself, must be keenly alert — for if I make a mistake woe is me. I send the pupils to the board to add columns of figures, to multiply numbers that they cannot do rapidly in their heads. Each step must however be explained in French. They are so intent on finding the correct answer that they forget to be self-conscious about the numerals. Never yet have I found a class that did not enjoy this exercice.

I let the pupils lead as often as possible. They like to do it, even tho it prove embarrassing. Everything interests them, pictures, maps, short stories, even bits of conversation that I may chance to carry on with another French teacher who comes into the room for a moment. After studying the parts of the body and the names of various articles of clothing, an excellent exrcise is to have each pupil draw a picture, or cut one from a newspaper or fashion sheet of a man, boy, woman or girl; then describe the personal appearance and clothing. I really find some very clever ones. I even become a sort of cheer leader at times when we are drilling on forms. Ensemble work in beginning classes is very effective because the pupils are naturally timid about venturing too soon to pronounce the words alone. I have them give a sentence slowly at first, then speed up a bit, all the time keeping them together. They want to see how fast they can give it without making a slip. Their censure is very severe for the pupil who continues to make the same mistake after having been corrected several times. After they master the pronunciation, I can teach them to group the words of a sentence intelligently. These then are a few of the devices that I use for first year classes.

As we go on, the first real connected story always arouses interest and enthusiasm. First reading books may well be short stories, but to read a "connected, continued story," as one girl recently expressed herself, is truly inspiring. Even tho a class may be accustomed to ordinary simple questions, it is difficult for them to follow at first the more complicated questions that inevitably result from the connected text and idiomatic expressions of a story-book. This term I was having considerable difficulty in getting the class to understand my questions, so I hit upon this expedient, not a new nor an original one, to be sure; each member of the class was assigned a definite paragraph or two for concentrated effort. He was to form five questions based on the text of his paragraph. Then he was allowed to call on whomsoever he chose as he gave his questions directly to the class. This is an approved pedagogical device, but I mention it because it chances to be fresh in my mind and I have not yet recovered from the storm of interest it roused from all the 2-1 pupils who had not had much experience along that line. I was rather timorous about the result, but on the whole the questions were not so bad. (It was amazing how easily the class understood what the other members meant by a question even tho it was incorrectly formed.) But the exercise had the desired result. The pupils wanted to know how to ask the question correctly and after each pupil had given his questions and mistakes had been gently but persistently corrected — there had been quite a background formed. There was my opportunity to drive home the interrogative pronouns, and forms of questions in general. Now what a difference when I ask the questions! I seldom have to repeat a question, when before, it was, "Je ne comprends pas"; "Voulez-vous bien répéter la question ?" You may imagine the psychological effect on the class, when I tell you that one boy with immense assurance and unblushing conceit said to me, "Why, our questions sound just like yours, Miss Huckans."

Verb blanks are like new toys to the pupils. I could almost say with reason that they want to take them apart to see how they run. By means of these blanks they soon gain a surprising proficiency in writing verb forms — which is not, to be sure, all that is essential. So I have prepared some stencils of drill sentences, short and snappy, for each irregular verb. Sometimes we translate these orally and at other times they are written. These sentences may also serve to bring out some of the special idioms with certain verbs. In this case I usually have them given orally and then written either at the board or as home work.

Second year people especially like to be asked for information which they have secured from other sources, from history, from English or from general outside reading. A few days ago we came across a reference to the story of Roland and the cleft he was supposed to have made with his sword in the mountain. I asked casually how many knew the story and there was a near riot as to who should tell it. The person I called on first did not relate it to suit the others so one and another added details until we had some that I must admit I had never heard before. There is one boy who could and would, if permitted, go on forever entertaining us from the wealth of his knowledge. He can be decidedly interesting and it is a problem to know just when and how to curb his enthusiasm.

Dictation proves to have a peculiar fascination for everyone. In choosing dictation for second and third years, I like to choose material that will be interesting and helpful from another point of view than merely to write correct forms. This means endless searching, revising, abridging. But I am rewarded by the attention with which the pupils follow the meaning of the dictée.

With third years classes, I have tried using one story for dictation and comprehension, alternating from day to day, but keeping the thread of the story to connect them. This worked very well as far as being interesting was concerned, but it does not afford so great a variety of theme and form. For drill in comprehension, I do not always, during the term, use set exercises. For instance, twice a week I like to talk to the class on some topic outside of their reading or one suggested by their reading. Not always do I question them directly on what I have said — I can often tell by their expressions whether they have understood. At other times I question them indirectly. By that I mean, refer question to their own experience, has such a thing ever happened to you, etc. Then I tell by the replies that my own story has been understood. When starting a new book, I sometimes introduce the author by telling them a few facts about his life and work instead of having the pupils read it themselves. This is a more formal exercise because they know that I expect them to remember more of what I have said. With a third year group this can be assigned to a pupil and he must make the other members of the class understand. All oral reports by pupils count for comprehension. Formal exercises occasionally to accustom the pupils to the form for the examination, I believe advisable.

Dramatization by the pupils especially in the third year aids materially in stimulating the boys and girls to renewed effort in conversation. Books of short plays are easily handled in this fashion. With some classes I use model conversations which I have the pupils learn just as a part in a play. These are presented before other members of the class. The point of this is to see if they can present it in such a way that they can be readily understood. Variety is secured with these people by having them question each other. They are sufficiently advanced in this art, so that I can trust them to form their questions correctly at least and it is surprising what "thought-provoking" queries they can present.

In all the advanced classes, that is beyond the first year, I like to have my assignments organized so that the pupils may know with a fair degree of accuracy what sort of work is due each day. But I refuse to be bound absolutely by the way I have done a thing before. I learn to my horror at intervals that some precocious individual has tried to do three or four lessons in advance, following the regular schedule without waiting for the help that each day's class work brings. So I often vary not the nature of the assignment but the method of approach, not simply to vary the monotony, but to give the added stimulus of several view-points, and to prevent the pupil from trying to do too much at any one time.

I used to think that third year classes must have just so much formal history, willy-nilly. I have preserved now in my private museum some elaborate history outlines that I used to present religiously to all third year pupils. Of course, they should have some history and they enjoy it, but I no longer assign it in such a bald way. To give the background for a book they are reading, such as Hugo's "Quatre-Vingt-Treize," a general notion of the trend of events is all we can hope to give now that there are so many demands put upon us.

In the last term of the third year, I require that each person read one book outside of class and report on it. I have quite a number of texts that I loan to the pupils and others can be found in the library. As far as possible each is allowed to choose his own book or at least the type of book that he likes. The reports are sometimes written and sometimes oral, but always there are a few questions of my choosing to be answered about the book.

After I had finished writing this article, I casually asked all the pupils in my classes to tell me, in writing, of course, what they found most interesting in their French work. It is rather a doubtful experiment at best and I suppose that I scarcely expected any valuable contributions. But I was curious to know what they would write and greatly to my surprise they took it seriously. I believe from the earnestness with which they set to work and from what they wrote that most of them were quite sincere.

There was perhaps an overwhelming vote for connected reading, stories particularly, altho quite a number chose the historical readings. Then the testimony bore out what I was sure I had already discovered, that dictation offered a strong attraction to practically everyone. Only a few failed to mention it and over half gave it first place. Conversation was a favorite, a surprising number expressed their pleasure in the use of verb blanks and a few mentioned grammar drill.

From the third year group I was rather agreably surprised to find about half who really liked to do composition work, not so much the original composition writing, but the formal translation from English to French, based on a definite text. But what surprised me most of all was the large vote cast for actual translation from French to English -- the sort of exercise that most of us avoid for one reason or another and one which I thought the pupils detested. Sight reading and translation were also mentioned.

I thought a few of the shorter answers I received were amusing and surprising enough to warrant passing them on to you:

"I like translation of stories best — especially funny ones and ones that turn out unexpectedly (so as to vary the monotony)."

"I like the questions in class from one pupil to another because they are hardest of all for me and I have to listen so carefully and think so hard to understand that it makes it interesting."

"I think I prefer taking dictation to anything else. It seems I get more benefit from it. However, I see, "translation from reading books" peeking over my shoulder for first place in my preference."

"The most interesting thing in studying French is when you come across some French phrases in American books to see if you understand them."

"French is very musical *if* one can learn the correct pronunciation."

"In French, I like to learn the habits of the *queer* French people."

"Translation, if we don't have too much of it."

"In music there are a great many French terms used and it is very helpful to know the meaning. Some of the Italian terms resemble the French and it is easier to guess their meaning if you know French. I like French, anyhow."

"I find the grammar most interesting. It always seems to hold my interest more than the reading which seems so dragged out and boresome."

(This last speaks well for the teacher.)

"I prefer to read from "Le Beau Pays de France." My taste for history is a sufficient explanation of this unusual phenomenon.

I may say that the notes in "Le Beau Pays" are valuable and interesting."

"The more I learn and understand French the better I like it. I find it interesting to be able to read a story in French as tho it were an English story — not having to look up every word and doing it for pleasure rather than as a lesson."

DISCOURS DE M. MONGENDRE

Consul Général de France

prononcé à la première réunion annuelle de l'*Association Américaine des Professeurs de Français*

Vous savez tout l'intérêt que je porte aux Membres de l'Enseignement, et plus particulièrement peut-être encore, à ceux qui se sont consacrés à l'enseignement de la Langue Française.

Aussi c'est avec le plus grand plaisir que je prends part aujourd'hui à la première réunion annuelle de la *Société Américaine des Professeurs de Français* représentée ici avec tant de distinction, et je vous adresse à tous mon salut le plus cordial.

Je tiens à vous féliciter de l'heureuse initiative que vous avez eue de constituer cette intéressante association et en particulier votre éminent président le professeur Charles Downer ainsi que mademoiselle Pauline Gray, dont on ne peut que louer hautement le zèle et l'activité.

Je sais en effet, quelle tâche est celle des professeurs et je puis dire qu'il n'est pas à mes yeux d'association qui soit plus sympathique et plus digne de tous les encouragements que la vôtre.

On ne saurait assez apprécier tous vos efforts, le soin consciencieux que vous apportez dans l'enseignement de la langue française, et pour répandre autour de vous la pensée française dans ce qu'elle a de plus noble et de plus élevé.

Vous êtes aussi, de ce fait, les artisans du rapprochement de deux grands peuples, les Etats-Unis et la France — rapprochement pacifique destiné à faciliter dans l'avenir, une Paix Générale, préparée et forgée par nos deux grandes Républiques sœurs.

On pourrait appeler cette première assemblée de votre honorable association, le congrès préparatoire de la pacification par l'éducation des nouvelles générations américaines, appelées à collaborer demain à cette grande cause.

La pacification du Monde par des discours, dans des Banquets ou à des Conférences, ne semble pas avoir produit, jusqu'à présent, les résultats attendus avec une impatience bien compréhensible.

Vous, au contraire, professeurs et instituteurs, vous êtes les porteurs de la parole, les auxiliaires de l'action et les nobles interprètes, — par la langue française que vous enseignez, — de la pensée, de la littérature et des Beaux-Arts — de la toujours belle France.

Vous êtes les premiers — après la mère de famille à servir la cause de la pacification, parce que vous versez dans les veines, dans le cœur, dans l'âme et dans le cerveau de la jeunesse, les germes du sentimentalisme, par les idées françaises qui ont toujours été protectrices de la famille, seules armes efficaces pour la défense de la vie.

Oui, mes cher professeurs, vous savez comme moi-même que la langue française a cette importance. Vous savez qu'elle représente une civilisation pratiquée par presque tous les peuples, parce que la civilisation et la culture française symbolisent toute une religion.

Et cette religion, par l'influence de sa douceur et de son harmonie, rend encore plus importante et plus belle, la noble tâche que vous accomplissez.

Vous préparez lentement, mais sûrement, la pacification de l'humanité par l'éducation, comme le font eux-mêmes aujourd'hui les grands hommes d'Etat qui travaillent sans relâche, avec espoir et tenacité, pour arriver au but.

Leurs discours ont été puisés dans le berceau de la langue française, puisque c'est par cette langue que les citoyens de toutes les nations arrivent à s'entendre et à se comprendre.

Et c'est à vous, modestes et infatigables travailleurs, que nous devons ces miracles.

La langue française a été adoptée, depuis des siècles, comme langue de liaison entre les peuples. Son expression, son harmonie et sa clarté ont rendu des services considérables en dissipant tant de malentendus entre les peuples, dans maintes conférences et en établissant l'ordre nécessaire dans les relations politiques et économiques par des traités de relations amicales.

Les hommes d'Etat se sont toujours efforcés d'insérer dans ces traités les principes d'amitié. Ils l'ont fait dans le but d'assurer une existence utile et pacifique à la famille du lendemain, afin qu'elle puisse vivre en paix et sans la crainte continuelle d'être surprise un jour — en plein travail — par la ruine et par la mort.

Le rôle de la langue française — qui est de servir de trait d'union entre les peuples, a été de tout temps important dans les cinq parties du monde.

Il n'est jamais arrivé à qui que ce soit de remplacer la langue française par une autre langue, dans les relations internationales.

Un jour, cependant, peu de temps après la guerre de 1870, le Prince de Bismark pensa remporter aussi une victoire, dans le domaine diplomatique, en substituant la langue allemande à la langue française.

Il écrivit, à titre d'essai, au Prince Gortchakoff une note quelconque en allemand.

Le Prince Gortchakoff, comprenant la manœuvre répondit à Bismarck en langue russe.

Vous voyez d'ici l'effet produit par cette réponse, et depuis cette aventure la langue française est demeurée la langue de rapprochement entre les peuples.

Vous, mes chers professeurs, puisque vous êtes des amis de mon grand peuple, vous faites mieux.

Vous dites, comme l'avait fait autrefois à la Chambre des Députés le Ministre Charles Dupuy, après l'explosion d'une bombe lancée par un anarchiste : "La Séance continue".

Vous continuez, en effet, la diffusion de la langue française pour faire mieux connaître, aimer et apprécier, la pensée et l'art français.

Vous atténuez ainsi, peu à peu, les frontières intellectuelles nées de la diversité du langage qui se sont élevées à travers les peuples.

On ne saurait donc être assez reconnaissant à tous ceux qui, comme vous le faites, tous, avec tant de conscience, prêtent leur concours dévoué à la diffusion du français.

En ce qui me concerne, je n'ai pas besoin de vous assurer que vous me trouverez toujours prêt à seconder de mon mieux votre travail et vos efforts.

La langue française, que vous enseignez, est demeurée la langue universelle, parce qu'elle est restée ce qu'elle était autrefois, parce qu'elle est, comme jadis, dans tous les pays, la langue de ce qui prétend à la clarté comme à la nuance.

Les services rendus par cette langue universelle sont incalculables, parce qu'elle est élégante, gracieuse et charmante, et qu'elle est apte, en même temps, à l'expression scientifique, à la délicatesse, à l'urbanité, à la douceur et à l'harmonie.

Que Dieu me garde de mettre dans l'ombre les autres langues, telles que la langue anglaise qui possède une si belle littérature, ou la langue allemande qui tient une des plus honorables places dans la science, dans la poésie et dans l'art, une langue avec laquelle on peut "Alles Vergöttern", comme on dit en allemand. De même pour les autres langues qui sont aussi belles et aussi puissantes que la langue française.

Mais la langue française a monopolisé, semble-t-il, par la force des éléments, l'expression de la spiritualité latine et de la beauté antique.

Le terrain que sa logique, sa probité et sa grâce lui ont conquis dans les siècles précédents, le français le défend aujourd'hui par sa précision, sa rectitude, son harmonie.

Le Chevalier Rivarol, littérateur français connu par son esprit, dans son célèbre discours disait déjà : "On demande souvent ce que c'est que le génie d'une langue," et il est difficile de le dire. Ce mot tient à des idées très composées ; il a l'inconvénient des idées abstraites et générales, on craint en le définissant de le généraliser encore.

Si, en Angleterre, vous consultez l'éminent philosophe et historien Bodley, vous l'entendez parler dans une communication à l'Institut Français "de la noble langue française, précieuse possession que vous avez héritée de vos aïeux... le plus bel organe pour l'expression des idées que le monde moderne ait connu...

Votre illustre compatriote, l'éminent savant Murray Butler, dans un discours à l'Académie Française déclare à son tour, "L'homme civilisé conserve soigneusement les modèles qu'il a créés. Le modèle de la langue française, dont vous êtes les conservateurs privilégiés, ce manteau si vrai de la pensée et de l'imagination d'un peuple, est un instrument merveilleux, si flexible, si juste, si riche, qu'il est capable de... etc..."

Un autre grand Américain, M. Théodore Perrin écrit : "Prenant la parole au sujet de la langue qui pourrait être adoptée comme étalon mondial, je demande la permission de proposer la langue française, car elle est, et probablement restera, le meilleur moyen de communication, grâce à la simplicité et à la précision de son vocabulaire de travail."

La France est le berceau des idées de pacification, justement parce que sa langue est devenue la manivelle des évènements et le ciment de rapprochement entre les peuples.

Avec le travail de vos prédécesseurs, chers Professeurs, et avec celui que vous poursuivez avec tant d'élégance et de charme, nous espérons que les générations de jeunes gens éduquées par vous et vos successeurs, seront assez fortes pour forcer l'union générale, afin d'écarter de l'avenir, tous les malentendus néfastes.

Le grand homme d'Etat français, Briand, a tracé l'avenir par Locarno — c'est à vous d'utiliser ce terrain dans l'intérêt du bien-être de la famille universelle.

Et soyez heureux d'être à même d'accomplir une si noble tâche.

Je ne saurais enfin terminer sans exprimer mes vœux les plus cordiaux pour la prospérité de la *Société Américaine des Professeurs de Français* et pour la grandeur de la Nation Américaine, comme en faveur de la fraternité qui nous a de tout temps unis, et qui en tout temps nous unira, pour le plus grand bien des idées de Paix, de Justice et de Liberté.

L'ÉTAT ACTUEL DE LA FRANCE[1]

Par ALBERT FEUILLERAT

Je suis quelque peu effrayé, en commençant, par la difficulté de la tâche que j'ai assumée. Lorsque par ce souci français de précision dont on vous a entretenu tout à l'heure, je téléphonai à votre Vice-Présidente pour savoir combien de temps je devais parler, et qu'à ma demande je reçus en réponse : vingt-cinq minutes, je devinai bien à la vivacité du ton avec lequel ces mots étaient lancés au bout du fil qu'on n'avait qu'une peur — c'est que je fusse trop éloquent. Je me rends compte qu'un programme est avant tout réglé par le temps, et vingt-cinq minutes, ce sera donc. Mais parler de l'état actuel de la France en vingt-cinq minutes, quelle gageure ! Et je me demande comment j'ai pu me lancer ainsi à la légère dans pareille aventure. Je croyais que l'audace était un privilège de la jeunesse : serais-je par hasard resté si jeune ?

Jamais, en effet, nation n'a eu à résoudre de problèmes plus graves et plus complexes. Voilà neuf ans que la guerre est finie et la paix est plus difficile que la guerre. Il y a eu pendant quatre ans une destruction effroyable, non seulement de choses matérielles, mais encore de vies humaines. Si la Pennsylvanie avait été bouleversée de fond en comble, si vos usines avaient été vidées de leurs machines, si vous aviez à recréer la puissance de cette région, quelle ne serait pas votre tâche ! Or le Nord de la France c'est notre Pennsylvanie, la partie la plus riche de notre pays, celle où se trouvent concentrées les plus puissantes de nos industries, à proximité de nos mines de charbon. Et nous avons eu à reconstruire cette région presque en entier. Treize cent mille hommes ont été tués, environ six ou sept cent mille sont mutilés ; au total deux millions d'hommes retranchés de la population française. Deux millions d'hommes en pleine force, car ils auraient aujourd'hui

[1] The following paper was read at the first annual meeting of the A. A. T. F. held at Hunter College, New York City, March 10, 1928. Mr. Feuillerat is Professor of English Literature at the University of Rennes and is this year Visiting Professor at Columbia University.

entre vingt-sept et quarante-cinq ans. Autant dire que la fleur de la nation a été emportée par la tourmente.

Cette destruction est à l'origine des difficultés au milieu desquelles nous nous débattons. Mais ce qu'il y a de plus tragique, c'est que les problèmes soulevés, déjà suffisamment graves en eux-mêmes, sont gros de répercussions et engendrent de nouveaux problèmes, à leur tour source de nouvelles difficultés. Vous avez parfois vu des enfants jeter des pierres sur un étang. Si la pierre est projetée selon un certain angle elle rase la surface liquide, rebondissant plus ou moins selon l'habileté de celui qui la lance. Cela s'appelle faire des ricochets. Ainsi en va-t-il des effets de cette abominable guerre. Ces effets ne sont pas seulement terribles dans leur portée immédiate, ils le sont peut-être encore davantage par ce qu'ils entraînent. Laissez-moi vous donner quelques exemples.

Prenons la question de la population. En 1911, sur 39.191.143 Français, on comptait 19.254.444 hommes et 19.937.689 femmes, soit environ six cent mille femmes de plus que d'hommes, proportion nullement inquiétante, extrêmement favorable même si l'on songe au surnombre de femmes que l'on constatait en Angleterre avant la guerre. Au recensement de 1921, sur une population de 38.797.540, il y avait 18.444.656 habitants du sexe masculin et 20.352.884 habitants du sexe féminin. C'est-à-dire qu'il y a en ce moment près de deux millions de femmes de plus que d'hommes, deux millions de femmes qui doivent renoncer à fonder un foyer, et dont un grand nombre remplacent les hommes dans des métiers pour lesquels elles ne sont pas faites. J'ai entendu certains Américains s'étonner que l'on confie nos tramways, par exemple, à des femmes. Mais nécessité fait loi ! Cela n'est pas normal, assurément, et le travail en souffre. Car je ne crois pas faire injure aux dames ici présentes si je constate que dans les emplois exigeant de la force musculaire les femmes ne rendent pas autant que les hommes. D'où une diminution considérable du pouvoir producteur de notre pays.

Voilà une première répercussion du mal initial. Mais cette conséquence a, à son tour, créé un autre problème : celui de la main d'œuvre étrangère. Pour suppléer au manque d'ouvriers, nous avons dû faire appel au surplus de population d'autres pays, l'Italie, la Pologne, l'Espagne, etc. Je n'ai pas de statistiques très récentes. Celles que j'ai sont d'ailleurs incomplètes, car il est difficile de suivre les immigrants dans toutes leurs pérégrinations. Nous avons en France cette idée que nous n'avons pas le droit d'attenter à la liberté des autres. Nous laissons entrer les étrangers trop facilement, ce qui rend le contrôle exact presque impossible. Quoiqu'il en soit, en 1926, d'après les rapports de la police, sur une population de 40.743.851 nous avions 2.498.230 étrangers contre 38.245.621 Français, proportion énorme et dangereuse. Car la plupart des travailleurs étrangers ne sont attirés que par l'appât du gain ; ils n'ont nullement l'intention de devenir citoyens de notre pays. Et l'argent qu'ils gagnent ils se hâtent de l'expédier dans leur pays d'origine si le change y est plus bas que le nôtre. Il en résulte que tous les ans des millions quittent la France, nous appauvrissant encore, à un moment où nous aurions, au contraire, besoin d'importer des capitaux.

Car notre situation financière, vous le savez, est des plus délicates. Voilà encore un des effets immédiats de cette destruction dont j'ai parlé au début. Nous avons dépensé pour la reconstruction des pays envahis près de cent milliards de francs. Dans ce gouffre nous jetons le peu qui reste de la fortune de la France. Et ce n'est pas fini. Ainsi l'appauvrissement du fait de la guerre se double du nouvel appauvrissement occasionné par la nécessité de réparer les pertes.

Pour trouver l'argent nécessaire nous avons eu d'abord recours à l'emprunt. On a retourné les poches des Français et nous y avons pris les quelques francs qui s'y trouvaient encore. Notre dette intérieure se monte à environ 150 milliards. Ces 150 milliards s'ajoutent aux 150 milliards que nous devons à l'étranger. Soit en tout trois cents milliards ! Si en 1913 on nous avait dit que nous pourrions être débiteurs de sommes aussi prodigieuses personne n'aurait voulu le croire. Nous estimions alors que notre dette qui ne dépassait guère cinq milliards était insupportable. Trois cents milliards de francs-papier cela équivaut à environ soixante milliards de francs-or, c'est-à-dire que notre dette actuelle est douze fois plus grande que notre dette d'avant guerre. Dette en vérité écrasante, qu'il faudra bien payer, que nous voulons payer. On a dit sur la question de nos dettes, aussi bien en France que dans ce pays, des choses regrettables. La France est composée d'honnêtes gens pour qui ne pas faire honneur à une signature serait la pire des hontes. Et à ce propos laissez-moi vous conter une anecdote, car elle me paraît en quelque sorte symbolique de cet état d'esprit du Français "moyen". J'ai connu un paysan d'une probité si entière qu'on l'avait surnommé "l'honnête Mathieu". Il était encore en pleine force quand il fut pris d'un mal qui ne laissa bientôt aucun espoir. L'homme le comprit et l'on vit sur l'oreiller son visage tanné se rembrunir. Etait-il tourmenté par l'idée de sa mort prochaine ? On le croyait et quelqu'un pour le rassurer lui dit: "Ne vous tracassez pas, père Mathieu, vous avez eu une si belle vie que vous êtes sûr d'aller en Paradis "! Et alors l'honnête Mathieu de répondre : "Je vas vous dire : j'ai récemment emprunté de l'argent et je n'ai pas de quoi le rembourser avant de m'en aller. Voilà ce qui m'attriste ". Et une pensée traversant subitement son lent cerveau, son visage s'éclaira d'un rayon d'espoir et il ajouta : "Dites-moi, oui, bien franchement... Croyez-vous que je pourrai payer cet argent de là-haut ?" Quand un pays est composé de pareilles gens il n'y a pas à avoir de doutes sur sa probité.

Nous avons encore essayé de combler le déficit par les impôts. En 1927 nous avions un budget de 40 milliards. Pour cette année, en raison de l'augmentation du coût de la vie, et malgré de sévères économies notre budget a été arrêté aux environs de cinquante milliards. Pour trouver ces cinquante milliards on s'adresse naturellement au contribuable que l'on soumet à un système de pressoir, à vis semble-t-il sans fin, et dont chaque tour est, je vous l'assure, extrêmement douloureux pour des gens dont les ressources sont le plus souvent réduites au minimum. On est déjà allé si loin que l'impôt atteint le point où il va cesser d'être productif. Selon une loi souvent constatée l'impôt excessif "se dévore lui-même". Un exemple entre mille. On a mis une taxe sur les mutations de propriétés. Toutes les fois qu'un immeuble change de main, l'acheteur doit payer au fisc 22 % de la valeur de la propriété. Résultat : la vente des immeubles a tellement diminué que cet impôt sur lequel on comptait beaucoup ne produit presque rien et l'on se demande si le mieux ne serait pas de le supprimer. Ces appauvrissements successifs ont à leur tour entraîné d'autres appauvrissements. C'est toujours cette suite de ricochets dont je vous ai parlé. Notre franc a perdu les quatre cinquièmes de sa valeur nominale. Et voilà peut-être le plus difficile des problèmes que nous ayons à résoudre. A vrai dire quelle que soit la solution adoptée elle sera détestable. Le gouvernement se trouve en face du plus angoissant des dilemmes ; et tout ce qu'il peut faire c'est de choisir entre deux maux. Ou bien il décrètera que le franc doit être stabilisé au taux actuel de vingt-cinq francs au dollar, c'est-à-dire qu'il décidera que dorénavant le franc ne vaudra plus que quatre sous au lieu de vingt. Et alors il consacre du même coup la ruine de tous les petits possédants, de ceux notamment qui ayant fait confiance à l'Etat français lui ont prêté des francs-or et devront abandonner 80 % de leur fortune. C'est une faillite morale. Ou bien pour tenir compte des droits de ces épargnants il revalorisera le franc et alors il bouleversera toute notre économie, mettra nos industries et notre commerce en péril : le réajustement des prix ne pourrait se faire qu'après de dangereuses convulsions au travers d'une longue période de chaos. Sans compter que par un phénomène inverse l'Etat français se trouverait chargé d'une dette fabuleuse. Car si les trois cents milliards de notre dette qui n'ont en ce moment qu'une valeur papier se trouvaient transformés par la revalorisation en milliards or ils constitueraient un fardeau écrasant pour la nation. On comprend que notre Grand Argentier hésite entre ces deux solutions. On nous dit : "Décidez-vous tout de suite". Cela est facile pour ceux qui n'ont pas de responsabilités ou raisonnent dans l'abstrait. Mais la vie d'un pays n'est pas réglée par des plus ou des moins ni par des signes algébriques. Il y a des réactions psychologiques, morales et sociales dont le gouvernement doit tenir compte et surtout qu'il doit prévoir.

La situation est donc difficile. Mais elle est loin d'être désespérée. Nous nous relèverons. La France a en elle un merveilleux pouvoir de récupération. Souvenez-vous de notre histoire. Que de fois nous avons été jetés à terre, piétinés ! Chaque fois on nous croyait abattus pour toujours et chaque fois nous nous sommes miraculeusement sauvés. Sans doute aucune de ces catastrophes dans le passé n'est comparable à la situation actuelle. Nous sortirons néanmoins de nos difficultés. Et déjà l'on peut voir des signes surprenants de notre redressement. Vous savez comment l'état de notre trésorerie, si inquiétant il y a un an et demi, s'est transformé du tout au tout. Notre gouvernement n'a plus d'appréhensions pour l'avenir immédiat. Cela ne veut pas dire que nous ayons surmonté tous les obstacles. Surtout ne nous laissons pas prendre à des apparences. Les étrangers qui visitent la France, voyant la vie normale reprendre, constatant surtout une circulation très active de la monnaie, s'écrient : "Mais la France est plus riche que jamais!" Comme je voudrais que ces étrangers eussent raison! Ce dont ils ne se rendent pas compte c'est que, en raison de la dépréciation du franc, les billets de banque sont anormalement nombreux. Mais tout cela c'est de la monnaie papier. La France, hélas! n'est pas plus riche d'un sou parce que des mesures intelligentes ont été prises pour préparer la voie du salut. Ce qui est vrai, c'est que notre trésorerie, c'est-à-dire l'administration qui règle pour l'Etat les dépenses courantes, est fort à l'aise. Par un procédé ingénieux nous avons pu acheter une quantité considérable de monnaies appréciées, — livres, dollars, couronnes, francs suisses, etc — qui constituent une masse de manœuvre permettant de déjouer les complots de la spéculation internationale contre le franc. En outre la dette flottante en Bons a été en partie transformée en annuités amortissables. L'Etat a déjà remboursé plusieurs des milliards avancés par la Banque de France. Nous sommes entrés à pleines voiles dans la période d'assainissement monétaire et les résultats obtenus sont si merveilleux qu'ils font l'étonnement du monde entier.

Nous sommes donc sur la bonne voie et nous gravirons les derniers kilomètres de la rude montée avec d'autant plus d'aisance que nous trouverons plus d'encouragements chez nos amis. Et c'est ici que vous pouvez prendre part à notre relèvement. Vous tous ici présents vous vous intéressez aux choses de France, vous aimez la France, pourrait-on dire, par définition. Répandez cet amour parmi vos élèves: soyez les artisans de la confiance. Que dans ce pays si beau et si puissant nous sentions partout des sympathies. Nulle affection ne nous est plus chère que la vôtre et de nous savoir soutenus par vous triplera notre fermeté. Ce que vous pouvez faire est indicible. Vous avez assisté parfois à cette scène, hélas! fréquente. Dans une chambre de malade un être tracassé par la souffrance lutte contre la mort. Et sur son front pâli se lit peut-être l'angoisse des ultimes incertitudes. Tout à coup une personne aimée entre dans la chambre et le malade se met à sourire, les couleurs remontent à ses joues, le désir de vivre reprend ses droits : c'est le miracle de l'amour ! Soyez la jeune sœur, pleine de vigueur et de santé qui, en se penchant sur le visage de la France encore gravement blessée, lui versera au cœur l'espoir et le courage.

QUELQUES RÉSULTATS OBTENUS
DANS UN COURS DE COMPOSITION AVANCÉE

Par Felix Weill

Le temps assigné à ma causerie étant limité, et l'heure déjà avancée, je ne m'attarderai pas à un long préambule. Je tiens cependant à remercier votre président, M. Downer, des paroles fort aimables qu'il a prononcées à mon égard, et à féliciter votre association de l'extension qu'elle a prise en si peu de temps et de l'intérêt que présente, au point de vue pédagogique et littéraire, sa publication périodique: The *French Review*. Je tiens également à vous dire que je suis de cœur avec vous : j'ai été un des premiers à adhérer à votre groupement comme j'ai été un des premiers à organiser, en 1904, la *Société des Professeurs Français en Amérique,* dont le président actuel, M. Zacharie, est présent parmi nous ce matin.

Cela dit, je passe à mon sujet. Il s'agit des résultats qu'il me semble avoir obtenus dans mes classes de composition au Collège de la Ville de New York. C'est donc de ma propre méthode que je m'aventure à parler, et c'est de quoi je veux m'excuser tout d'abord. Mais s'il est bon dans une société comme la nôtre d'exposer des théories générales et de présenter des statistiques impersonnelles, je crois qu'il est également utile de traiter des questions pratiques, et que chacun de nous dise à l'occasion ce qu'il a fait, ou, du moins, ce qu'il a tenté de faire, au cours de son enseignement.

J'avais été frappé, et je le suis encore, de l'incapacité presque générale où se trouvent des élèves ayant déjà deux, trois, et même quatre années d'études françaises, à construire une phrase correcte en français, à plus forte raison, à rédiger un simple récit de quelques lignes. J'en ai cherché les causes. La cause essentielle, qui est certes à l'honneur des maîtres de nos écoles, me paraît être le souci qu'ils ont de viser à la perfection. Ils veulent que leurs élèves sachent tout : toutes les formes des verbes, même les moins employées ; toutes les subtilités de la syntaxe, même celles qui ne sont jamais, ou rarement, observées par d'excellents écrivains français ; tous les mots du dictionnaire, alors qu'on peut s'exprimer correctement avec un vocabulaire limité ; toutes les expressions idiomatiques, même celles tombées en désuétude et qui ne sont que des curiosités linguistiques, à côté de celles de la langue la plus vulgaire, et qui ne sont que pur argot. Il est hors de doute cependant que le Français moyen — l'homme de la rue — parle et écrit sa langue sans connaître tous les verbes, sans se soucier des chinoiseries de la syntaxe, avec un vocabulaire souvent fort restreint, et avec un minimum d'expressions idiomatiques.

Vous me permettrez une comparaison. L'idéal du maître me paraît être trop souvent d'introduire ses élèves dans un magasin d'outils perfectionnés, dans un arsenal contenant des machines de précision délicates et compliquées, dont il prétend leur expliquer et leur apprendre le mécanisme. Je crois qu'avant de former un spécialiste, un ingénieur savant, il faut former un simple ouvrier, un bon charpentier, un bon maçon, et lui enseigner l'usage des instruments les plus ordinaires, lui apprendre à manier habilement les outils les plus communs. C'est en somme ce que je me suis proposé dans mon cours de composition : je ne cherche pas à produire des artistes, mais à faire de bons ouvriers.

Pour éviter tout malentendu, il me paraît nécessaire de préciser ici ce que j'entends par *composition*. Vous avez tous entre les mains des livres de composition. Ces livres, pour être franc, je ne les aime pas ; j'irai jusqu'à dire que je les ai presque tous en horreur, bien que j'admire la science de ceux qui les ont édités, et que je rende hommage à leur bonne volonté, à leur ingéniosité. Mais je trouve qu'ils font fausse route. Ces livres sont ce que nous appelons en bon français des livres de thèmes, instruments de torture pour les malheureux élèves, et parfois aussi pour les maîtres ; sauf pour ceux qui, paresseux de nature, trouvent le livre de composition un instrument admirable pour diminuer leur tâche, et se contentent d'écouter leurs élèves d'une oreille distraite et de corriger presque mécaniquement leurs traductions, grâce à un corrigé établi une fois pour toutes par eux-mêmes, quand il ne leur est pas fourni par l'auteur du livre.

Je ne suis pas partisan de la méthode directe absolue, mais la méthode du thème est assurément la plus indirecte, la plus ingrate qui soit, la moins productive de résultats permanents. C'est par cette méthode que nous avons étudié le grec et le latin ; ce n'est pas celle à employer pour enseigner une langue vivante. Je crois qu'au début des études, et pour un certain temps, il est essentiel de faire du thème afin d'enseigner les éléments de la grammaire. Je crois d'autre part qu'à la fin des études, il faut mettre les élèves avancés en présence de textes anglais et leur demander d'en tenter la traduction en français ; car c'est un travail profitable par l'étude des ressources variées des deux langues et la comparaison de leurs moyens d'expression.

Voici en substance ce que je dis à mes élèves au début du cours de composition : "Ce que je vous demande avant tout, c'est de faire, non de la traduction, mais de la composition directe en français. Je vous rappelle que la composition est à la fois l'art de penser et l'art d'écrire. Je n'ai pas la prétention de vous apprendre à penser, ni même à disposer les parties d'un travail écrit en un ordre logique ; cela viendra naturellement, il me semble, si vous vous inspirez des modèles sur lesquels j'appellerai successivement votre attention. Ce que je vous demande avant tout, c'est d'employer un langage simple, naturel, clair et correct. Je ne prétends pas vous enseigner l'élégance ; elle viendra peut-être par surcroît, si vous êtes bien doués".

Je leur dis aussi : "Jusqu'à présent vous n'avez fait que du travail passif. Vous avez lu des centaines, peut-être des milliers de pages de français. Vous avez, de gré ou de force, emmagasiné beaucoup de matériaux, mais un peu au hasard ; votre mémoire est encombrée de mots, de règles, et d'exceptions ; c'est un amas confus, mais qui sera pour vous d'une grande valeur, lorsque vous y aurez apporté un peu d'ordre. C'est à quoi je veux vous aider. Ce que je me propose de vous apprendre, c'est à faire bon emploi de ces matériaux qui sont déjà en vous, à les utiliser pour élever une construction qui tienne debout. Vous ne pourrez évidemment pas construire d'abord un grand édifice ; ce ne sera peut-être qu'une masure ; plus tard vous bâtirez une maison à plusieurs étages, puis, l'audace vous venant en même temps que l'expérience, vous réussirez à édifier un palais, à le décorer avec goût, avec style. Ce que je demande de vous, c'est de faire du travail, non plus passif, mais actif ; de faire un effort réel pour utiliser les matériaux que vous avez amassés en grand nombre et que vous possédez souvent sans en avoir conscience ; il est inutile d'en chercher d'autres. C'est pourquoi je vous interdis l'emploi du dictionnaire anglais-français. Si vous voulez vous assurer de l'orthographe d'un mot, ou même, s'il en est besoin, vérifier une forme verbale, ouvrez un dictionnaire tout entier en français, le seul qui doive être en permanence sur la table de l'élève, le Petit Larousse par exemple. Et maintenant, pour vous faciliter votre tâche, je vais vous lire un récit en français, que je vous demanderai de reproduire du mieux que vous pourrez".

Le point de départ de ma méthode est en effet l'imitation d'un modèle français choisi avec intention pour la simplicité du sujet et la parfaite logique du récit. Ce procédé assurément n'est pas nouveau ; il est universellement adopté pour l'enseignement de la composition dans la langue maternelle ; je l'ai simplement modifié pour ce même enseignement dans la langue étrangère.

Je lis ce premier récit avec soin, deux fois s'il le faut ; en m'abstenant naturellement de traduire, mais en soulignant la valeur et la précision des expressions ; je ne néglige pas, en passant, de faire remarquer la manière dont l'auteur a présenté son sujet. Pendant cette lecture, les élèves peuvent prendre des notes, et même interrompre pour demander une explication si quelque passage leur paraît obscur. Ils rédigeront leur composition, chez eux, à loisir.

A la classe suivante, je demande à l'un d'eux de lire son travail à haute et intelligible voix, et à ses camarades de suivre, le crayon à la main, afin de relever ce qui leur paraîtra digne de remarque, c'est-à-dire, d'éloge aussi bien que de blâme. J'en fais autant de mon côté. Cette première composition lue, elle est discutée, en français naturellement ; et je ne saurais assez insister sur l'utilité de cette critique orale au point de vue de la prononciation et aussi de la conversation. Il faut que l'élève qui lit sa composition se fasse comprendre, non seulement du maître, mais aussi de ses camarades, qui souvent sont plus difficiles à satisfaire que le maître ; il s'entraîne ainsi à mieux prononcer. La discussion qui suit présente les avantages d'une conversation naturelle. En passant, je dois dire que je ne crois pas aux cours de conversation proprement dits. Pour arriver à un bon résultat, il faut que la conversation porte sur des sujets qui intéressent directement les élèves, et c'est le cas quand on discute leur manière de s'exprimer et surtout leurs procédés de raisonnement.

Il est difficile de lire et de critiquer en classe plus de deux ou trois compositions. Je me réserve d'ailleurs quelques minutes à la fin de l'heure pour relever les fautes qui ont pu échapper aux élèves, et aussi pour donner quelques éloges, car il est bon d'encourager les élèves, quand l'occasion s'en présente. Je fais aussi, surtout au début du cours, une critique générale, qui porte sur les points que je considère essentiels, car d'année en année je retrouve dans les copies d'élèves les mêmes erreurs, si bien que je suis arrivé à instituer des mesures préventives pour en diminuer le nombre. Je suis persuadé en effet qu'on peut, et qu'il faut, enseigner aux élèves l'art de se corriger eux-mêmes. J'insiste par exemple sur la connaissance exacte de la valeur des modes et des temps. Les élèves ont souvent des idées peu nettes à ce sujet, surtout en ce qui concerne les temps du passé ; et malheureusement certains exercices dans ces livres de composition auxquels je faisais allusion tout à l'heure contribuent à donner aux élèves l'idée néfaste que les temps du passé sont interchangeables ; par exemple, quand on leur demande de mettre à l'imparfait tous les verbes qui, dans un texte donné, sont au passé défini ; ou inversement, ce qui n'est pas plus raisonnable. Par l'emploi de modèles spécialement choisis, qui présentent des exemples variés et frappants des temps et des modes, j'obtiens très vite des élèves qu'ils aient conscience de la valeur des formes verbales, et qu'ils écrivent selon une perspective exacte des différentes phases dans lesquelles se passe un récit.

Il y a d'autres mesures préventives à prendre, que je n'ai pas le temps d'énumérer. Je conseille par exemple de s'abstenir de phrases longues, et fais remarquer que la phrase courte est un bon moyen d'éviter maintes occasions de faire des fautes. Je critique l'emploi des vieux clichés qui se trouvent dans les textes étudiés dans les classes, mais qui ne sont plus de mise dans la langue d'aujourd'hui, et surtout l'usage d'expressions idiomatiques mal comprises, insuffisamment assimilées, qu'on enfile, comme on ferait des perles, pour éblouir le lecteur. Ces expressions ne s'enseignent pas au moyen de listes apprises par cœur. Elles s'acquièrent par la lecture, et, une fois assimilées, viendront naturellement sous la plume de l'élève.

Après la correction orale vient la correction par écrit. J'emporte chez moi les compositions des élèves, et je les corrige avec soin, sans ennui, et parfois avec enthousiasme. J'avoue en effet que lorsqu'il s'agit de lire une trentaine de fois le même thème ou la même version, où les mêmes fautes se répètent à satiété, le plaisir du maître est mélangé d'un peu de dégoût. Mais quand on lit des copies où les fautes ne se répètent pas identiques et où se manifeste souvent quelque originalité, l'intérêt persiste, et l'on résiste beaucoup plus facilement au sommeil. Tout en lisant je prends des notes, ayant soin de classer, sous des rubriques diverses, les fautes de même nature, afin de pouvoir, à la classe suivante, dire aux élèves : "Voici ce que j'ai trouvé ; je vous apporte le produit de ma chasse". Ces listes constituent ce que j'appelle mon "Musée des Erreurs" depuis l'année dernière, époque à laquelle a paru en France, sous ce titre, un livre amusant (de Curnonsky et Bienstock). J'ai mentionné ce livre à mes élèves, et l'un d'eux s'est empressé d'en transformer le titre ; il en a fait le "Musée des Horreurs". Erreurs ou horreurs, je demande à chacun des élèves de faire le relevé de celles dont il s'est rendu coupable, et que j'ai soulignées dans sa copie, afin de les éviter à l'avenir. Je les prie aussi de me remettre une édition revue et corrigée de chacune de leurs compositions, persuadé que je suis que ce n'est pas la quantité des sujets traités qui importe, mais la qualité du travail et le souci de la perfection. Très rapidement je note des progrès, parfois surprenants, non seulement en ce qui concerne la correction des formes grammaticales, la construction des phrases, mais aussi dans l'agencement général d'un récit, dans la présentation des faits ou des idées. Et à ce propos je me permets de mentionner que plusieurs de mes élèves m'ont informé que leur cours de composition française leur avait facilité leur tâche quand ils écrivaient en anglais. Et cela me rappelle une anecdote concernant le grand Arnauld. Quelqu'un lui demanda un jour ce qu'il fallait faire pour bien écrire en français. Arnauld répondit : "Lisez Cicéron. — Mais c'est en français que je veux écrire, non en latin. — Je vous entends, dit Arnauld; lisez Cicéron". Il en est de même de nos élèves ; la pratique de bons modèles français leur facilitera la composition en langue anglaise.

J'ajoute que les élèves s'intéressent à un cours organisé de la sorte. Preuve en est l'émulation qui règne parmi eux. C'est à qui écrira la composition la meilleure ; et je m'empresse d'ajouter que ce n'est pas pour obtenir une note élevée qu'ils font cet effort. En effet, je n'ai pas l'habitude de donner de notes pendant le semestre. Ce qui importe dans un travail de genre, c'est le point de départ et le point d'arrivée ; et ce n'est qu'à la fin du semestre que je puis apprécier la courbe des progrès, après avoir revu la série des compositions écrites par les élèves et constaté les différences entre les essais souvent piteux du début et la perfection relative des derniers efforts.

Le temps me manque pour indiquer ici les sujets que je choisis. Je ne m'en tiens pas à la reproduction d'un texte lu en classe. Peu à peu je permets à l'imagination des élèves de se donner libre cours, et, plus tard, je donne des sujets à développer, sous formes variées : lettres, dialogues, rapports, dissertations.

J'aurais voulu également vous soumettre quelques copies d'élèves ; j'en possède une collection assez étendue, car si j'ai un Musée des erreurs, ou horreurs, j'ai aussi formé un Musée, non pas de chefs d'œuvre, mais de souvenirs ; et le mot est plus juste que je ne croyais, car dans cette collection qui s'accroît d'année en année, j'ai retrouvé des compositions d'élèves disparus et aussi le compte rendu d'une conférence faite il y a quelques années, au Collège de la Ville de New-York par le Professeur Feuillerat, que nous avons l'honneur d'avoir parmi nous ce matin. Je pourrais encore lire à Mrs. Dickson, également présente ici, une appréciation d'élève sur les mérites de sa publication scolaire : Le Petit Journal.

Si les élèves me paraissent s'intéresser à leur travail de composition, y prendre un réel plaisir, ce plaisir est partagé par le maître, dont la satisfaction est grande, lorsqu'il trouve — et cela est fréquent — non seulement un travail consciencieux de la part de l'élève, mais aussi de l'originalité et de véritables promesses de talent. Dans cette collection que je mentionnais tout à l'heure j'ai remarqué en la feuilletant, que, parmi les compositions que j'ai conservées, il y a celles de jeunes gens qui sont aujourd'hui professeurs dans les High Schools de New-York, et dont quelques-uns sont mes collègues au Collège de la Ville. Je suis heureux d'avoir été un des premiers à reconnaître leur valeur, d'avoir encouragé et facilité dans une certaine mesure leurs efforts méritoires pour se perfectionner en français, et d'avoir contribué à faire d'eux les excellents maîtres qu'ils sont aujourd'hui. C'est peut-être le plus beau résultat dont puisse se vanter un professeur.

College of the City of New York

LE CENTENAIRE DE JULES VERNE

Par Robert Fouré

On vient de fêter, en France, le centenaire de Jules Verne. C'est à Nantes qu'il vit le jour; c'est à Amiens qu'il est venu se fixer et qu'il a achevé son existence. Tout l'invitait à vivre à Paris, notamment la défense de ses intérêts de librairie et de théâtre. C'est un fait bien connu que, lorsqu'ils n'aiment pas les cités trop bruyantes, c'est dans leur ville natale ou en pleine campagne que les hommes voués à des travaux sédentaires vont généralement planter leur tente, la jeunesse envolée. Qu'est-ce donc qui attira Jules Verne vers Amiens, vers cette Picardie qu'il aima tant? La réponse est simple, quoique bizarre. Etudiant à la faculté de droit de l'Université de Paris, Jules Verne fut invité comme garçon d'honneur à un mariage, à Amiens. Il tomba amoureux de sa demoiselle d'honneur. C'est cette affection brusquement éclose qui devait retenir le jeune homme sur les bords de la Somme. L'amour lui avait choisi sa petite patrie dans la grande. Il y voulut vivre et mourir. Et c'est aux Amiénois qu'il a légué le soin de veiller sur ses cendres.

On aurait beaucoup étonné, il y a quelque trente ans, les Américains de passage dans la cité picarde si on leur avait dit, en leur désignant le bon bourgeois qui se promenait sur les boulevards ou dans ces délicieux jardins qui sont la fierté d'Amiens: C'est Jules Verne.

Jules Verne, ce bon vieillard, qui s'en allait d'un pas tranquille, pensant et rêvant sans doute, mais pensant au cours de la Bourse et rêvant de quelque partie de chasse ou de pêche bien plus qu'aux audacieuses aventures dont ses livres sont remplis. Jules Verne, cet homme d'aspect si modeste et qui jouissait d'une gloire quasi universelle? Jules Verne en personne. Et on eût bien d'avantage étonné les étrangers en leur révélant que Jules Verne, membre de l'Académie d'Amiens, président des Rosati Picards, ne manquait aucune réunion de ces sociétés distinguées; que Jules Verne, membre du Conseil municipal d'Amiens, était exact à toutes les séances du conseil et qu'il y présentait, sans se croire le moins du monde diminué, des rapports qui n'avaient qu'un intérêt tout local ; que Jules Verne, enfin, le soir venu et sa tâche quotidienne achevée, s'asseyait volontiers, entre quatre ou cinq amis de choix, pour faire une honnête partie de cartes, au Café Dufourmantelle, de la rue des Trois Cailloux, établissement traditionnel que les obus et les bombes détruisirent en 1917. Mais alors "*Vingt mille lieues sous les mers, Les Enfants du capitaine Grant, Cinq semaines en ballon, De la terre à la lune, Michel Strogoff*", et tant d'autres ouvrages célèbres et lus pourtant, il les avait composés sans courir le monde, sans se mêler si peu que ce fût à tant d'entreprises étranges et magnifiques ! Mais, oui ! Son cabinet de travail lui suffisait. Son imagination si diverse faisait le reste. Sa documentation aussi, car il ne faudrait pas croire que Jules Verne fût un conteur qui ne demandait rien à sa fantaisie. Imagination, documentation, ainsi procédait Jules Verne dont la vogue n'a pas diminué, encore que certaines de ses "anticipations" aient perdu quelque peu de leur attrait, étant devenues les réalités du jour après n'avoir été que le paradoxe de la veille. L'obus des monstrueux canons allemands, ces horribles Berthas, ne porte certes pas encore jusqu'à la lune ; mais nous savons — et trop douloureusement — qu'il porte beaucoup plus loin qu'on ne l'aurait supposé il y a seulement vingt ans, que dis-je ? qu'on ne le supposait jusqu'en mars 1918. Aucun aéronaute encore n'est resté cinq semaines en ballon ; mais Linbergh, et d'autres après lui ont franchi l'Océan d'un seul bond. D'autres aviateurs, tels les capitaines Costes et Lebrix, ont bouclé, ou presque, le tour du monde en moins de quatre-vingts jours. Aucun sous-marin n'a fait jusqu'ici un voyage de vingt mille lieues; mais les longues croisières n'effraient pas les équipages des submersibles. Ce jovial journaliste Jolivet ne pourrait plus dire aujourd'hui : "Le télégraphe est coupé" ; il se servirait de la T. S. F. (télégraphie sans fils). L'œuvre du grand imaginatif n'a donc plus tout à fait ce caractère "d'exploration dans l'inconnu" — on disait même au temps où elle était publiée : "dans l'impossible" — qui a tant contribué à son succès. Elle n'en vaut pas moins comme le témoignage des fièvres et des inquiétudes d'une époque, et si elle ne gardait d'innombrables lecteurs en dépit des inévitables injures du temps, ne devrait-on pas la considérer encore comme annonciatrice?

Cyrano de Bergerac, qui ne fut qu'un écrivain très ordinaire, est admiré pour son extravagant beaucoup plus que chimérique voyage dans la lune. Charles Perrault, dont on fêtait dernièrement le troisième centenaire, doit une gloire durable à ses contes d'enfants qui ne sont guère cependant que de faux chefs-d'œuvre. Ce n'est pas être trop exigeant que de demander pour Jules Verne un meilleur rang dans l'admiration des hommes. Il a amusé et bercé plusieurs générations. Il a été pour un certain nombre de jeunes hommes un véritable initiateur. Combien, en effet, ont puisé dans ses ouvrages le goût de l'action et de la recherche ! Et même s'il n'avait été que l'auteur qui nous a fait accomplir de beaux voyages à sa suite n'aurait-il pas droit encore, le bon, le charmant Jules Verne, à la plus chaude estime et à une infinie gratitude?

On lui reproche parfois d'avoir manqué de ce qui rend la gloire littéraire durable : le style. Mais Charles Perrault, dont je viens de parler, en a-t-il donc mis beaucoup, de style, dans ses contes d'enfants ? Pourtant la Fontaine "prenait un plaisir extrême" à la lecture de Peau d'Ane. Et, comme la Fontaine, ne peut-on trouver un heureux délassement dans la lecture des romans "extraordinaires", même quand on a des cheveux grisonnants et qu'en fait d'aventures, on ne peut plus avoir que le recours de celles qu'on n'a pas courues ? Jules Verne, au surplus, ne voulait pas être qu'un simple amuseur. Son ambition était certainement de servir la science dans laquelle il avait une foi absolue. Et il y a vraiment beaucoup d'injustice et une certaine puérilité dans l'attitude des savants qui lui reprochent de n'avoir rien prévu. Accordons-leur, s'ils y tiennent que Jules Verne n'a pas "annoncé" expressément la navigation aérienne, la navigation sous-marine, la télégraphie avec ou sans fils, ni tant d'autres applications de la science dont nous ne nous émerveillons plus depuis qu'elles sont devenues d'un usage courant. D'autres, à ce point de vue, ont été plus prophètes que lui, au sens qu'on donne communément à ce mot. Mais ils n'ont été que des visionnaires plus ou moins perspicaces et plus ou moins inspirés. Tandis qu'il a été, un réalisateur, j'entends qu'il ne s'est pas borné à affirmer qu'un jour, par exemple, l'homme voguerait sous l'eau comme les poissons, mais il nous l'a montré explorant déjà les profondeurs marines. C'est là sa grande qualité personnelle. Je me rappelle comme il nous mettait en confiance, quand nous étions jeunes, au lycée, dès les premières lignes de ses livres. Entraînés à la suite de ses personnages, nous avions bientôt l'impression, non pas que cela pourrait bien arriver quelque jour, mais que "c'était arrivé". H. G. Wells, qui le continue en Angleterre et qui est lui-même un grand imaginatif, avec beaucoup d'idées profondes ou simplement hardies, y compris quelques idées fausses, est loin de nous donner semblable sécurité. Son domaine, d'ailleurs, est plus vaste que celui de Jules Verne : Wells est avant tout, derrière le décor ultra-merveilleux de ses récits, un psychologue, un moraliste et un réformateur. Mais comme Jules Verne a su, tout en circonscrivant volontiers son propre domaine, l'animer, le peupler, et, sans sortir du possible, nous découvrir tout ce qu'il nous cachait encore et que nous tenions précisément pour impossible !

Là est son grand mérite et, peut-on dire, sa marque personnelle. Venu à une époque où la littérature avait exploité à peu près tous les genres et où le roman d'aventures brillait d'un éclat qu'il n'avait jamais eu, il a jeté le roman d'aventures dans une voie qu'il n'avait pas explorée : il l'a renouvelé. Cela lui a valu d'enchanter plusieurs générations d'hommes, et c'est un titre à la reconnaissance des générations qui sont venues après celles-là. Qui sait, d'ailleurs, si elles ne lui doivent pas beaucoup, et un peu plus qu'elles ne pensent ? On prétend qu'elles sont romantiques dans une certaine mesure, mais romantiques autrement qu'on ne l'était en 1830. Ne le seraient-elles pas à la manière de Jules Verne, qui semble bien avoir discerné que si l'esprit lui-même a ses frontières, elles sont du moins assez larges pour qu'il découvre encore de nouvelles joies et de nouveaux moyens d'action sous le double signe de la science et de la raison.

Ohio State University.

ITEMS FROM FRANCE

By Harry Kurz

The Dearth of Teachers in France

The papers frequently publish lists of places in lycées that are not filled by men. There was recently much commotion over the fact that the students in *première* at the lycée of Puy had not had any Latin or Greek since the opening of sessions in October, because there was no agrégé available for the post. There is also a vacancy in German. The problem of carrying on the work in classics has been solved temporarily by dividing the work among three already overburdened teachers. The situation is worse at the lycée of Saint-Brieuc where there is no agrégé available for four posts in languages, two in history, and three in mathematics. All this work is being carried by substitutes. Even in a large city like Rouen, a post in history recently vacated by an agrégé, had to be filled by a "délégué."

An Anti-classicist

M. Gustave Hervé in his paper "La Victoire", declares that times have changed as well as men and insists that the old classics—Latin and Greek—while useful formerly, are not at all necessary to-day to train men and women. His diatribe has this significant paragraph:

"Mais aujourd'hui, où l'on peut trouver pour les Humanités modernes un personnel de professeurs aussi distingué que pour les Humanités anciennes et où laissés à eux-mêmes, les sujets d'élite vont aussi volontiers aux Humanités modernes qu'aux Humanités anciennes, qui peut assurer que l'enseignement classique donne de meilleurs fruits que le moderne?"

L'Anglais tel qu'on le parle

On the Champs Elysées with its perfumeries, automobile stores, and modistes, there are more signs worded in English than French. "Afternoon dress" vies with "evening dress". "Smoking" for tuxedo is the universal term. I saw "mantles" for manteaux, which sounds odd. "Latest creation" is a hybrid frequently met. "Smart Tailor" abounds. A night restaurant near the Place Pigalle has dubbed itself "Elite's Rendez-vous", apostrophe and all. "Trench coats" are still in evidence of the war, also "Rushian Coat". M. André Fribourg, deputy from Aix, has proposed half seriously to tax signs in English—an annual duty of 1 franc for each letter. If this goes through, signs in English will multiply—but what English? Not certainly, as she is spoke chez nous.

ITEMS FROM FRANCE

Foreign Students at the Sorbonne

The following percentages are informal but sufficiently accurate.
50% of the foreign students are Americans.
20% " British

The majority of the remainder come from Germany, Scandinavia, China and Japan. There has been a falling off in registrants from the central European states. Perhaps owing to the recent official efforts at rapprochement between France and Italy, there has been a notable increase in the numbers coming from Italy.

Most of the Americans are college graduates pursuing work that will help them in home universities. The groups from the University of Delaware and from Smith College, all undergraduates, are prosperous and hard-working. Every American student here feels a current of friendly welcome and interest inviting him to the various university centers.

An Odd Contrast

In America, the parents may complain that the high schools do not exact enough intellectual labor from their children and overemphasize athletics, manual occupations, and social relationships. Two French fathers have recently written letters to the *Figaro* in which they express sentiments probably totally unknown to-day to American fathers.

One writes: Ma fillette ne connaît pour ainsi dire plus le délassement des jeudis et des dimanches. Elle néglige la musique, car le piano lui prendrait trop le temps, et je suis stupéfait bien souvent par la difficulté des questions qu'on lui pose et qui embrassent tantôt tous les ordres de connaissances.

The other writes: Mon fils est demi-pensionnaire. Tous les soirs, malgré les heures d'étude, il rentre à la maison chargé de devoirs et de leçons, et veille fort tard. Bien souvent, il aurait plaisir à sortir avec sa mère et moi. Mais il lui faut rester à travailler.

The hue and cry in educational editorials is that the "programmes sont trop chargés." A serious effort will eventually result to find out what might be termed the useless baggage in the curriculum and to discard it. It is safe to say that the next few decades will see many changes in French elementary and secondary instruction. The emphasis, however, will never be removed in France from where it belongs—namely the training of the faculties of the mind—first and foremost—in the educational process. The French lycée to-day is still the institution where the best secondary instruction in the world can be found.

Knox College.

VARIA

By J. F. Mason

In *School and Society* of Feb. 18, 1928, Professor B. G. Morgan of the University of Wisconsin, Editor-in-Chief of the *Modern Language Journal,* has written an excellent defense of the study of modern foreign languages in the article entitled, *The Place of Modern Foreign Language in the American High School.* Mr. Morgan gives us a résumé of all the best arguments in favor of retaining the instruction of modern foreign languages in our curricula. While we teachers of French are only too ready to admit all that Mr. Morgan brings forth in support of our subject, we should do well to read and assimilate this article, in order that we may use its arguments when confronted by those who wish to drop modern foreign languages from the high school.

Mr. Morgan, in conclusion, gives three separate and important grounds for justifying the study of the modern foreign languages in the high school curriculum. "First, foreign language mastery is a skill which is a professional requirement for a considerable percentage of our high school graduates, and calls for a training which the high school can give better than any other part of our educational system. Second, the study of foreign language is particularly adapted to promote proficiency in skills which are involved in many other high school and college branches. Third, a knowledge of a foreign language contributes in an unusual degree to the making of internationally-minded, broad-thinking, intellectually resourceful and contented citizens."

"In defending our subject, therefore, against the attacks which have been rather freely directed against us of recent years, we language teachers may justly feel that we are not only serving the best interests of the secondary schools, as well as of the pupils enrolled in them, but also of the nation in whose life they are being prepared to participate."

* * *

Dr. L. A. Wilkins, Director of Foreign Languages of the high school of New York City, has supplied us with the following statistics:

Enrollment in foreign languages in the senior high schools of New York City:

	French	German	Greek	Italian	Latin	Spanish	Total
March, 1927	42,709	6,438	188	1,593	27,289	32,244	110,224
October, 1927 ...	43,964	6,602	180	1,606	27,399	30,411	110,162
February, 1928 ..	47,200	7,388	201	1,743	28,077	31,251	115,860

VARIA

Mr. Jacob Greenberg, Director of Foreign Languages in Junior High Schools of New York City, has given us similar statistics for the junior high schools of New York City.

	French	German	Italian	Latin	Spanish	Total
March, 1927	26,943	229	745	3,708	4,809	36,434
October, 1927	27,915	511	843	3,235	4,737	37,241
March, 1928	29,213	907	968	3,687	4,880	39,655

Statistics of this sort perhaps mean little without considerable explanation as to distribution, ratios, etc., but all teachers of modern foreign languages who retain a modicum of linguistic idealism will be glad to learn that there are still five high schools in New York City teaching Greek.

* * *

The *German Quarterly,* the official organ of the American Association of Teachers of German, has published its first two numbers which contain a number of very interesting articles. In the first issue Professor R. H. Fife, in wrting on *Some new paths in teaching German,* insists upon a fundamental truth which all of us should constantly remember: "The modern language teacher cannot take as his first ideal a greater number of pupils in French, German or Spanish, but better pupils and better opportunities to achieve something with those whom he has." To German teachers who sigh for the ante-bellum days, Mr. Fife says: "Much time and energy has been wasted in bemoaning the loss of the former position of German studies which after all had many illogical aspects, some of them actually harmful to American education."

Mr. Fife points out the importance of prognosis in the solution of American secondary school problems. "From this standpoint the attitude of a great many Latin teachers undoubtedly rests on a fallacy, the historical illusion, nourished most actively in the South and Central West, that every secondary school pupil should study Latin." In this connection it is interesting to note how little importance the Classical Investigation gave to the question of prognosis.

Mr. Fife concludes with advice which we should all take to heart. "It may safely be said at the present time that nothing in the teaching of modern foreign languages is fixed. The greatest need, especially for the German teacher, is to keep an open mind for the new and to experiment intensively in order to find new ground."

The second number contains a symposium on *Shall German be taught in our high schools?* Governors, college presidents, lawyers, editors, bishops and archbishops, actresses and men of affairs, etc., speak more or less strongly in favor of restoring German to the high schools. The important question, however, is not that of German but rather of the right of the public to make a snap judgement in regard to an educational matter. It was most unfortunate from every point of view that German should have been so quickly withdrawn from the high school curriculum for such specious reasons. The public must recognize that curricula should be altered only upon advice of the specialist.

* * *

Professor E. C. Hills of the University of California has called our attention to the following interesting quotation taken from an article of the well known Italian scholar, Guglielmo Ferrero, in the *Illustration* of February 11, 1928.

"Le monde est plein d'étranges contradictions. Autrefois, dans les classes supérieures de toute l'Europe, nombreux étaient ceux qui savaient le latin et aimaient lire, dans le texte original, les écrivains de Rome. Aujourd'hui, le latin n'est plus connu que de ceux qui font profession de l'enseigner. Parmi leurs élèves, il n'en est pas un sur mille qui, ses études finies, n'oublie tout ce qu'il a appris et qui serait capable de lire une page de Cicéron ou une ode d'Horace. C'est ce qui explique pourquoi on publie depuis un certain temps tant de nouvelles traductions des auteurs anciens, avec ou sans texte. C'est la dernière chance qu'ont encore ces écrivains de demeurer dans la circulation intellectuelle.

"On peut discuter si l'étude des langues classiques est utile ou non: mais le débat est superflu parce que les étudiants des deux mondes ont déjà résolu le problème d'une manière définitive. Ils étudient encore le latin et le grec dans la mesure où les programmes les y obligent, mais ils ne les apprennent plus. C'est la suppression des études classiques réalisée par en bas."

Teachers of modern foreign languages should always remember that the fate of Greek and Latin may come to their sujects as well, and it is only by holding the interest of the pupil thru excellent teaching that we can retain the modern foreign languages in the high school. The unprogressive teacher who does not keep abreast of all the developments in his field has no right to complain if his pupils desert him.

* * *

In the January-March number of *La Revue de Littérature comparée* (vol. VIII, no. 1) we can see how close is the relationship between France and the United States. The entire number is given over to our country and a group of eminent scholars, both French and American, have contributed very interesting articles on such topics as Franklin et Mirabeau collaborateurs, Chateaubriand et la littérature des Etats-Unis, le Suicide de Prévost-Paradol à Washington et l'opinion américaine, l'Initiation américaine de Georges Clémenceau. Teachers of French must never fail to point out to their pupils how many evidences France has given us of her friendship not only in the nineteenth and twentieth centuries but also in the eighteenth when we, as a struggling young nation, needed both sympathy and assistance.

VARIA

All teachers of French who are constantly seeking new methods of presenting the drier aspects of paradims and formal grammar will welcome this suggestion from *Les Nouvelles Littéraires* of March 31, 1928.

"Une institutrice des Vosges apprend à ses élèves la grammaire par la dance. Le thème étant par exemple l'indicatif, chaque élève représente un temps de ce mode. Le 'présent', l'"imparfait', le 'passé simple' et le 'futur' donnent le bras à une compagne désignée d'avance qui figure le temps composé correspondant.

—Présent, avancez dit l'institutrice.

Le 'présent' s'avance en chantant: 'Qui prenez-vous pour cavalier!'

—Le 'passé composé', dit le 'présent'. Le 'passé composé' s'avance en chantant; 'J'ai chanté, tu as chanté . . .' Les couples s'unissent, se déunissent. Voilà un système auquel Lhomond n'a pas pensé."

Molière's famous "Maître à danser" of *Le Bourgeois Gentilhomme* extolled the art of dancing, showing how useful it was to statesmen and generals to prevent them from making a "faux pas"—"Sans la danse, un homme ne saurait rien faire"—but he apparently overlooked this Terpsichorean method of teaching French grammar.

* * *

To students and teachers of French who should be interested in any manifestation of the French genius, we strongly recommend a visit to the Ile de France of the French Line which offers one of the finest examples of contemporary French decorative art that we know. A card of admission, free of charge, may be secured at Pier 57, New York City, whenever the ship is in dock.

* * *

Henry Holt & Co., the well-known publishers of New York City, are to be congratulated upon their new venture, the publication of *Foreign Language News,* the first number of which appeared in January and the second in April. It serves not only to advertise most attractively the publications of Henry Holt & Co. in the modern language field but also gives space to news of interest to modern foreign language teachers.

In the April number, for example, we find some very interesting information under the following titles: American Students in France, Writers wintering on the French Riviera, The Three Musketeers have an anniversary, A Memarial to Anatole Le Braz, etc.

The *Foreign Language News* is sent free of charge to teachers upon application to Henry Holt & Co., New York City, and additional copies are furnished to any who wish to distribute them among their students.

RECENT TEXTS

WOODBRIDGE, Benjamin M.—*La Semeuse.* The University of Chicago Press, Chicago, Illinois, 1928, xiv-182 pages. Price $1.50

Professor Woodbridge's *La Semeuse* is the final volume of the University of Chicago Junior College Series in French. It is intended to be "the logical conclusion of a course that visualizes the ability to read French as a major aim." It has been compiled for the use of second year college French classes or for the advanced course in modern French literature.

One might differ with the editor of the series as to the adaptability of the text to courses in modern French literature; the reader lacks too many important names to be considered an anthology of modern French literature: Flaubert, Zola, Baudelaire, Verlaine, Hérédia, Mallarmé, Becque, etc., are not represented in it by selections. But whereas the value of this new reader as a representative anthology is questionable, it is no doubt an excellent guide to modern French civilization. Professor Woodbridge must be congratulated on his good taste by which he was led in the selection of the texts: Maeterlinck, Hugo, Sully Prudhomme, A. Daudet, France, Leconte de Lisle, Lemaître, Hémon, Lamartine, Chateaubriand, Michelet, Rostand, Balzac, Vigny, Renan, Sand, and others have been chosen as interpreters of the French mind. Prose and poetry have been used in a well-balanced ratio in the reader, which, thus, has become an ideal anthology for advanced college students. The two eighteenth century selections might have been omitted for the sake of unity, and the value of the work would have been enhanced by some systematic grouping of the texts.

Every selection is followed by exercises, all arranged according to the same principles throughout the whole work, and thus likely to prove somewhat monotonous in the classroom. They consist of drill in idioms, English sentences to be translated into

French, and brief questionnaires. The notes are scanty, perhaps too scanty for the taste of many instructors. Slang and patois forms and expressions have frequently been explained in the texts themselves, a device which is likely to break up the unity of the texts. The note on *je die* (p. 43) is inadequate: "on dit en prose *dise",*— the form *je die* is archaic, whether used in prose or poetry; *adorner* (p. 103) is not French; *beaucoup des auteurs* (p. 37) stands for *beaucoup d'auteurs.* A brief note in French points out the literary qualities of every author quoted. Although these notes are too concise, they are suggestive and will certainly stimulate the student. From the note on Sand, it is hard to guess that the "*grand romancier*" (p. 113) was a woman; "*femme romancier*" (p. 50) evidently means *romancière; "emporter* de *grand succès*" (p. 69) should be "*remporter de grands succès.*" The vocabulary is exact and complete. A few errors could have easily been avoided: *Buter* means "to stumble," and not "to reach one's goal"; *cramponnez-vous* (p. 148) is a popular expression, meaning "do not stagger," and not "to fix attention"; *hurluberlu* means rather "madcap" than "unconventional." *La belle avance, sentence* — "maxim", — *mâtin, éventuel, métier* — "technique", — *messire, bistro,* are not found in the vocabulary, and are not explained in the texts either.

A number of misprints have remained uncorrected; especially, the accent marks have been treated rather carelessly. Only the most important ones should be noted: on p. 24, the plural of *chef-d'œuvre* is spelled with a final s; on p. 24, *dimanche* is treated as a feminin noun; "abbreviation" should be spelled with one *b* in French (p. XIV); it is difficult to recognize the name of Shakespeare from the disfigured spelling on p. 43; *mélancolique* (pp. 44 and 53) is spelled without *h* in French. These exceptions are, however, insignificant details in view of the fact that *La Semeuse* is one of our best French readers available at present for college students. In a second edition, it might be advisable to replace the present illustrations by others, preferably reproductions of the works of French artists.

Arpad Steiner.

Marquette University.

FRANCE, Anatole. *Abeille et Autres Contes,* with Notes, Direct-Method Exercises and Vocabulary by George Neely Henning. D. C. Heath & Co., 1927, v-260 pages.

About four years ago Professor Henning achieved the distinction of presenting the first important American edition of Anatole France selections, in the organization of which he was obviously appealing to the advanced student. Professor Henning now offers a second collection of France stories which apparently is intended to reach a less scholarly level of students. Curiously enough, more than half of the latter duplicates material (the story *Abeille*) found in the earlier volume. It is only fair to state, however, that the notes applying to *Abeille* have been re-written in order to give greater stress to grammatical constructions and idioms—a preoccupation conspicuously less present in the notes to the other stories in the new book.

Anatole France is recognized as being of fairly difficult access to the average undergraduate, and unfortunately the stories of this latest edition—gleaned mainly from collections of the pre-Dreyfus France—are less famous and less strikingly representative of the mature author than the stories of Professor Henning's first choice. Therefore we venture to question the unqualified success of the book among the very students for whom it seems to have been designed.

The book is edited according to the recognized text-book ritual of the day; ample exercises are provided for practice in conversation, grammar and composition, although the subject matter and vocabulary of many selections lend themselves rather awkwardly to practical oral work and composition.

Aside from *Abeille,* the book includes the following stories: *Les Blattes; La Caution; Les Pains Noirs; L'Aube; La Fée* (extract from *Le Crime de Sylvestre Bonnard*); *Histoire des Trois Chevaliers d'Eppes; Les Contes de Maman; Jessy.*

B. R. JORDAN.

Duke University

BIBLIOGRAPHY

TEXT BOOKS

CHINARD, G. *Petite Histoire des lettres françaises.* Ginn and Co., 1927, viii—328 pp. Price $1.48.

GRAEME RITCHIE, R. L. *A First Book of French Poetry.* Thomas Nelson and Sons, 1927, xxi-198 pp. Price $1.00

A Second Book of French Poetry. Thomas Nelson and Sons, 1927, ix-144 pp.

HUISMAN, M. and G. *Contes et Légendes du Moyen Age français.* Edited by Hélène Harvitt and Julien J. Champenois. Charles E. Merrill and Company, 1928, x-212 pp. Price $0.96.

LEMERCIER, Nepomucène. *Christophe Colomb.* Edited with Introduction, Notes and Vocabulary by Charles Grimm. The Century Company, 1928, xix-114 pp. Price $0.90.

WILSON, F. B. *French Humor.* Edited with Exercises and Vocabulary. Ginn and Company, 1928, v-140 pp. Price $0.80.

PEDAGOGICAL ARTICLES

LEAUTIER, Marie Louise. *Secondary Education in France.* The High School Teacher, March, 1928, pp. 98-103.

REINHARDT, Emma. *French Textbooks used in Secondary Schools.* The Modern Language Journal, Vol. XII, No. 6, March, 1928, pp. 446-450.

FOREIGN PUBLICATIONS

Articles

DUNCAN, Isadora. *La rencontre de la Duse et de Gordon Craig.* Nouvelle Revue Française, Mars, 1928, pp. 372-377.

MAUDOUL, Jean. *L'Amitié franco-américaine.* La Grande Revue, Fév. 1928, pp. 643-650.

VALLÉE, Gustave. *Les Etats-Unis d'aujourd'hui.* La Grande Revue, Fév., 1928, pp. 629-642.

Books

ANTOINE, André. *Mes Souvenirs sur le Théâtre Antoine et sur l'Odéon.* (première Direction). Grasset, 1928.

BAUCHE, H. *Le langage populaire.* Payot, 1928.

CARRÉ, J.-M. *Les Deux Rimbaud.* Cahiers libres, 1928.

DURTAIN, Luc. *Hollywood dépassé.* Nouvelle Revue Françaís, 1928.

Encyclopédie de l'Education. Editions du Loup. Vol. I, April, 1928.

French-English, English-French Dictionary. Larousse, 1928.

JOLAS, Eugène. *Anthologie de la nouvelle poésie américaine.* Kra, 1928.

SILAINE, Gabriel. *William Dixon et son Amour.* Calmann-Lévy, 1928.

TREICH, Léon. *Histoires américaines.* Nouvelle Revue Française, 1928.

THE FRENCH TEACHER'S FORUM

THE CLASSICS NOT TO BE READ IN HIGH SCHOOL

In our first number we proposed the following resolution: Resolved that students in our High Schools are not sufficiently advanced to read with profit the French classics of the seventeenth century such as Corneille, Racine and Molière. If we are to judge from comments received, the opinion of our teachers is decidedly in favor of the resolution: 62% of our correspondents believe that the classics should not be taught; only 25% are against the resolution; and the rest either take no definite position or make an exception in favor of Molière. The Forum has already published in former issues of *The French Review* certain communications typical of the various points of view received up to that time. We add the following which takes up the question from an angle not yet represented:

Dear Mr. Editor:

It would not occur to anyone to give a course on the French classics to students who have not had a preliminary survey of French literature. Corneille, Racine and Molière represent some of the culminating peaks in the living chain of French literary history. To get used to their pure but rarefied atmosphere, students require a preliminary journey through the less arduous and, to the mind of the modern American youth, more pleasant and more frequented hills and dales of modern and contemporary French works. The classics represent the essence of the French spirit purified to its highest degree. We cannot expect students in High Schools to understand and appreciate it without a preliminary initiation into its secrets. Even if they had the taste for it, it is doubtful if they could assimilate it outright. Neither linguistically, nor spiritually are they prepared to do so. The ability to read French with the aid of a dictionary is not a sufficient garanty of this. Hence students should first become acclimated to French civilization by frequenting the more accessible great and near great of modern French literature. They will then be better prepared to enter the treasure-house of the spirit when they get to college.

Sincerely yours,

S. A. RHODES.

Rice Institute.

CLERICAL WORK BY TEACHERS

In our last issue we quoted the complaint of a teacher who stated that in her school half of a teacher's time was taken up with clerical work. Her contention is that much of this work might better be done by other persons, allowing the teacher to devote her energies to the task for which she has been trained. It would seem from comments so far received that this teacher's case may not be exceptional, especially in some of our bigger High Schools. The editor of the Forum invites the members of the A. A. T. F. to send him definite data upon this matter. He will be glad to print comments (not exceeding 200 words) and requests that each correspondent take as his basis a typical 5 day week, giving 1) the number of hours which the correspondent must spend on clerical work and 2) a brief description of the nature of this work. No anonymous data will be accepted; but the name of the correspondent will not be printed, if he so desires.

TOPICS OF DISCUSSION: LES "TOLÉRANCES"

As our Association grows, we are receiving from various quarters requests for the discussion of questions, often of a "practical" nature, which are of special interest to teachers belonging to certain groups e. g. what attention, if any, should the teacher pay to the grammatical *"tolérances"*. At the same time we learn that certain chapters, at their last meetings this year, may decide on some subject to be discussed on the resumption of their meetings in the Fall. If the editor is informed of any topic interesting a reasonable number of our readers, he will announce it in these pages and, should conditions permit, propose this subject for discussion and comment. As for the particular matter of the *"tolérances"*, it is hoped that we may print a short article upon them in the not too distant future.

A. A. T. F. NEWS

NATIONAL CONFERENCE ON EDUCATION

to consider present conditions in professional training and modes of its future development in response to new social demands.

Held at Teachers College, Columbia University, April 10 and 11, on the occasion of installing the Dean of Teachers College.

Group Conferences: Wednesday afternoon, April 11.

There were 24 Group Conferences, attended by College Presidents, Deans, Professors, Superintendents, Supervisors, Principals, Heads of Departments and Teachers.

Conference on Modern Languages

At 2:30, Professor Cru opened the meeting; there were about 60 persons present. After having told of the occasion that brought us together he deplored the fact that modern language teachers had altogether too few opportunities to meet and discuss their problems. There are many problems, the most important being that of the adequate preparation of modern language teachers. He urged the teachers to spend at least one summer term in Spain, Germany or France and mentioned the co-operative plan worked out by Teachers College and the Sorbonne for the training of teachers of French.

He, then, introduced the speaker of the day, Mr. Jacob Greenberg, Director of the Foreign Languages in the Junior and Junior-Senior High Schools of New York City. Mr. Greenberg spoke on "The Problems of the Teaching of Foreign Languages in the Junior and Senior High Schools."

Mr. Greenberg developed his subject in the most interesting and forceful manner. The seven problems he stated and analised were:

1. Who shall study the Foreign Languages?
2. What language shall we give our pupils?
3. What is our main objective? What shall we teach?
4. The measurement of results.
5. The question of correlation between the Junior and Senior High School work.
6. The problem of the Junior High School pupil in a new environment (entering the Senior High School).
7. The problem of the Teacher. How shall we keep the Teacher working at high efficiency? The well-prepared Teacher.

A round-table discussion followed the report of Mr. Greenberg. The first question asked was: "Has it been proved that an examination does more than making the teacher work in view of that examination?" The value of uniform tests and State examinations for the pupils was discussed. Opinions differed widely. Mr. Greenberg answered the objections by saying that we have to face facts as they are. In an ideal school with only ideal teachers, only the best kind of work would be accomplished; but he believes that if the examinations are taken away, 50% of the teachers will be lazy. The question was raised: "Has there been any falling off of the quality of teaching since the successive changes that have taken place regarding regents Examinations? Are not the best results obtained in regents examinations by the students of teachers who knew less about French, but are willing to drill their students for the purpose of taking those examinations?" Mr. Greenberg's conclusion was that although examinations are not perfect, the good by far exceeds the numerous ills. Uniform tests in different schools are an incentive for the teacher to do the best kind of work. Examinations should never be used as a whip, as an instrument of promotion for the pupils or of dismissal for the teacher; they should be used for diagnostic purposes only.

The suggestion was made that the best way to relieve the friction that may exist between Junior H. S. teachers and Senior H. S. teachers is to have them meet and discuss their common problems. It has worked successfully in a school in New York City

The question of the preparation of the teacher was also brought out. What do we mean by a well prepared teacher? was the pivotal question of the discussion. Teachers Examinations were also discussed and criticized. Attention was called to the fact that even the best prepared teacher could not work at maximum efficiency when she has to be on duty in the classroom (teaching or study periods) 35 periods a week. This problem is not hopeless, said Mr. Greenberg. It should take only 250,000 dollars to relieve teachers in New York City.

Two European students gave their opinion on the teaching of modern languages in the United States, bringing out what they thought were the strong and weak points of such teaching.

There were some incidental remarks on several other problems. Mr. Cru closed the meeting by reminding the group that watever we do for the bettering of the teaching of modern language, we must not be like La Fontaine's astrologer who was looking so intently at the stars that he fell in a well he had not happened to notice. He expressed the appreciation of the group to Mr. Greenberg for his thought-provoking address, and considering the success of the meeting, he expressed the wish that language teachers meet oftener.

M. Tamin.

THE AMERICAN ASSOCIATION

OF

TEACHERS OF FRENCH

President Charles A. Downer announces that the following have accepted his invitation to become Honorary Directors of the Association:

Professor James Geddes, Jr., Boston University, Boston, Mass.

Professor Christian Gauss, Princeton University, Princeton, N. J.

Professor Harry Kurz, Knox College, Galesburg, Ill.

Professor Hugh Allison Smith, University of Wisconsin, Madison, Wisconsin.

The following list contains the names of officers of the various chapters whose names were omitted inadvertently from the list published in the second number of *The French Review* or who have been elected subsequent to the publication of that list.

Metropolitan Chapter

Directors

Miss Jeanne Lanz, 1140 Pacific St., Brooklyn.

Mr. Victor Chankin, Seward Park High School, New York City.

Mr. Aaron Tomberg, 2715 Grand Concourse, Bronx, New York City.

Brother Francis Borgia, St. Ann's Academy, New York City.

Westchester Chapter

First Vice-President: Miss Caroline A. Burgevin, Portchester High School.

Second Vice-President: Miss Catherine A. Eastman, Gorton High School, Yonkers.

Third Vice-President: Miss Lula A. Carpenter, Washington Irving High School, Tarrytown.

Fourth Vice-President: Miss Sarah T. Baker, Peekskill High School.

Director: Dr. Clifton T. Edgerly, New Rochelle High School.

Hudson Valley Chapter

First Vice-President: Professor Arthur de Pierpont, Rensselaer Polytechnic Institute, Troy.

Second Vice-President: Miss Genevieve Brooks, Schenectady High School.

Third Vice-President: Miss Louise Stocker, Arlington High School, Troy.

Treasurer: Miss Emily Cavanaugh, Troy High School.

Directors: Professor Florence B. Hayes, Russell Sage College, Troy.

Professor Charlotte Loeb, State College for Teachers, Albany.

THE AMERICAN ASSOCIATION OF TEACHERS OF FRENCH

Rochester Chapter

Director: Professor E. J. Williamson, Hobart College, Geneva.

The membership of the various committees of the Association is as follows:

State and Regional Membership: Edmond A. Méras, *chairman*, Jacob Greenberg, Simeon H. Klafter, Edward O. Perry, William R. Price, Lois F. Strong.

Finance: Jacob Greenberg, *chairman*, Mary M. Fay, Simeon H. Klafter, Jeanne Lanz, Miriam Mahler, Charles Sueur,

Professor Albert Cru is in charge of both the Library of the Association and the Student Correspondance.

The Board of Directors of the Association is now composed of the following members:

Officers of the Association:

Charles A. Downer, A. G. H. Spiers, Raymond Weeks, Claudine Gray, Edmond Méras, Simeon H. Klafter.

Editors of the French Review

James F. Mason, Edward O. Perry.

Quota Directors:

Metropolitan Chapter, William R. Price, Jacob Greenberg, Colman D. Frank, Jeanne Lanz, Victor Chankin, Aaron Tomberg.

Long Island Chapter, Mary Louise Smith, Freeport, N. Y.

Westchester Chapter, Clifton T. Edgerly, New Rochelle, N. Y.

St. Lawrence Chapter, Sarah Plaisance, Canton, N. Y.

Hudson Valley Chapter, Florence White, Vassar College.

Rochester Chapter, C. H. Holzwarth, Rochester, N. Y.

Utica Chapter, F. M. Jones, Colgate University.

Western New York Chapter, J. P. Rice, University of Buffalo.

Fingerlake Chapter, E. Margaret Grimes, Elmira College.

Central New York Chapter, L. W. Crawford, Syracuse University, A. D. Menut, Syracuse University.

Ohio Chapter, E. B. de Sauzé, Cleveland, Ohio.

A. A. T. F. NEWS

A meeting of the Hudson Valley Chapter was held on March 17, at the State College For Teachers, in Albany, with the following program:

9:30—10:30 How Shall We Measure Achievement in Modern Languages? W. C. Decker, Professor of German, New Yok State College for Teachers.

10:30—11:30 Discussion.

a. Time for Aural Comprehension and Dictation Questions in Regents' Examinations.

b. French Book Clubs.

c. Use of the Victrola and Moving Pictures in the Class-room.

During the general discussion Dr. W. R. Price explained several points having to do with the Regents Examinations.

* * *

The first meeting of the BOSTON CHAPTER of the A. A. T. F. was held Saturday, April 21, at 2:30 in the Gamma Delta Room of Boston University.

Professor Geddes, whose untiring efforts made possible the organization, was in charge and introduced as the first speaker, Professor Charles A. Downer, President of the A. A. T. F., who came on from New York to bring greetings to the new Chapter and its founder. Professor Downer outlined the aims and ideals of the Association, whose membership is well on the way to 2,000 with 32 states represented. Monsieur J. C. Flamand, French consul at Boston followed Mr. Downer, welcoming the new Chapter to Boston. M. Flamand has always shown keen interest in all the French societies of the city, of which he is an honored member.

Professor Louis J. Mercier of Harvard, of the editorial board of *The French Review,* spoke of the advantage of the separate associations for the teachers of modern languages, but also dwelt upon the advantage gained by being a member of the wider associations. Two thirds of the members of the Boston Chapter are also members of the Modern Language Association.

Very helpful and interesting papers on "Evolution du langage" by Professor Louis C. Lambert, "La Méthode semi-inductive pour les commençants" by Professor P. H. Churchman, "Les Romans d'Erckmann-Chatrian" by Professor Henri Bourdin, "L'Entente Cordiale" by Professor de Andria were thoroughly appreciated by the audience.

Madame Jeanne Blondel-Allen delighted with her "Chansons françaises." The meeting closed with the singing of the Marseillaise.

The success of the first meeting was impressive and augurs well for the continuance of the aims and ideals of the Association so admirably explained by the President. M. Flamand was elected honorary president, Professor Geddes, president and Miss Frances B. Wilson, secretary.

May 28

The New S. S. Ile de France

2307 359

PRINTED IN U. S. A.
FRENCH PRINTING & PUBLISHING CO., 149 W. 24TH STREET, N. Y. C.